D1544376

A

MANY-MINDED HOMER

by the same author

ACCENTUAL SYMMETRY IN VERGIL
ROMAN VERGIL
POETIC INSPIRATION: AN APPROACH TO VERGIL
ST AUGUSTINE'S 'DE MUSICA': A SYNOPSIS
VERGIL—THE AENEID: TRANSLATED INTO ENGLISH PROSE
VERGIL: EPIC AND ANTHROPOLOGY

MANY-MINDED
HOMER

An Introduction

BY
W. F. JACKSON KNIGHT

EDITED BY
JOHN D. CHRISTIE

BARNES & NOBLE, INC.
NEW YORK · NEW YORK

FIRST PUBLISHED IN 1968

© *George Allen and Unwin Ltd., 1968*

*First published in the United States, 1968
by Barnes & Noble Inc.
New York, New York 10003*

PRINTED IN GREAT BRITAIN
in 11 point Baskerville type
BY C. TINLING AND CO. LTD.
LIVERPOOL, LONDON AND PRESCOT

for
Hugh Stubbs

EDITORIAL PREFACE

When Jackson Knight's *Roman Vergil* appeared in 1944, to be met with general acclaim, it must have seemed obvious to many that a comparable book on Homer by the same author would be of immense value. Only a few knew that there already existed in typescript an extended essay on Homeric poetry, drafted by him in 1938 and 1939. Arrangements for its publication had in fact been made but for various reasons these had been abandoned.

After the successful publication of *Roman Vergil* by Messrs Faber and Faber, the Homer-script was submitted to T. S. Eliot as a director of the firm. He read and greatly liked it. He suggested, however, that the author should consider amplifying it, to match in scope his book on Vergil. This suggestion was accepted; and Jackson Knight began to conceive the idea of a full and comprehensive work to cover the whole field of Homeric studies, embracing the latest researches as well in oral epic as in Homeric language and archaeology.

Now it so happened that the post-war years saw a remarkable florescence of new and challenging work in these fields, and all this Jackson Knight absorbed with intense interest and eager delight: evidence may be seen in his lectures, reviews, and other articles of the time, as well as in the copious notes found among his papers. But—such is the complex and elusive nature of Homeric studies—the projected book became more and more intractable as the scope widened and the quantity of material grew. The postponement of the writing from year to year was often a cause of severe anxiety to the author. T. S. Eliot, however, understood the position, and his interest remained firm, as is shown by a letter he sent to the author's brother, G. Wilson Knight, on August 12th, 1949, part of which I quote by kind permission of Mrs Eliot:

'I wish you would reassure your brother about the Homer book. All that we want is that he should produce a book as good as the Vergil book and that it should be a book such as only he can do, and we are not in the least anxious to hurry him over it. What you say about his researches makes me all the more anxious that he should not interrupt them and perhaps produce a book which might satisfy neither himself nor us. And he should not feel under any obligation to work at the Homer book continuously. When he feels that he must leave time for digestion of material already collected or when he is impelled to interrupt the work for some other task he should feel no scruple of conscience about doing so. . . . Assure him that my own interest in his book will survive any amount of delay.'

In 1953 he wrote to Jackson Knight sending his good wishes for 'a masterpiece'; and as late as 1963 he asked his secretary to say that he had 'never quite given up hope for his book on Homer'. But when Jackson Knight died in 1964 the book was still unwritten.

The loss can never be estimated; and yet it is not, by any means, all loss. For what has survived, and it might well have vanished as the more ambitious work came into being, is the original, shorter, work. Those of us who have read it feel increasingly convinced that it possesses, on its own scale, an attractiveness and intrinsic interest that should appeal to a wider audience than the projected, more 'learned', volume might perhaps have reached. So, though the author himself had for long regarded it as inadequate, it has nevertheless been decided to publish the earlier script, suitably edited, and to supplement it by two of the author's later statements composed while he was immersed in his reading for the larger work. The result is the present volume.

I have edited the main script, which dates from 1938-9, removing some duplications, inconsistencies and other small imperfections, but incorporating, where the text seemed to need strengthening, passages, some small, some quite large, taken from the author's other papers. Occasionally I have had to compose new bridge-passages or links, especially when I judged that a transposition of material would aid the flow of the book. It was mainly in the last chapter that such adjustments were needed. The translated extracts and brief commentaries upon them (pp. 161-8), though in the main carefully executed, had been left imperfectly, and it seems hurriedly, grouped, as though awaiting a revision. These I have rearranged, and linked.

The author's treatment of 'symmetrical composition' in

Homer was confined mainly to the *Iliad*, with only a brief mention of the *Odyssey*. I have ventured to expand this section considerably by incorporating some of the suggestions made by Sir John L. Myres in his article in *The Journal of Hellenic Studies*, 1952, and by C. H. Whitman in his *Homer and the Heroic Tradition*. Among other major revisions I should mention the various references to the Cretan scripts. As his 1954 reference in *Orpheus* (p. 176 below) indicated, Jackson Knight was convinced of the general correctness of Ventris's decipherment of the Linear B Script, and I have adjusted the earlier text accordingly (on pp. 36, 128 below). I should perhaps also insert here a general warning about 'name-equations' based on Near Eastern and Egyptian documents; scholars nowadays treat these with much reserve. (A good example of a moderate approach is Sir John Forsdyke's in his *Greece before Homer*; the extremity of caution is reached by Professor Denys Page in his *History and the Homeric Iliad*.) Furthermore, Minoan-Mycenaean chronology is once again in a fluid state. It begins to appear as if current developments in Aegean archaeology, especially at Santorini and at Knossos itself, may soon call for a drastic revision of early Aegean history.

The two additions to the main text are printed here as an Epilogue and an Appendix. The former appeared originally under the title 'Many-Minded Homer' in *Orpheus*, 1954; and the latter was the Presidential Address to The Virgil Society of London in 1950, first published in the Autumn 1950 issue of *The Wind and the Rain*. Some small inaccuracies in these versions have been corrected and the expression smoothed in a few places. These two additional pieces, used in conjunction with the Selected Bibliography, can provide a valuable guide towards further reading.

The Bibliography comprises not only most of the main works which I know the author considered to be important, but also full references to all his reviews of Homeric books. I would single out as being of special interest his long review of Nilsson's *Homer and Mycenae* in *The Classical Weekly*, 1936, and his review of the books by Pestalozzi and Howald in *Erasmus*, 1948. I have included a selection of more recent works which I have myself enjoyed and which will, I am sure, interest and reward those who are stimulated by this book to pursue their Homer reading further.

I know that the author would have acknowledged his debt to many, perhaps above all to Sir John L. Myres and Professor Martin P. Nilsson. For myself, my main debt is due to Wilson Knight who, as ever, has been of inestimable help to me at every stage in the preparation of this volume; he has suggested many solutions of editorial problems and whenever re-writing was needed, he created turns of phrase perfectly in tune with his brother's spirit. Had I been able to prevail upon him, he would be named as Joint Editor with myself: such is the extent of his contribution. We were both greatly helped by Mr Hugh Stubbs of Exeter University who scrutinized an early draft of the main script and sent us many useful comments. I thank my friend Dr T. D. M. Roberts for once again giving me valuable advice and his expert assistance with the proofs and index.

As I have worked with the three parts of this volume, I have come to feel that, as well as being a lively, and even exciting, book about Homer, it also reveals, in a fascinating way, the stages in one man's exploration, through twenty years and more, of Homer's poetry and its background. It is thus a valuable chart to the Homeric fields, a chart that could guide the steps of others who seek the sources of the magical stream of Homer's poetry.

University of Glasgow, 1968   John D. Christie

The book was originally called *Homeric Poetry*, but we have decided to let our volume carry the title used by the author for his *Orpheus* article. 'Many-Minded Homer' is a phrase coined by W. B. Yeats in his poem, 'Mad as the mist and snow', No. XVIII in *Words for Music Perhaps*, 1933.

The typescript of *Homeric Poetry*, typed on the occasion of its submission to Messrs Faber and Faber in 1945 and bearing corrections by the author, will be lodged in The Roborough Library, the University of Exeter. With it are placed certain items of which extracts have been used to supplement our final text. These include an essay in manuscript 'Are there different styles in Homer?' and (now our final paragraph on p. 170) an offprint of a press-report composed by Jackson Knight of a lecture on Homer delivered by him to the Exmouth Branch of the Virgil Society in 1946; and other relevant material.

CONTENTS

I

EPIC POETRY

With the exception of the Chinese lyric and the Japanese epigram, no literary form has had so long an active life as Greek epic. It was certainly alive, more or less as we know it, in 1000 B.C., and probably 500 years before; and in the sixth century A.D. it was still being composed in sincerity and energetic emulation, according to a tradition neither petrified nor lost. It is surprising that no books have been written on the whole subject of Greek epic. Perhaps such a book should really be written before yet another book on Homer.

Books have, of course, been written on parts of the subject, and on subjects of which Greek epic is a part. In the Bodleian more than one whole volume of the old catalogue is given to the name of Homer—about twelve pounds weight of the names of books written about his poetry. Homer is an obvious reason why books have not been written on Greek epic. They have been written on Homer instead, because he is far the best of all known Greek epic poets. There was a sharp distinction between him and the rest, as Aristotle clearly saw. That is well known. But it is not so well known, or so regularly remembered, that good critics narrowed the distinction, and placed unexpected names, such as Peisander and Panyassis, close to the name of Homer. It must be of interest to consider these poets, who existed in great numbers, and commanded much attention in their own day and for centuries after. Most of their work is lost. But that does not prevent the opinions of ancient critics about them from mattering. They show for one thing what Greeks expected from epic poetry, and how they were likely to have regarded Homer himself, a question by no means settled yet. The reasons why Dionysius of Halicarnassus blamed Antimachus of Colophon are much like the reasons, or some of them, why thousands of Greeks adored Homer. That is one point. But it is not really scientific to collect knowledge only because it is attractive. All knowledge that can be collected should be collected; it may have a use and an attraction never suspected till long after the collection is made.

Greek epic, besides Homer, is not all lost. Some of the most interesting poems are lost, however, and they have invited much investigation. This 'Cyclic' epic, apparently composed in the generations following Homer's own time, and next to Homeric epic in outlook and interest, was the main subject of Welcker's work over a hundred years ago; it has not been treated for itself on a large scale since, and in spite of countless small and not always progressive discussions Welcker's work has not been replaced.

Of this part of the subject there may be more to say, and in any case a new treatment is due. But it is only a part of the subject. There is later epic in at least three groups; epic of the revival about 500 B.C., a most interesting event; Hellenistic epic; and perhaps above all the late epic, of which many poems survive, especially from the fourth and fifth Christian centuries. These poems have their interest, not least as part of the whole long tradition; but they have normally been discussed only in special investigations, one at a time. As I said before, this whole immense poetic tradition deserves attention in a synoptic history, which at the least should be convenient for reference, and at best might enable progress in knowledge to be made, if an arrangement by sequence should fortunately disclose principles of development, or contrasts, or problems not formulated hitherto. It is probably worth while to collect the names of all recorded Greek epic poets and poems in one book of moderate size, and to emphasize the historical moments at which epic started into life. And, once more, such an attempt is necessary for Homeric scholarship, by strengthening, if only a little, the lines of the picture, the background and the foreground, however trivial all else may be in comparison with the central figure's majesty. But the book does not exist, and we must get on without it.

Epic poetry regularly starts in a 'heroic' age. That does not mean that it is only composed in heroic ages. A heroic age is short and destructive, a time in which a young virile culture, influenced by an adjacent culture more advanced than itself, generates an adventurous individualistic aristocracy which lives for war and honour. There have been many such ages, especially the ages in which the Teutons broke into the Roman South and then Roman Britain, and the age of Charlemagne. Ages can be classified, if only roughly. There have been heroic ages, in which conditions naturally and in fact have started epic. There have been ages in which tragedy, and comedy too, naturally arose. There have been satirical ages; and ages in which satire could never have become prevalent. Literature must be expected to emerge from social conditions, in accordance with them.

But a form once found survives. Greek epic, starting, so far as we can see, in the Greek heroic age, continued with scarcely a break for at least fifteen centuries, through ages of many kinds that were not at all, in any technical sense, heroic. Still, epic does seem to need something like a heroic age to start, and indeed might be thought the very justification, before Providence, of such ages. For if half-barbarous, arrogant, too individual, destructive heroes made or gave Achilles, Odysseus, and Homer, perhaps they gave or made for mankind a greatness and a usefulness beyond any they took or destroyed.

There is a view that it is as wrong to talk of an 'epic' or 'heroic' age as it is to talk of an age as 'tragic' or 'comic' or 'satiric'. The point is that these adjectives are descriptions of kinds of literature, and not of 'ages', and there is no such thing as an age which can be described by the sort of book it produces. There may be comedy in any age, and it is not true to say that there is a definite kind of age in which comedy can happen and that it can happen in no other.

This is a useful warning, because it is easy to collect and compare 'ages' according to their literary production, and argue falsely from one to another. It would be absurd to say that the age which produced Molière was a comic age; that Molière is in the tradition of Latin and Greek comedy; and that therefore Japanese comedy, also necessarily a product of a 'comic' age, was also in the Greek and Roman tradition. The fallacy is that analogy is not logical argument. If two things are alike in known respects, that does not, without further evidence, prove they are alike in other respects which may or may not be in logical relation.

On the other hand, literature is in a sense part of a set of mutually dependent social circumstances. It is one circumstance and it varies to some extent according to the others. It is safe to say that satire naturally happens when a 'classical' age, an age of careful form and respected convention, has reached a

B

stage in which it ceases to satisfy and give moral impulse to life, but has not yet led to the repression of criticism, and still less to an ensuing failure of repression with a consequent insurrectionary ardour. You do not expect to find prosperous satire when writers are full of enthusiasm for an established régime, or against a régime, formerly established, and now collapsing or collapsed. Satire needs dissatisfaction keen but not too keen, and a freedom which allows expression, but not the action to which expression is a second best.

So also there have been 'epic' ages, ages which are alike in many respects, including the production of epic poetry. You can consider these ages, and come to see that in one of them it is natural that there should be epic poetry, because this particular age is the kind of age in which epic is usually produced. It does not follow that you can always go further, and say, for example, of some new part of history you have just discovered, that it reminds you of ages which produced epic, and therefore it must have produced epic also. But you are quite safe if you let comparison suggest a frame of mind or even occasionally a hypothesis, all subject to careful testing. 'Analogy at least shews what is possible.'

There have been 'epic' ages in ancient Babylonia, Greece and India, among the Huns, in old Germany, Norway, Britain, Iceland, Ireland, France, Russia, in the Balkans, in Siberia, and in New Zealand. That is, in these places there have been periods, sometimes centuries long, in which a tradition of oral poetry concerning action and adventure existed.

This 'epic' poetry has been carefully and thoroughly examined in six or seven of its instances, and brought into more general comparison in many more, perhaps altogether in ten to twelve. Such work has shewn that a wide class of epic, oral poetry, all in some respects alike, has existed. The places of it are nearly all in Europe and Asia; except New Zealand, where epic tradition was introduced from Asia by the Maoris when they came, and Greek colonies in north Africa, where it was also intrusive. No strict epic is known to belong to the other continents, though they all have, of course, songs or recitations of various kinds. Epic has occurred in practically all times, from a period not long after the beginning of settled civilization in Mesopotamia, if the stories of Adapa and Gilgamish are rightly called epics, down to the present day; for the tradition of oral epic poetry still lives, especially among the South Slavs of the Balkans.

It is hard to be precise about world epic, and it would be absurd to generalize in any but the simplest way about it. On the whole something like this happens.

Everyone, in some moods, likes telling or hearing a story, with or without music and dance; and always has, from the neolithic stage, or before it, onwards. The reasons are complicated, but on the whole they are clearly present in the known nature of the human organism in which mind and body are interdependent. Instincts and tendencies, apparently developed for different ends in the evolutionary plan, demand satisfaction by verbal art. Some of the satisfactions are these. There is pleasure in imaginary wish-fulfilment, when you imagine that you are a conquering hero, whether you have yourself been allowed to be a conquering hero or not. There is pleasure in imaginary feasting and sex-gratification. There is, too, pleasure in curiosity about what will happen next in a tale, all the more if you know you are soon to be told. There is pleasure in admiring or ridiculing imaginary people; in the relief after an imaginary escape, in revelling in imaginary revenge; and in the recognition of an imaginary tale heard before, or of elements in your own experience somehow recalled by an imaginary tale. There are also more mysterious satisfactions; in the strong emotion and the rhythm which emotion creates and in the new strong emotion created by a rhythm; and in the sense of unity between personalities, which story-telling produces in the sympathy generated or restored between story-teller and audience, and between different members of the audience, under a single spell. Verbal art, like other art, gives us a rest from the torment of individuality, by restoring us to a more primitive undifferentiation. Not that it only looks back; for in looking back it looks forward too, and shews the way to the future out of the past.

These obvious gratifications soon create fairy-tales, which are very early, and world wide. They are nameless at first, but the characters in them are given the names of great men when great men begin to be remembered.

That is not all the use made of great men. A time often comes when people in an alert and active condition of mind and body, organized under the leadership of individuals, have exciting adventures, in battles and travels especially. The story of the adventures is told immediately they happen, and becomes saga; it is told again and again, with improvements, including the addition of other material, such as fairy-tales, at first about no one in particular, and myths, originally about beings who are not purely human and real.

It has been observed in six good examples that ages of epic have started in one particular way. A more backward people develops quickly by contact with a more cultured people. It then adopts a life of aggressive adventure, captures civilized territory, and gives free, glorious, but destructive play to its new found individualism, because it has grown up too quickly. That is a 'heroic age'. Heroic ages do in fact come that way. And heroic ages start epic ages. The deeds of the heroes are told in saga which develops an epic tradition in later generations.

German, Icelandic and French epics all have an aristocratic and warlike organization of society behind them; as in Homer, there is an overlord and many partly independent vassals, living with their retainers in castles, prepared for war, and spending their time in fighting and hunting, with feasting, quarrelling, and listening to minstrels for relaxation. There is even, at least in Iceland, an almost Homeric dignity of life, in the exclusion, either aesthetic or moral, of several kinds of unpleasant and indecent things. The epics last for centuries, and undergo changes, far more violent than the text of Homer underwent. The *Nibelungenlied* in the oldest manuscript is written in assonances, but in later manuscripts, apart from other changes, regular rhymes are introduced. In the French *Chanson de Roland* the metre changes still more, and twelve-syllabled lines are substituted for lines of ten syllables.

The French poetry is a specially close parallel in its history to the Homeric.

In France, in the eleventh, twelfth and early thirteenth centuries A.D., there was a Germanic aristocracy of Franks, dominating an older population, and attached by an uncertain loyalty to the king, their overlord. They lived in strong castles, hunted, fought, and listened to epic poems recited by jongleurs. Among this aristocracy the national poetry of France developed.

At first, apparently, some of the fighting men composed and performed poetry. But soon professional poets arose. Some were of gentle birth, and both composed and performed the poems. They visited the courts and castles. Later, they performed in open places, for the interest of the townspeople.

The French epics deal with legends of an age long past, and especially legends of Charlemagne, his wars, the brave deeds of his peers, and their quarrels, with him, or with each other. Saracens are introduced instead of the real enemies, and the Emperor, at first a prince of great nobility, is gradually degraded. Angels take part in the action, and dreams provide motivation.

The poems were much more than combinations of the early lays about Charlemagne which are known to have existed. They are not in ballad metre. When the *Chanson de Roland* first found a complete form about 1050–1070 A.D., that was by no means the end of its history. For several generations changes were introduced, especially expansions, compressions and adaptations to new ideas. Rhyme was introduced and the metre altered. Finally, new and more artificial poems were composed, in which, as in Greek Cyclic epic, new heroes, forced into genealogical connexion with heroes of the old epic, furnished subjects.

French epics were soon written down, at first in small volumes, meant for the use of the jongleurs themselves. They used the books to help them recite poetry which they or others had created. There was no reading public till later, when large folio texts were written. One of the jongleurs was Jendeus de Brie, who composed the first version of the *Bataille Loquifer*, in the twelfth century. He wrote his poem, but kept it secret, and, after making a good profit with it in Sicily, left it to his son when he died. It is supposed that after his death more copies were made, of varying fidelity to the original, and that the poem came into circulation at last in that way. Other poets also were jealous of their written copies.

All this, except the record of writing, is comparable to Greek epic history: original lays and the creation of poems about a legendary past with fanciful elements and divine action and sometimes an overlord who can be disparaged by his nobles; the succession of professional poets, like Homer's Phemius and

Demodocus, to fighting men like Achilles who were also poets; a certain amount of variation of the text as time passed; and finally a 'Cyclic' age, long after the poetry first began, in which poems were composed more artificially to complete the original epics. There is even a story about Homer which recalls Jendeus de Brie; for Homer was said to have written the *Cypria*, and to have given it to Stasinus, who married his daughter, as her dowry. Since the French evidence shews that such a thing can be natural in an epic age, it may be guessed that if poets in the Greek epic age had not had written texts of their poems for their own use the story about Homer would not have arisen.

In the history of French epic there was no school of epic poets comparable to the Greek school of epic poets, the 'Homeridae', till the fourteenth and fifteenth centuries. Then the jongleurs used to go to Beauvais in Lent, when they might not perform, to learn new poems. That was in the decline of epic, partly due to the circulation of copies and the rise of a reading public among the rich.

Original short lays, almost contemporary with the events which they describe, are known in many places. Sometimes, as in France, poets used them and went far beyond them in composing long epics. In Germany the *Nibelungenlied* never became a real whole. In Iceland the prose Eddas came nearer to unity but are not true epic poems. The Finnish peasant lays, the *Kalevala*, existed separately for centuries till between 1835 and 1849 Lönnrot combined them into something like a continuous poem by joining them and adding passages of his own. But that did not produce an epic poem, because the material did not come under a true poet's poetic control. The Russian *byliny* are long narratives of adventure and might be called epic poetry. They grew up between the tenth and the sixteenth centuries, and there occur together in them Viking ships, telescopes, fire-arms, and coffee, introduced by the reciters of different ages. The South Slavic epic consists of tales of adventure, especially in war, and the practice of it has continued in a single tradition from the thirteenth century till the present time. The form of the verse, the style, and a great number of set expressions, 'epic formulae', provide a means of relating great deeds alike of many centuries ago and of the last generation. So in 1942 a minstrel in Egypt sang an old song substituting Mr

Churchill's name for the name of the old hero. *Beowulf*, at first a pagan tale, was worked over by a Christian poet. It has a patterned construction like the *Iliad*, and was a favourite in England, where the people and places of the poem were unknown, as Homer's poetry was enjoyed by people who had no personal interest in Achilles or Odysseus. The Indian *Vedas* are very long, and were for centuries preserved and evolved by priests, in oral tradition, without writing. But they were not tales of adventure, and in fact existed for a religious purpose as a guide for life and ritual.

Of all this traditional poetry only some can be called epic, but the rest gives interesting and useful facts also. There emerge some general characteristics.

The poems begin mainly if not solely with saga, and are developed, for long periods sometimes, by people living in an uncritical age who confuse history by turning it into legend, but who are inquisitive about the past. At first anyone may recite or sing extempore poems, but there are soon professional poets. There is some national solidarity and uniformity, especially in religion. The poems deal with adventures often tragic and often far in the past. They are closely dependent on an aristocratic feudal organization, with an overlord, peers, and subjects. The age of adventure in which the poetry, or at least one of its more important phases, starts, tends to be an age in which a people has suddenly advanced in culture through contact with a more civilized race, and becomes violently expansive.

The poems, again, are full of formulae. They often combine metrical and grammatical forms, and references to thoughts and things, which belong to very different ages, because they grow continually. They exist in different versions. They present fact in a distorted shape. A king who ought to be young may appear old—Charlemagne at Roncevaux was thirty-seven but is represented as grey-haired. In *Thidreks Saga* Theodoric appears as quite different from his historical self. He is far more limited in the range of his activities, and his importance to a small circle of people is emphasized to the exclusion of his part in world affairs. Perhaps in this he is a useful parallel to Odysseus. Stories, again, are regularly compressed, and heroes who lived generations apart meet together.

The point of view in fully developed epic is royal or aristocratic. At first the poet praises the king. Later he may represent the nobility, and let them enjoy in his poetry thoughts of hostility towards an overlord. Or the royalist sympathy may be perpetuated, if the story is good enough. There exist also traditional poems which are not aristocratic epic but represent the views and interests of less exalted people. But on the whole strictly epic poetry gives to military, aristocratic audiences tales of chieftains at war, though often the poetry lives on to interest people of a different degree.

True epic poetry has a spirit of chivalry, and a code of behaviour. There may be much selfishness and arrogance and cruelty, but on the whole some things are not done and not mentioned, and the direction of the poetry, the implied moral of it, is towards a courageous and gentle ideal. The characters can, or should, see the ideal, but they are proud individualists, who often do not reach it, and for that or another reason come to disaster. There is a tendency to pessimism, and the faith that men have glory, and not much else, for which to hope. Therefore the heroes passionately love glory. The pessimism is partly mitigated by the Christian faith of the poets who handled earlier themes, some pagan, in North European epic.

Epic poetry lasts a varying time before it is written down. But it regularly, in all stages, shews signs of its oral origin. You can see that in the original plan it was meant to be remembered and meant to be heard. The recitations of it were a strain on both the minstrels and the audiences. So the minstrels did not normally try hard to find a different expression for a similar thing or event. In fact they were glad to make as much use as they could of set descriptions for subjects that recur, such as the arming of a hero, the beginning and ending of a speech, sunrise and sunset, meals, and washing. This is very general. Homer, the French *Chansons de Geste*, and South Slavic epic are very much alike, in spite of other differences, in this use of formulae.

The formulae remain, recalling the oral time, just as securely when the poems are written and widely read, if they ever are. At first it was simply not worth while to think out variations, an added burden to the inventive powers and the memory of the minstrel, and indeed no kindness to the audience, which was glad of a momentary rest in the familiar and known, and anxious to get on with the story, without wasting mental effort on understanding new impressions of sunsets or meals, of which really not much was left to say. It is true that there might be some inaccuracy, if formal phrases, verses, or, as in all epic, longer passages recurred in similar situations, which were yet not identical, as of course no two situations ever can be. But if so, it does not matter, especially when poems are heard, not read. Misfits are not noticed; all the less noticed when the audience is lulled into a temporary inattention by familiar phrases, in rhythm that is familiar and strong. After all, to be completely expressive we should need never even to use the same word twice; but we do. It is not really different in kind to use the same phrase, verse, or passage more than once. Like other practices, in some circumstances it is a good idea, but not in others.

As poetry gets farther from its oral origin, exact repetition becomes less. About a third of the *Iliad* consists of or contains phrases or verses used elsewhere. Yet Homer is very far from any primitive kind of oral poetry. Vergil, on the other hand, though he composed by ear, as the old, oral poets did, and remembered countless verbal combinations, made a point of changing them. In the *Aeneid* only about thirty lines are repeated exactly; and even for similar events such as sunrises and the beginnings and ends of speeches he nearly always says the same kind of thing in at least slightly different words, and in this is in sharp contrast with Homer. In Dante, Shakespeare, and Milton such variety has become normal and perhaps even spontaneous.

Epic heroes on the whole are not other-worldly. They have superstitions, but think little of ghosts, and are accustomed to fear disgrace more than danger, natural or supernatural. They are too busy with active life to reflect much, and are reconciled to the doubtful doom of human kind. An admired epic hero is strong and dangerous in battle, brave, courteous, obedient to the code; resentful of insult, and yet merciful when the code requires it; but limited to the outlook of his class and time. He is the more admirable to us if we think ourselves back into his position, and force ourselves to be more satisfied with the simple merits of strength and courage than now we naturally are. Moral advance and discovery, and the more complicated merits of a full human personality are not usually expected in epic heroes; even if they are really there, less apparent than real.

There are compensations. Humanity gains dignity for the very simplification. Issues are made more clear; and the mere plot, in so far as there is one, may reveal part of the world's nature by displaying the kind of thing that happens to people of a few broad types. Again, the progress of epic poetry, rapid and yet leisurely, with its time for ordinary routines, gives dignity to them, and reveals the important truth that to live life and be civilized you cannot always afford not to make the most of common things like meals and furniture and animals and the smaller parts of a home. Epic is full of zest, childlike often, and sometimes to us childish, as when it enumerates details of ritual and legalities and delays the story for them, or interposes lists, often genealogical, which are meaningless to us. Even Homer preserves such lists, the remains of a simpler age; but in his elaboration of details and zest for ordinary things he represents a healthy state of mind which persisted in his own time.

Greek poetry is well known to be unique in certain qualities. There is nothing so clear and direct and balanced and, on the whole, moralized. The moral issue, whatever it may be, seldom fails to emerge from a Greek poem. The Greeks found it natural to make the idea of the mind and the object outside in the world coincide so exactly in poetry that sometimes you hardly notice that it is poetry at all and imagine that it is plain prosaic statement. Perhaps that is the best kind of poetry; or perhaps there is no best kind, but many kinds can be good.

Of Greek epic poetry it is not easy to talk generally, because no typical Greek epic poetry is known, unless Homer's is typical, which is exceedingly unlikely. Greek epic poetry started well before 1000 B.C., and probably before 1500 B.C. It continued at least till the dark ages of the Christian era. So it had a life of not much less than two thousand years. There was, besides, a great deal of it. The names of eighty-three lost epic or didactic poems by fifty poets, all in the early part of the period, down to the fifth century B.C., are known. But this period has left only the Homeric Hymns, three or four didactic poems, some fragments, and the *Iliad* and *Odyssey*. Of the next period, from the fourth century B.C. to the third A.D., one epic poem survives, the *Argonautica* of Apollonius Rhodius, in four books, written early in the third century B.C. Then, near the end of classical antiquity, there are more epic poems, which, strangely, have survived. In the fourth century A.D. Quintus Smyrnaeus wrote fourteen books of Greek epic about Troy, *Posthomerica*; soon after him Tryphiodorus wrote a short *Capture of Troy* in one book; and about seven hundred years later Johannes Tzetzes wrote another short poem about Troy, in three books. There were other 'epic' poets also, among them Nonnus about contemporary with Tryphiodorus. Work by Nonnus, also, is extant; it is not so close to Homeric subjects. Not till Tzetzes does the Homeric ring quite disappear. Quintus and Tryphiodorus are soaked in Homer, and write in Homeric language and metre with freedom and eloquence and sometimes true poetry, though they have never been much admired. But Tzetzes is quite different. His Greek and his versification are ignorant and childish like his thinking.

Of these poets, Homer, the Hymns, Apollonius and the late epic writers are available to shew what Greek epic was like. The Cyclic epic of about 800 to about 550 B.C. is lost but for short fragments. So is any poetry which existed before Homer. We have not any of the Greek short lays which may probably have arisen before full epic, except in so far as traces of them can be found here and there in Homer. The later epic has in a way outlived the epic time, and has sustained influences from other branches of poetry. It can only help a little towards a general description, and the Cyclic fragments cannot do so very much more. Homer may or may not be quite exceptional; but that he was not quite exceptional is hard to believe.

Greek epic poetry is therefore not nearly so well known as other epic poetry, if Homer is not counted. The Cyclic poems (see pp. 63–5, 71 *ff.*, below) composed after Homer's work, to complete it, must have been very unlike it. They have too many incidents, and tell too much story. They do not develop and make clear the moral significance of what happens. They are more other-worldly than epic usually is, and have more fear of ghosts and guilt, more superstition, and more horrors. They are less aristocratic, and seem to belong to an age when the purity of aristocratic tradition had been influenced by a resurgence of popular life, with much folk-lore preserved from a Mycenaean or pre-Mycenaean time when Homer's Achaeans had not established their way of life over Greece. They are composed in order to give a complete if artificial story, rather than created in service to a single poetic vision of the condition of man.

Apollonius follows the custom of his time in filling his poem with mythological learning, and turning old stories to romance. His poem is about love, travel and wonders. It is enjoyable enough often, if sometimes slow. But it is scarcely heroic. There is not enough passion and will, especially in the hero, Jason himself.

Quintus also is inclined to be tedious, and to depend too much on pathos, for which he develops a great many situations, seeming to regard the intervening narrative as a means of getting from one pathetic scene to another.

Nonnus is liked for voluminous learning, but little read or admired.

Tryphiodorus is the second best extant Greek epic poet. He has force, music, control, and even tragic restraint. But he gives rather a glimpse than an imaginative and universal scheme of man's destiny.

Perhaps it is just possible to find a common quality for Greek epic. First is lucidity of language, simply built, one thought after another, with little subordination. Second is the swift balanced movement and inimitable music of the long hexameter verse; for all Greek epics, from start to finish, have it—the metre of 'How art thou fallen from heaven, O Lucifer, son of the morning!' Third is a humanization of everything. Gods, goddesses, men, women, monsters, powers of nature are all translated completely and convincingly, not merely into mythical personification, which is regularly crude and incredible, but into real humanity. Fourth is a certain homogeneity of circumstances. We are always in a heroic world, with the extravagances, perhaps, of fairy-land sometimes, but without violent aesthetic incongruities. There is always some dignity in simplicity. Characters and individualities may be weak or strong and weakly or strongly portrayed; but they generally shew up clearly in a typical epic simplicity. Fifthly there is a great wealth of mythology, and an ability, even when they are artificially manufactured, to tell mythological stories in a uniform, clear, and attractive way.

Greek epic lasted long, longer, I believe, than any other.
Perhaps it is in general more alert and full than other epic.
But if we had not Homer, we should find it hard to say sincerely
that Greek epic is greater than corresponding poetry of the
Teutonic or Celtic north.

II

HOMERIC EPIC

The greatest Greek epic, the Homeric poems, came into exist-
ence about half way between the beginning of advanced human
culture and our own time. They are the earliest European
literature; but not the earliest literature of the Indo-European
group of languages, for the *Vedas* in India are a little earlier,
parts of them, perhaps, earlier by two or three centuries. The
Homeric poems are very far from being the earliest literature
in the world. They were complete one or two centuries after
those Psalms which are actually by David. Some of the Bible
is, of course, much earlier than that. And in Babylonia and
Egypt literature of a kind certainly begins before 3000 B.C.;
before 2000 B.C. it reached an advanced development, and
came to be comparable in several respects with Homer, and
with literature as it is today.

The world in which the Homeric poems came to life was a
world of violent movement; but also a world which had had
long periods of peaceful development; a world in which many
races, nations, and tribes, of very different histories and levels
of culture, met in harmony or more often contention.

The area is the south-east of Europe and lands to the east
and south, called 'the fertile crescent', where civilization grew
very early between deserts and mountains principally along
river valleys.

First of all in time, as far as is known at present, was the
culture of the Ganges valley and Turkestan; then, soon after,
and akin to it, the cultures of Mesopotamia, Sumer in the
south and Babylonia further to the north, in the valleys of the
Tigris and Euphrates. Later on, but before 3300 B.C., Egypt,
influenced from Mesopotamia, became a unified and civilized
state under the first king of the first Dynasty, usually known as
Menes. By 2000 B.C. settled civilized life in strongly built cities
had started in Crete, several Greek islands, Syria, and here and
there in Asia Minor too.

Copper, writing, and the potter's wheel had been used in
Mesopotamia and Egypt well before 3000 B.C. By 2000 B.C.

the bronze age was in full progress not only there but through the whole area as far as the Greek islands.

In Europe however conditions were less advanced. The settled but slowly developing life of the new stone age was still continuing generally; until pressure of population and climatic change began to cause violent migrations in Europe as elsewhere.

Between 2400 B.C. and 1600 B.C. there were two main movements, which continued to exert force on history for centuries after the first impulses were spent.

The first movement came from Asia towards Europe. At least one part of it is quite clear. Asianic pottery and placenames were carried to Greece. Other effects are possible; even the physical type of human remains has been thought to prove immigration. There is less doubt about the habit of constructing round stone buildings, as at Tiryns in southern Greece, and very strong stone defensive walls, as at many other places in Greece, and also at Troy, in Asia, near the Dardanelles.

There was also a spread of Semitic people from Arabia. They came into Mesopotamia, and also Palestine; their influence may have spread north-west also, carried by the Phoenicians. Certainly there was a great invasion of Egypt in the eighteenth century B.C.; for there the Hyksos, 'Shepherd Kings', gained control and ruled for more than 200 years. The Egyptian Dynasties numbered XIII to XVII are dynasties of the Hyksos. But Egyptian rule was re-established in the sixteenth century by strong kings of the XVIIIth Dynasty, who created an Egyptian empire in Syria also.

Independent of these movements were others from the north. In south Russia and western central Asia population expanded, and tribes speaking Indo-European dialects came down into India, Persia, Asia Minor, Greece and Italy. They brought the horse with them, and like the peoples of the south they used bronze. Their first known representatives were the Kassites, who captured Babylon and established a government there soon after 1900 B.C. The Kassites were followed by the Hittites, who created an empire in central Asia Minor in about 1800 B.C. At this same time there is no doubt that kindred tribes entered Greece, and the Greek language began to be spoken in Greek lands. The first Greek invaders were followed by other waves, one about 1450 B.C. and another about 1100 B.C. The first main wave cannot be described safely by a name; it has been called Ionian. The second can more safely be called Achaean. The third is the Dorian wave of invading immigrants. The Homeric poems tell the adventures of the Achaeans between about 1250 and 1150 B.C., not long before they were overthrown by Dorians. The poems are rooted in the Achaean age. They remember conditions at least as far back as the fifteenth century, and perhaps earlier. But there is in the poems material belonging to the eighth and conceivably even the seventh centuries B.C. It took nearly a thousand years to make our Homer.

The world in which the Greek race and Greek epic poetry was born was a world of contrast and conflict. The principal conflict was between north and south. The northern invaders were less cultured, and younger in spirit, than the people into contact with whom they came. Mesopotamia, Egypt and Crete had cultures already thousands of years old, which had reached a high level at least a thousand years before the northern invasions, and had become fixed in many particulars. The northern men had their own traditional culture, but it was far more rough and simple and less settled, except in so far as influences from the south reached and affected it, as in Bohemia about 1400 B.C. and at Hallstatt a few centuries after.

The southerners had elaborate systems of religion, law, administration, medicine, agriculture, trade, and architecture. The northerners may be guessed to have been horse-riding, cattle-owning nomads, who had a simple faith in a few gods, who lived by custom rather than law under a simple organization of kings and aristocracies, who buried their dead in barrows, and who were used to trusting the arbitrament of the sword. They seldom lived in cities, and had not long left the age of stone behind them. In Asia they soon met the older civilization face to face, and partly wrecked it, but still more assimilated it. In mainland Greece they came into a land whose inhabitants were in touch with people of high culture, but were themselves simple and backward agriculturists. In 2000 B.C. there was considerable culture in several Greek islands, such as Melos and Rhodes, and a brilliant and advanced culture in Crete. But it was only after the first northerners had arrived that a brilliant culture developed in mainland Greece—

the culture called Mycenaean after the city of gold, Mycenae, near to Tiryns in the north of the Peloponnese, where that culture had its richest prosperity and the centre of its power.

After the Dorian invasion about 1100 B.C. the Mediterranean world became more parochial, broken up into isolated communities little exposed to external influences, except when they were raided by marauding enemies. The many different local styles of pottery prove that. But in the full bronze age the world of the eastern Mediterranean was much more nearly one. Even Italy, Sicily and Spain came to share the same great bronze-age culture. The world of which Homer tells knew the west and the south too, as the world in which his poetry came near to its perfection did not.

The Heroic Age of Greece, the age in which Homer's heroes lived, was a time when old cultures of the south and east met one another, and met the new, rougher culture from the north as well. The contacts were creative, and in mainland Greece they formed the Mycenaean culture of the Homeric heroes.

The Mycenaean culture was composite almost from its start. In Crete a neolithic culture, perhaps 6000 years old, had, about 3000 B.C., been vitalized into new activity by influence from north Africa. This influence may be called Egyptian, but a better name is Egypto-Libyan. The very ancient culture of Libya was one ingredient in the life of Egypt; first it passed into that life, and helped to form it, and then across into the less mature life of Crete. There it fitted in with native tendencies and conditions, and changed them greatly, to make what is called the Minoan culture. The Minoan culture is the first advanced and metal-using culture of Greek lands. It lasted from about 3000 B.C. till about 1200 B.C., in its three periods, called Early, Middle, and Late Minoan, corresponding roughly with the Old Kingdom, Middle Kingdom, and New Kingdom in Egypt, and divided at about the dates 2500 B.C. and 1600 B.C. Early in the Middle Minoan period the spread of population and influence from the east reached Crete, and helped to form the later Cretan culture. The next influences came from the Achaeans, who must have visited the island about 1400 B.C. or before, and from the Dorians, who settled there after 1100 B.C. What the Achaeans did in Crete is not clearly known; they may have had something to do with the partial collapse of

c

Cretan organization and culture about 1450 B.C., contributing to the effects of civil war in the island, and of an earthquake, which destroyed the great palace at Knossos, the chief city, situated in the centre of the north coast.

On the mainland also events are obscure, but conditions for much of the period are clearer. In about 1700 B.C. centres of high culture began to appear amid the simple and backward people of the Greek mainland. These centres were 'Mycenaean' fortresses, sited for defence on high ground, surrounded by immense walls constructed of large squared or variously shaped blocks of stone without mortar, and containing principally a royal palace. The fortresses could cover towns built below them, in the sense that they threatened attackers with counter-attack, and could at need admit the townsmen for temporary refuge. But they were not themselves cities; they were not large enough to contain many houses.

In North Greece Thebes, Orchomenos, and Athens and in the Peloponnese Mycenae, Tiryns near it, Corinth to the north-west of them, Pylos to the west, and Sparta to the south, are known now by excavation as important Mycenaean centres. There were perhaps twenty others, but they were smaller, and less is known from excavation about them; among them is a site in the island of Leucas, to the north-west of the Peloponnese, where according to some authorities the palace of Homer's hero Odysseus stood. Strictly Mycenaean fortresses are not known outside Greece. There are however comparable fortresses in the Troad, on the south coast of the Dardanelles. There in several places were settlements of Mycenaean date, and some had strong walls not unlike Mycenaean walls. The only site, here, which has yielded much to excavation is Hissarlik, now almost, but not quite, universally supposed to be the ancient Troy. Hissarlik was inhabited before 2000 B.C., when no Mycenaean fortresses existed yet. But later the inhabitants were in touch with the Mycenaean world, and imported Mycenaean pottery. The Greek islands also have comparable settlements, again however not strictly Mycenaean, but more satisfactorily described as Helladic. The chief sites are Thermi in Lesbos, not far from Troy, and akin to it in culture, Phylakopi in Melos, and Ialysos, Cameiros, and Lindos in Rhodes. Apparently the pre-Mycenaean Helladic culture of the islands, in touch with the Cretan, Minoan culture but different from it, had not reached any advanced stage in mainland Greece when the strictly Mycenaean culture began there; such culture as there was has to be called Helladic in the Peloponnese, though in north Greece 'Thessalian' is the name used for the most characteristic remains of that area.

When the northern, 'Greek' invaders came, they brought with them some customs which survived, especially a northern kind of house and a northern kind of dress. They could not write. They also brought the horse, and Indo-European speech. Some, at least, burnt their dead. They had and retained certain religious ideas of their own.

The Cretans built palaces of a peculiar pattern; it was certainly a southern pattern. They wore a southern dress. They could write. They did not know the horse, and their language can scarcely have been Indo-European. They always inhumed their dead. Their religious ideas owed something to Africa and the east, and were in many particulars quite different from anything European.

Somehow the Cretan and the northern influences coalesced in Greece to form the Mycenaean culture of the Homeric heroes. How this happened is not known. Greeks may have sailed to Crete and learnt from the Cretans, or brought Cretans back to work for them. Or Cretans may have settled in Greece and planted their culture there about 1900 B.C., not very long before, or after, the Greeks arrived to assimilate it, and change it. Or the Cretan ideas and practices may have spread to Greece by what is called 'culture creep' without any considerable movement to Greece of actual Cretan people. Or the immigrants from Asia who gave an impulse to the Middle Minoan age in Crete, and perhaps a little later imposed on Greece their characteristic place-names, and besides more doubtful contributions, the methods of building which were developed in Mycenaean fortresses, may have imparted also, before or when the first Greeks came, other elements of culture which are now naturally regarded as Minoan. However it happened, the Mycenaean culture is clearly a blend of Cretan, and perhaps also eastern, with northern ideas and traditions. Nearly everything in it can be traced to the north, to the east, or to the south; and though there are still plenty of obscure details, the obscurities are no argument against the main truth.

That was the world in which Greek epic poetry arose, and gave Homer to the future.

Speakers of Indo-European began entering Asia Minor and Greece and Italy not very long after 2000 B.C. Linguistic research has proved so much, and other evidence, not quite so conclusive, supports the linguistic. Mycenaean culture on the Greek mainland, almost from its appearance in the eighteenth century, develops rather differently from the parent Minoan culture of Crete. Northern influences seem to have been at work already. The Greeks were coming into Greece; probably they came in successive waves: first speakers of Arcadian and Ionic, and then speakers of West Greek dialects, Achaeans about 1400–1200 B.C., and a century later Dorians. The sequence is doubtful, but it is clear that the Greeks were arriving in those centuries, and at many places and times the conditions of a heroic age must have occurred. There is little doubt that something like epic composition must have been practised quite early in those centuries; but the circumstances of it are obscure.

Greek was spoken in Greece not long after 2000 B.C., but scarcely everywhere, or by everyone, until centuries later. Presumably there survived also the language of the earlier neolithic population, or the language of the invaders from Asia Minor who just before 2000 B.C. left place-names of the type of Corinth and Parnassos in Greece. Greece was until recently thought to have had a long bilingual period, when Greek and Minoan were both spoken side by side; and the discovery of 620 tablets, inscribed with a form of writing known as Linear Script B, at the newly-found palace of the Southern Pylos in 1939 seemed for a while likely to reinforce strongly the belief, which had been growing rather precarious, that the Minoan language persisted effectively among Mycenaeans. We now have reason to suppose that it did not. The partial decipherment by Ventris shews the language of the tablets to be Greek, not 'Minoan' (see Preface, p. 11 above).

This question affects the problem of the origin of Greek epic. Homer has been supposed to depend considerably on Minoan originals, current in the Peloponnese during Mycenaean times (Nilsson). There is no doubt that many or most of the important Greek myths go back as far; they may be called Mycenaean, but it is uncertain that they were ever related in the Minoan language. It is likely however that among Homer's sources, direct or indirect, was material, oral or written, in other than the Greek language. An example is the fourteenth century 'catalogue of ships' on a document from a place in northern Syria, Ras Shamra, obviously belonging to a type of list, current in the Mediterranean long before Homer, to which Homer's catalogue of ships ultimately belongs. Without exaggerating Phoenician or other Semitic influence on Homer, it is legitimate to see in the *Odyssey* a form derived from eastern poems, especially the *Journey of Ishtar* and *The Epic of Gilgamish*. The Hittites had two languages in use, a 'language of men', their own which they had brought with them, and a 'language of the gods', which they found in Cappadocia, and continued to use for religious observances. There are in Homer several pairs of synonyms given, the one 'in the language of men' and the other 'in the language of the gods' (*Il.* 1. 403; 2. 813–14; 14. 291; 20. 74: cf. *Od.* 10. 305; 12. 61). These languages have been supposed the incoming and the indigenous; but here the language of the gods is now generally attributed to the invaders, though not by every one. Homer may be in contact with an Eastern source; or there may be evidence here that Mycenaean Greece was bilingual.

The Greek epic tradition is in any case old, and, whether it was in any sense affiliated to the Minoan language or not, it belongs mainly to the Greek language. The hexameter was old when the Greek poet Callinus, about 700 B.C., mentioning Homer for the first time in extant records, attributed the old epic poem, the *Thebais*, to him. It is not easy to doubt that hexameters like Homer's, if not Homer's own, were composed in 900 B.C., and had taken many centuries to reach such perfection; the evolution is not fully understood, but it is supposed that the hexameter grew slowly from two or more simple and shorter elements.

There are indications in Homer, who cannot with probability be dated much later than about 800 B.C., that the Greek language in association with the hexameter had already had a long history. A theory that Homer's poems, surviving in Ionic, had been translated from Aeolic is now discredited, but like other discredited theories it contains important truth. There are Aeolic survivals in Homer. In the *Odyssey* (24.305) there is a joke. Odysseus pretends to be the son of Apheidas, who is called Polypemonides, 'son of "the man of many possessions" '. This name in its Ionic form, Polyktemonides, will not scan, and is accordingly left in an original but not so certainly intelligible Aeolic form. There are in Homer Ionic words with Aeolic terminations, as if at some time a poet familiar with Aeolic began to compose in Ionic and let the Aeolic terminations which were fixed in his memory become attached to Ionic words. It has been shewn that the Aeolic which lies behind Homer is not the Aeolic of early historic times, known from Sappho and Alcaeus to have been spoken in seventh century Lesbos, but an older Aeolic, spoken in the Greek mainland before Asia Minor was colonized. In this direction, too, point old words, of forgotten meaning, found in Homer and elsewhere only in Cyprus, where they must have been carried in very early times, perhaps the twelfth or thirteenth centuries, before the historical distribution of the dialects became fixed.

Homer certainly shews much knowledge of very ancient conditions, even going back to early Mycenaean date, the time of the 'shaft graves' of the earlier dynasty of the two which can be traced at Mycenae. He knows of Egyptian Thebes as a great and wealthy city, referring clearly to the fifteenth century, for after that time Thebes suffered a serious eclipse. In some of Homer's descriptions the memory of Mycenaean articles such as the 'Cup of Nestor' and Mycenaean helmets and shields is clear. It is reasonably certain that such knowledge must have been transmitted in something like Greek epic verse.

It is perhaps nearly or quite as likely that Greek epic verse was the vehicle of mythical and legendary tradition about heroic personalities. It is important not to confuse myth with poetry. It is possible and usual for a myth or legend to exist in one form in general belief and in quite a different form in the poetry of an actively artistic poet. In Homer especially anything may happen to a myth; it will be reproduced as Homer heard it only if he has no particular reason to change it. Such stories, then, must not be assumed to have a rigidly continuous identity in poetry, and the fact must be faced that poetry is their normal vehicle of transmission. A myth or legend, as it is in itself, that is, as it is without any alteration by an artistic poet, is often hard to identify. And it is not known how many artistic poets had handled Homer's myths before him.

Myths are often the verbal form which corresponds with ritual as part of a religious observance. A true cult myth, known from the cult which started it or from its recitation as part of the cult, can be trusted to be free from purely poetic distortion. And mythical or legendary genealogies in early documents, not far from the times at which the personalities have lived, or known to have been used for their practical value as records or title deeds, provided that they are coherent with themselves and any other known evidence, may also be trusted, but more guardedly. The question is whether mythical or legendary traditions can help to date or otherwise elucidate the origins of Greek epic.

Greek genealogies are some help. From the care with which heroes in Homer describe their descent in order to explain themselves, and perhaps too from the habit among later Greeks of supporting political claims by references to Homer, it is natural to infer that genealogical material was used for practical ends by early Greeks, as it was by other simple peoples such as the old Icelanders, and also the Maoris, whose genealogies, going back six centuries, were till lately used as title deeds. It is further natural to suppose that early Greek genealogies were conveyed in hexameter verse for centuries before Homer and the didactic poets wrote, as they were for generations, if not centuries, after their time. This is not certain, but nearly certain; and the probability is increased by the success with which genealogies, recorded in epic verse and by later prose writers, can be traced coherently to very early times indeed. This method is not of course entirely secure. Some genealogies involve contradictions and shew signs of arbitrary manipulations. It is never safe to think that artificiality and falsification did not intervene till in the sixth century prose writers began to edit traditional material; for though in earlier ages before writing began genealogies may have been jealously preserved as records of high practical importance, it is seldom certain that any particular genealogy is entirely accurate.

The heroic genealogies of the chief Homeric Achaeans only
go back a few generations; very often three are known.
Apparently Homer is reproducing without artistic manipula-
tion material which gives the descent of heroes from ancestors
who first entered Greece about a century before the Trojan
war, and honestly stops there. These 'divine born' dynasties,
such as the dynasties of Peleus and Tydeus, and of others,
many of whom have this same termination to their names,
appear to have come south as the last wave of immigrants
before the Dorians, a fact faithfully represented by their
genealogies. Other genealogies are longer. The Perseids are
traced to the sixteenth century, and there are lines which go
back even to the eighteenth or nineteenth centuries, at Argos in
the Peloponnese to Phoroneus, and at Athens to Cecrops.
There was an early Greek epic called the *Phoronis*, describing
the reign of Phoroneus and the establishment of early culture,
apparently Mycenaean culture, at Argos. In this poem, and in
many others too, it is hard to deny that much material survived
from very early centuries. There is little reason to doubt that
genealogical material, in something not entirely unlike the
form of ordinary Greek epic verse as we know it, began to be
generated as early or almost as early as the beginning of
Mycenaean times, and was retained in circulation.

This genealogical material in verse was not epic in the
strictest sense. Perhaps that can be said of nothing on earth
except the *Iliad* and *Odyssey*. But it is wisest to allow the word
epic to remain comprehensive. By derivation it means at first
a unit of any kind of talk, perhaps 'a mouthful', then a line of
verse, and lastly and particularly a hexameter line. Epic must
include for the present anything in Greek hexameters, or
whatever their ancestors in metrical form may be guessed to
have been.

But this assumed prerogative to use the word epic so compre-
hensively does not excuse distinctions. There is little doubt that
genealogical and other practically useful verse was composed
far back in the Mycenaean age. That is a constituent of
Homeric poetry, and has been noticed as an early characteristic, for early poetry is known to be fond of lists, genealogical
and other. It is not the main constituent, however. Much more
important is saga, stories of adventurous deeds by real men

who lived. It is saga, and the expression of it in the form of long or fairly long poems for recitation, which are characteristic of heroic ages, partly because they are adventurous ages, with plenty of stories to tell. The question is when Greek saga is likely to have begun. What is usually known as the Greek heroic age lasted between about 1300 and 1150 B.C., including the two wars of Argos with Thebes, and the war of a Greek confederacy with Troy. The heroic age is said to have had no other 'history'. From the traditions, it is clear that this was an age of adventure, individualism, military aristocracy, and minstrelsy, and so technically a heroic age. It generated epic poetry about its own adventures, which is remembered and to some extent reproduced in Homer and later Greek poetry. The proof of this is in Homer's knowledge, undeniable in spite of his manipulations of inherited story, of detailed facts about the Trojan war, such as the topography of Troy. Epic, though not Homeric epic, existed in the thirteenth and twelfth centuries. Whether in the sense of poetic saga it existed before, is less certain. The history is not known, and there may not have been men of adventure and minstrelsy. More probably there were, however.

Mycenaean culture looks, from excavation, fairly secure and settled, though heavy fortification was necessary, and there are breaks in continuity, especially in the fifteenth century. It is to be supposed however that at least sometimes there were waves of immigrants from the north, at longer or shorter intervals, and unsettled conditions. Archaeological hints are indecisive, except for certain signs of destruction and new arrivals at the ends of the early and the middle Mycenaean periods. It is not easy, either, to find genuine traditions of events, as it is for the twelfth and thirteenth centuires. The stories are much affected by pure myth, that is, the spoken part of religious cult which takes narrative form and comes to seem an account of an adventure which happened once to historic individuals, instead of the ritual speech and prayers, and the directions for performing ritual, which in fact it is. It cannot be assumed that we have traditions of adventures earlier than the First Theban War. Some stories may well contain them, for example stories of the Danaids and Perseids, and the relations with Egypt which appear to reflect history; but the intervention of myth, and confusion of chronology, make all confidence precarious.

The earlier centuries, then, may have produced saga, and there is one apparent origin for it which is exceedingly likely. It is possible to infer that Minyans living at and near Iolcos in north-eastern Greece in the fourteenth century or soon after had traditions of the voyage of the Argo, and to see the effect of these traditions in the *Odyssey*. The *Odyssey* in its earliest form can be traced to Boeotia in northern Greece, where the name of Odysseus, and other names belonging to the story, are at home among people of Minyan connections. The Minyans, as tradition in Homer and in later writers attests, sent some of their members to Arcadia, to western Peloponnese where the Minyan Nestor ruled, and probably north-westward from there to the Ionian islands, including Ithaca. Then came the Trojan War, and a prince returning from Troy, whose real name may or may not have been Odysseus, was made to carry the circumstance of older legend and myth. The Minyans, then, may be the first known creators of epic in Greece, first by saga, and then by myth overlaid on saga, which in turn came to be overlaid on saga of a later day. But, as ever, folk-tale entered too, and the *Odyssey* is built of many stories that are world wide beyond the saga and myth which are perhaps, but only perhaps, primary in it.

The history of Greek epic then begins with genealogical material, and perhaps other kinds which can only be guessed, probably in the early generations of Mycenaean times. Saga becomes clear about the thirteenth century, though it may have existed before. The great age of epic in its earlier stage lasted till the twelfth century. Contemporary events were recorded, and the saga grew from complication to complication by accretion of myth, folk-tale, and other kinds of material.

Homer himself indicates some of the poetic history to which his work belongs.

There are three stages in the composition of epic poetry. The first stage is contemporary and may be almost immediate. Lays about a battle are composed, often extemporarily on the very day of the battle, or the day after. Minstrels are recorded to have performed such immediate lays to Attila the Hun; and Achilles in the *Iliad* (9. 186) seems to be doing much the same when he stays in his tent, performing lays to himself and to his friend Patroclus, with a harp. Elsewhere in Homer the minstrels Phemius, in Ithaca, and Demodocus, in Scheria, perform lays which seem to belong to a set repertory, but they none of them seem old; the ministrels have made them up themselves, possibly with help from lays which they have heard other minstrels perform, all within a few years. The principle is even stated in Homer that the newest lay is usually liked best (*Od.* 1. 351).

But Phemius and Demodocus are really in the second stage, the stage of later creation, repetition, or adaptation, the stage in which Homer is himself. This is the stage of memory and tradition, not direct description of events which have just occurred, but their preservation and revival. Court poets had a repertory. There may still have been kings and chieftains, before whom the lays were performed. Often, and by Homer's own time generally, kings had given place to aristocracies. Conditions were more settled, and it was no longer a 'heroic age', with exciting events, fit to be related in lays, occurring almost daily. So old events were retained; it is noticeable that the heroes of epic are people about whom good stories happen to exist, not people who in themselves were likely to interest the audiences of later times.

The third stage is after Homer. The epic art ceases to be aristocratic, and comes to be enjoyed by the poorer classes. Minstrels perform to them, sometimes perhaps because economic and political changes have taken their aristocratic employers away. The minstrels may perform the same poems; or they may adapt the epic style to impart useful knowledge. This is what the chief didactic poet, Hesiod, did, and the other poets of his school. There was a similar stage in England in the dark ages, when the Church was anxious about the interest taken by the poorer classes in recitations of epic poems, with their pagan associations. The Church prevailed, and the recitations died out; but before they did a Christian colour was overlaid on some of the poetry, and is in fact clear in the poem *Beowulf.*

Homer comes at the end of a long poetic history. Greek epic verse was hundreds of years old when he used it in the ninth or eighth century B.C. It may have been a thousand years old, and have begun its life at about the time, not many generations after 2000 B.C., when Greek was first spoken in Greek lands.

Analogy suggests that epic tradition is generally long; but even if it is long everywhere else, it still may not have been long among the Greeks. The Anglo-Saxon epic had an active life of three centuries, and the Russian, of which the poems called the *byliny* are the example, of twelve. The South Slavic epic is still a living art after a life of six centuries; and in New Zealand the Maoris have still, or had till very recently, a tradition about as long.

It must have taken a long time for the Homeric metre to reach its final grace and power, but there is no way of saying how long. The language of Homer gives a similar indication but more definite. It is Ionic, one of the three main dialects, at a distinctly earlier stage than that found in any other Greek writer except Hesiod; and even the language of Hesiod is clearly later, if not much later. Homer's language is mixed. It has forms of words and words which are otherwise unknown or scarcely known. Some of them either belong to a much earlier stage of language than most of Homer's Ionic dialect, or to a different dialect altogether. There are the Aeolic forms and the words which were already obsolete when Homer used them (p. 38, above). It is practically certain that these signs mean that Homer includes in his verse elements of language which had been maintained in the epic tradition and had formed parts of hexameter verse for at least two hundred years before his time.

Homer in part describes the world of his own day but in part a much earlier world, not merely of Mycenaean times but even of the earlier period of them. As we have seen (p. 38, above), he tells of Egyptian Thebes as it was in the fifteenth century, and there are memories of objects in Homer which go back to the earlier, 'shaft grave' dynasty at Mycenae, before the 'beehive tomb' dynasty succeeded it about 1400 B.C. All this applies to things remembered, not necessarily epic tradition, or the preservation of the memories in hexameter verse; it is likely that that is how the memories were retained, but not certain.

The things which Homer says about Troy, Ithaca, and other places which concern him prove that some details were remembered very accurately, and many not so accurately, but with considerable precision. It is hard to see how details could have been remembered so well without the epic verse to retain them in their fixed form; if they had been preserved in ordinary talk, they must surely have been dislocated and falsified, just as Homer's more general account of larger matters has been altered and adapted by poetical design, or by the inaccuracy of tradition, when it is a question of keeping parts of the story, probably contained previously in different poems, in their original relation. The verse itself will preserve a small detail, but not a large expanse of narrative, if there is a reason to reorganize the narrative for the sake of a different plan.

There is little doubt that Homer knew Greek epic poetry in hexameter verse which was composed within a generation of the Trojan War, and that he incorporated in the *Iliad* and *Odyssey* many lines of it almost or quite unchanged, and perhaps some quite long passages. He probably included parts of a great number of poems of various ages, some composed not long before his time, and very possibly some even older than the Trojan War. Such a long tradition so used is usual in epic poetry; and Homeric poetry shews many signs that it is normal in this respect, and none which prove that it is not.

Lately traditional heroic songs still being sung by the Bosnian Moslems, especially those on the old Montenegrin border, have been collected and examined (Abbott). They are the only songs known which approximate in length to the longest Greek heroic poems. From them it appears that oral poetry need not be recited by whole poems at one session, that Homeric poetry need not necessarily be composed of separate lays each complete for a single occasion, and that the scale and to some extent the internal distribution of Homeric poetry is compatible with and quite probably characteristic of oral poetry.

It has been well stated: 'To oral antecedents Homer owes traditional formulae, the groups of words, especially nouns, and above all proper names, with fixed epithets, which recur again and again. These formulae do not prove that Homer was illiterate, or that his poetry is the work of many poets rather than one; it is even maintained that the repetitions in Homer are entirely explicable on the assumption that they have a meaning as parts of a poetic whole; and since they can be thus explained, it is quite unnecessary to assume that they were forced upon a series of singers because of their inability to write.'[1]

Homer himself may certainly have been able to write. There was writing in Minoan Crete, and it has been preserved in quantities on clay tablets. There was writing among the Mycenaeans; but till the recent finds of tablets at Pylos and elsewhere, it was known only from certain marks, apparently alphabetic, on vases of about 1230 B.C., and an inscription from Asine in Argolis, a line and a half long, and of about the same date. The Hittites wrote, and more than 20,000 of their clay tablets are preserved. Many of them have been read with some degree of security. In Babylonia writing was common from well before 3000 B.C. In Egypt writing begins quite suddenly with the First Dynasty and can scarcely be said ever to have stopped; hieroglyphics were still written in the early centuries A.D. There were many systems of Syrian writing. In or near that area writing has begun by about 2000 B.C.

For the Greeks, Syrian writing is the most relevant, for three reasons taken together. It continues through into the dark ages, and the Syrian writing used before and after the Dorian Invasion about 1100 B.C. is not very different. The Greeks were never quite out of touch with Syria, as they were out of touch with Egypt, probably from the twelfth century, until the revival of trade relations in the seventh. Thirdly, the alphabets of ancient Greece and Italy, and of Europe and America today, are inherited from the alphabets of Syria, especially the Phoenician.

The names of the Greek letters are unintelligible in Greek but not in Hebrew, where most of them are found. A, *alpha*, A, is *aleph* in Hebrew and the word means an ox. B, *beta*, B, is *beth* in Hebrew and means a house; to us the word is best known in Bethel, Beth–El, House of the Lord, and to the Greeks it was further known in βαίτυλος, baitylos, which means a meteoric stone, regarded as containing supernatural power, and so a kind of 'House of the Lord', like megalithic menhirs, often called 'spirit houses'. G, *gamma*, Γ, is *gimel* in Hebrew,

---

[1] I have been unable to trace the author of this quotation.— J.D.C.

and means a camel; the word came into Greek twice, first as the letter and then as a name for camel, κάμηλος, kamēlos, the same word as our own. One of the most interesting letters is the *Digamma* or *Wau*. The sign of the letter in Hebrew gave us, through the Greek F, our F, and its Hebrew name, *Wāw*, gave one of the names by which the Greeks called the letter.

The Greek alphabet was said to have been brought to Greece by Cadmus, the Phoenician, when he came from Phoenicia to settle at Thebes in Boeotia. The traditional date is 1430 B.C., too early for Phoenicians, but not for Minoans, and Cadmus may have been a Minoan. Herodotus (V. 59) claims to have seen three tripods bearing inscriptions in 'Cadmean letters'. They would not, at that date, have been obviously antecedents of Greek letters. But there is a time at which a Phoenician, or at least a Syrian, alphabet comes very close to the earliest forms of the Greek alphabet. That is about 1000 B.C. It is possible enough that a southern or eastern alphabet was introduced into Greece twice, once before the end of Mycenaean times, and again after the Dorian invasion. The earliest Greek inscriptions, from the island of Thera, belong to the end of the eighth century. The comparison of alphabets makes it very likely that 'Phoenician' writing had been known in Greece for perhaps about two centuries before, that is from about the tenth century.

There now exists a solution of at least part of the problem, by the help of the Pylian tablets which belong apparently to a date about 1200 B.C., the end of the Mycenaean Age, within about a generation of the Trojan War. They prove that writing could be freely used in Greece at about Trojan times, and that a former opinion, that Minoan Crete was contrasted with Mycenaean Greece through its habitual use of writing, can no longer stand.

Homer gives no proof himself that he knew of writing. He mentions something like it twice, marks of identification scratched on lots, pebbles to be tossed out of a helmet to decide which hero should fight Paris, and 'tokens of destruction on a tablet', some sort of message taken by Bellerophon to Lycia and meant to make his host there work his death. The 'tokens' were understood, though Bellerophon managed to escape; but they were not necessarily writing, and may have been pictures, like the pictures of unauthorized killing and legal execution by which the Maoris of New Zealand were first made to understand that under British rule there was the same law for white men and coloured men alike.

It is also by no means necessary that Homer should have had to use writing to compose and remember long poems, an argument which was used by Wolf about a hundred and seventy years ago. The South Slavic poems, comparable in length to Homer's, and certainly composed and preserved orally, prove that Greek epic does not presuppose writing. Instances are recorded of Greeks who knew the *Iliad* and *Odyssey* by heart, and there are many examples in ancient and modern times of such great powers of memory among both literate and illiterate people. There is a modern instance of a Balkan minstrel who knew a hundred thousand verses by heart, and that is more than three times as many as there are in the *Iliad* and *Odyssey* together.

Minoan and Mycenaean writing may have been forgotten in the dark age after the Dorian invasion, and there is no proof of Greek writing before the inscription at Thera. Homer himself certainly did not necessarily know how to write. But there is little doubt that he either did know, or could have learnt. He certainly lived between 900 and 750 B.C., in the period in which the Phoenician alphabet was introduced from Syria to Greece. It is likely that Homer used his memory and imagination to create his poems, without help from writing, but also likely that he himself used writing to preserve the poems for his own use, and that his school of followers, the Homeridae, did so also. Very old official texts of Hesiod and also the Homeric *Hymn to Apollo* are known to have been preserved, one in Boeotia in North Greece and the other in the island of Delos. They may have been started by the original poets.

The poetry in Homer is, or is near to, oral poetry and has the qualities of oral poetry. These qualities are what would be expected. The poetry is stirring, rapid, and never dull to a listening audience. It has many passages which are longer than they have to be, in order to give the audience time to follow the story without becoming exhausted by perpetual crisis and excitement. It is careless about details, such as strict metre, and even grammar, sometimes; it does not worry very much about what would not be noticed in a recitation. The words are put together as they come, controlled by the poet's sense of rhythm, and by his memory of the story, and of great quantities of poetry about the story, which he is telling, and about other stories also. Words attract other words, and are remembered together with them; many lines are built not so much of words, as of groups of words, which come again and again. Many whole lines come again and again, and are in fact groups of words which have grown together, and stay together. In particular the same adjective is found time after time with the same noun. The metre helps this to happen. Only a limited number of expressions will fit into the metre, and the poets were accordingly controlled. Control is good for poetry. In this sort of poetry there is necessarily what might now be called a free use of clichés. Clichés are sometimes very bad, and always need care, or they run away with you. But they are often very useful and indeed necessary, to save strain and time and to be communicative. They are much more general than they look, for when they are good they are not called clichés. All Latin prose, our Church services, and the newspapers, including the leading articles of the best papers, are full of them. They are useful if only to reduce the attention given to the ordinary parts of the thought in order to direct it to the special, new, part or purpose which the ordinary parts serve. In oral poetry generally, including Greek, something like the cliché happens to be particularly good and useful. It is part of the way the poetry comes to the mind of the poet, and also, by the mystic unity which governs these matters, part of the way an audience can best listen.

Oral poetry is a kind of communal sacrament, in which the minstrel, the audience, and the 'god' or 'muse', as Homer calls the mysterious impulse to poetry, all share. There is a complicated system of reactions between minstrel and audience, and to a certain degree the god or muse is a name for the system. There is intense pleasure and exaltation, for many reasons. The minstrel enjoys the sense of power, his own delight in the poetry, the sympathy of the audience, and the anticipation of great effects to come after suspense. The audience enjoys the sound and rhythm, the beautiful pathos, the triumph of right in the story, admiration for gods, heroes, and the minstrel himself, the thrills of imagined love, and relief after danger. Both sides enjoy a mental release from practical restrictions. They love thinking what they cannot or may not do or suffer. And both sides react on each other and increase each other's emotion and exaltation.

Obviously, subjects which fit in best with this situation are preferred. So the nature of oral poetry controls its subjects; so, also, does the nature of the society in which oral poetry occurs, for it is always a not very advanced society, in which a certain few interests are stronger than others.

Oral poetry is therefore about travels, wonders, quarrels, battles, exciting love affairs, admired and dreaded heroes, who are brave and strong, wealth and works of craftsmanship; lists of people and places in which the audience can recognize, with joy after a wait, the ones which are known to it; and restful ordinary things, like the preparation of dinners, and washing, and changing your clothes.

In the long centuries in which Greek oral poetry developed, there must have been many kinds of poem. There were the lists, some genealogical. There were tales of quarrels and love affairs. There were war stories of great deeds and victories. There were travel stories, fairy-tales, and short romantic novels. Epic verse was used for almost every purpose, but especially for sagas of real events, fairy-tales of wonders, and folk-tales sometimes developed into romance. The single stories, designed for one recitation of one or two hours, were liable to much mixture and combination.

The complicated and little-known history of Greek oral poetry allows two certain statements. There were short poems, handed down orally for centuries; and there presently came a time, perhaps in the tenth century or even long before, when a new and different art began, the art of constructing long poems, giving a complete story of about the scope of a modern novel. One way was to join existing stories of events into a longer whole in their natural sequence, without going far from the facts as they were known, but with the inclusion of wonders, such as divine interventions, and other additional material, principally through the natural tendency of stories to attract or develop fictitious enlargements. The Homeric poems go farther than this. They each tell a story planned not to give a mere account of events, but to be a real work of art in the full, almost modern, sense; a work of art shewing what men and their fortunes and characters are like, and how the divine world controls the world of time, and how through all the confusion of living a kind of eternal pattern runs.

The Homeric poems, the *Iliad* and *Odyssey*, have sources in many earlier poems of very varying length. Homer (to call him the poet of both *Iliad* and *Odyssey*, which is exceedingly likely, but not quite certain) used his sources in the same or nearly the same way as other poets have used theirs. The poet's mind stores impressions, some gained from thought and direct sense-perception, but many from former poetry, or at least partly from it. Remembered words and rhythms and sounds control and direct thought and feeling long after they are heard. Impressions of all kinds linger in the poet's unconscious mind, and combine together. At the moment of creation the poetry comes, telling a new story in words and combinations of words, and in sounds and rhythms, that are partly old.

There is a development in this method. Minstrels of oral poetry might use old poems unchanged, though at least small changes were likely at every recitation. A good performance was wanted rather than definition of authorship. The impressions might be all or nearly all from earlier poetry, and they might come out exactly as they went in, without even any rearrangement or recombination. At the other extreme are Vergil and Coleridge, who wrote poetry with several spontaneous verbal echoes of earlier literature in every line for perhaps pages on end, but scarcely leave any two or three words without some alteration.

Homer is in between, but nearer to the later poets. He makes little attempt to keep to the traditional sequence, significance, or motive of actions. He introduces names, and even events, from anywhere, and makes quite new uses of them, provided that they catch his imagination and help his artistic design. His major technique works by such integration of former elements. But his minor technique, in matters of single verses or words or word groups, may or may not work that way. There may be much less change. Homer may use hundreds of lines at a stretch, as they were left by some other poet, and either unchanged or little changed. But he often gives us verses which seem to be his own, perhaps containing old formulae, but melted and fused anew in his own mind. It is very unlikely that he was sure which of his verses had been used by himself first, and which by another poet before him. All this fits well with the conditions of oral poetry, which was meant for general effect, not examination on a written page. It was right and reasonable not to waste time on recomposing verses which were easily good enough; and it would have been very difficult to recompose in different words, but so as to tell the same story, a passage already running unforgettably in your head.

In reading Homer now from printed books, we sometimes notice a change of style and mannerisms which we are not expecting, as we come to a new part of the poetry, taken from a different source. We may object to this, as to other consequences of the oral tradition. This does not mean that we do not and cannot like Homer, but simply that we have to learn the grammar of the criticism which will help us to like him most. You have to get used to any poet and know something about him to like him as much as you should. With Homer, it is necessary sometimes to imagine that the reading is a recitation; that is, to keep the whole picture and the larger meanings of the story in view, and above all go quickly, if possible listening to the sound of the verse and not stopping at what is a little strange. There is no need to let yourself disagree with a world of poets and critics and readers who have let Homer gain and keep a sovereign supremacy.

It is now too late to doubt that Homer is incomparable, unique, and supreme. Anyone with a little trying can reach the frame of mind, and acquire the small amount of mental furniture, which are needed before the immense revelation of Homer's grandeur and loveliness will flash upon him.

You may or may not like poetry or languages. Andrew Lang was compelled to learn Greek, and at once developed what he called 'a hissing and malignant hatred' of it—till he chanced to see some lines of Homer, and then immediately changed round, and devoted his life to him. Schliemann did not know Greek, had never started it. When he was a boy, he heard an eccentric customer in his father's shop start reciting Homer suddenly. The effect on him was violent. He made it his aim to dig up Troy, which no one then thought even historical. He started with nothing, made two fortunes—the second was needed because he lost the first,—learnt twelve languages, and won. He started Homeric archaeology.

Homer is like other epic poets in aristocratic dignity, force of will, and courage against man and fate and gods above; like them in gentle courtesy and forethought, and in delight in ordinary things and zest for life, grand and simple, the sweet and the bitter too. Homer is like other epic poets in these ways, however much he excels them. There are other ways too. Homer shews man in danger, his one hope honour and maintenance of the code. He shews him almost hopeless in this life, yet winning and saving something, perhaps almost all; and quite hopeless before the world to come, a world containing only misery and passive weakness, just what a Homeric hero would hate. And all around and through is the strong winged music, now dainty and marvellous, and now furious, like seas and winds on rocks, at the need; and also the clear sharp precision of human forms, lovely and terrible, speaking out of the stream of time, and giving meaning to the world for man. This part perhaps belongs to all Greek epic, however much Homer's may excel the rest.

It comes to this. Homer can be a great epic poet, and then too a great Greek epic poet, before he has fully begun to be Homer. What it is to *be* Homer is hard to say.

Homer has grandeur, rapidity, directness. That is well known. In a way the rapidity and directness are there to help the grandeur, and grandeur is a word for a very great deal that Homer is.

The earliest European literature is Homer's poetry, and many people think it still the best. Homer left two long poems, the *Iliad* of 15,693 lines, and the *Odyssey* of 12,110. They are known to have existed before 700 B.C., and they are probably a century or two centuries earlier than that date. So they are now not many centuries less than three thousand years old.

The *Iliad* is a tale of war, how when Greeks from Greece were attacking the city of Troy on the south shore of the Dardanelles about 1200 B.C., a quarrel between Agamemnon, the supreme king of the Greek confederacy, and Achilles a subordinate chief led to terrible consequences, till the two leaders were reconciled. The *Odyssey* is a tale of travel and home life, how Odysseus, the wisest man among the Greeks, had terrible adventures on land and sea during his return, but came to his home in Ithaca, an island a few hours' sail south of Corfu, in the twentieth year, and found his wife Penelope waiting faithfully for him.

The poems are works of the greatest splendour, and have had much to tell all humanity since, not least ourselves, today. They were 'the Bible of the Greeks', and helped the Greeks to make Rome create out of Greece a world of harmony. They can help us now by shewing how great and wonderful are some simple things, above all the will to forgive and the will not to despair. The poems compel us to love and value such things, not by telling us to, but by shewing pictures, which we must believe. They are full of things that are a joy to hear and a peril to miss, from the clear vision of the value, greatness, and difficulty of human harmony, to be reached in the simplest and most natural, but never in the rough and most obvious way, to the right vision with which to look at the sea in storm, the stars, and the birds, and the pigs, and meals and tables and baths. Homer puts zest into everything, however simple, and gives us small excuse to miss anything, however sublime.

Homer is even more necessary than that. He is already part of us and we can be helped by being conscious of it. He singles out the great things of human experience, the strong main lines of the picture, and in them we can see ourselves, identify past and present, know the essential from the accidental, and take active and hopeful pride in holding membership in the pageant of man. Never was a great poet so simple, direct, clear, and utterly musical, as Homer, perhaps the greatest of all. So no other poet can have so much to tell that all people can easily understand. Most poets require special knowledge and a taste often hard to gain. There are conventions without obvious reasons, and strange, apparently needless, ways of expression. You have to learn to live in the poet's world, and sometimes that needs a lifetime.

The organization of Homer's world is feudal. Princes or barons lead their followers in the service of an overlord. They occupy land, on what right is uncertain, but it seems to be ultimately right of conquest. They rule over subjects, some or all of whom may have been members of an old population;

for it is usually supposed that the 'Achaean' barons of Homer were invaders from the north, who seized land in Greece from earlier owners, some of them earlier Greek invaders from the north but not Achaean Greeks, and others not Greek at all; for all Greeks in Greece came down from the north at some time.

These Achaeans lived in a 'heroic' age, an age of violent disturbance. Greece had had a high civilization for about five centuries before the Trojan War of about 1200 B.C. It owed much to Crete, and something to the north, whence several waves of invaders came. The Achaeans were violently expansive, and indeed destructive. But they had a real and admirable culture, with a finished code of chivalry. They lived in homes of wood and stone, like northern halls, within defended courtyards. They fought partly with bows, but more with spears for thrusting or throwing and swords which could cut or give point. Bronze was the metal of war, and gold and silver were plentiful; iron was little used yet, except perhaps for tools, where tempering, not yet understood, was less necessary. Ships were sailed and rowed. They had a mainmast with one square mainsail and fifty oars. They were narrow in the beam, and designed to be fast cruisers or corsairs. Chariots drawn by a pair of horses were common, but horses were not normally ridden.

You can picture a Homeric hero in different ways. The turnout varied. The older style included a large shield as big as a man, the newer a smaller, round shield. There was a helmet and plume, hard to describe; it may or may not have been like the later Greek helmet which has left some of its shape to the helmets of Italian and French cavalry. There were tunics cut to shape, and mantles, squares of cloth draped and pinned, white or coloured. Swords were worn from a shoulder belt. Women had simple straight frocks.

Homeric heroes, unlike later Greeks, seem to have lived mainly on roast meat. They ate bread, and also cheese. They drank wine from grapes. They wiped themselves with olive oil after their frequent hot baths.

They worshipped a sky-god, Zeus, with prayers and burnt sacrifices of animals. Zeus was a guardian of morality, especially towards the helpless, beggars, strangers, and all who appealed for mercy. There were other gods and goddesses. The Achaeans believed in dreams and other prophecy, but Homer in general displays them as in the main free from ghost-worship and magic.

Homer's world is easy. There is always a little mystery and surprise, habits, conventions perhaps, not quite obvious. A certain amount of that is an immense help to poetry, because it keeps wonder alive, and dramatic illusion. Even to us, Homer has only just enough of the puzzling things, usually. He is so very natural and direct, using universal forms of thought and seeing, for all his majesty and for all his humour.

To read Homer, in Greek or in translation, not much is necessary in advance. You must remember that the story matters most, and that what the people are like and what happens to them are questions full of significance. It follows that the best translations are the simplest, which do not interfere with your attempt to follow the story by extraordinary and artificial words. Prose translations are better than verse translations. Your own imagination must be given its chance, and you must be allowed to follow the story quickly. Next, it is wise, and quite easy, to know enough Greek to listen to the music and force of the best passages. It is also a good thing to know enough Greek to read all Homer in Greek. If you do not know Greek, but have learnt, a little, how to listen to Homer and have had a chance to get to like Homer, the rest may be expected to follow spontaneously.

It is, too, best to be ready for Homeric conditions of life. Homer's world is spacious, full of variety, and with many of the broad facts and departments of interest that are to be found in any one's world, today or at any other time. Homeric people are people of refinement, usually aristocratic lords and ladies, in baronial halls; but they delight in the simplicities of the farm and the home. The men are fierce in war and proud and often self-willed; but hearts that seem stern are soft really, and melt for sympathy, fidelity, and love within a home. You might say that Homer's life was given to shewing that the gentle things are sovereign; it is a true paradox to say that both his great poems are really poems of love.

III

THE TIME AND PLACE OF HOMER

The greatest things have many times been done by men under the shadows. Long stress, and the habit of conflict, makes tension in the spirit, and active force.

The tension and the force were there in the age of the heroes, and also in the age of the Homer whom they found.

The Greeks thought Homer specially wise. For them that was what a poet ought to be. He should communicate some mental or spiritual possession, which could enrich the recipient, not only in static quality, but in action also. If you heard Homer, your state ought to be better, and your actions ought to be better, also.

That leads to difficulties when totally different and much more complicated analyses of the human life-principle are reached. In a developed philosophy of knowing and acting, distinctions arise, and a poet, in the light of them, does not communicate the newly defined critical, scientific knowledge, or present directly rules of conduct either morally or economically of peculiar value. This has no effect on the incontestable truth of what the Greeks thought, that Homer communicated, as he communicates still, a kind of wisdom. It simply happened that when other kinds of communication and other mental attitudes to reality were separated from the undifferentiated activity of life and examined, the precisely poetical kinds of communication and wisdom, which offer unusually hard problems, were not equivalently clarified and defined.

Greek history depends for its dates on Greek contemporary record. There were records in writing, in which holders of offices and victors in the games were listed. The priestesses of the temple of Hera at Argos, the kings of Sparta, who go back to the ninth century, and the victors at Olympia, beginning in 776 B.C. at the first accurately remembered occasion of the four-yearly Olympic games, provided the time-sequences most used for fixing dates. The three scales are sometimes all used for one event, if it is important. Thucydides does this. Besides these very well known sequences there were others, local records of officials, secular and religious. There were also family traditions, going still farther back.

Chronology becomes fairly trustworthy from the start of the Olympic sequence. From there on, most events can be brought into relation with each other, and their years can often be fixed. Before the Olympic and other known sequences which were recorded in writing, there is traditional material, orally transmitted so far as can be known, and concerned principally with genealogies. Some of the genealogies are very long indeed. They may even go back far into prehistoric ages. The 'heroic' genealogies of Athens and Argos even reach into the eighteenth century B.C., that is, nearly or quite to the time when Greek was first spoken in Greek lands, and the civilization of Mycenae began.

The preliterary, mainly genealogical, material includes much that is accurate and valid, in Greece, as elsewhere, especially in New Zealand and Iceland, where orally transmitted genealogies were accurately preserved for centuries, and served practical ends as title deeds for the possession of land. But in Greece at any rate the genealogies cannot always be trusted. They have contradictions; they have been adjusted to cohere with other kinds of record, especially myth; and they have been edited again and again by the genealogists and chronographers, to bring them into agreement with themselves and other kinds of statement. These processes started very early, and it is often impossible to say where genuine 'folk-memory' ends and the results of adjustment begin.

But adjustments, or rather inferences from the inherited material, were not always misleading. Careful Greek writers worked out useful schemes of chronology from the Trojan War. The Parian Marble gives such a scheme; and Eratosthenes another. From such computations the Greeks themselves agreed that the Trojan War was fought about 1200 B.C. The date given by Eratosthenes, 1193 to 1183 B.C., is widely accepted. Even now, as discoveries of many kinds are made, they do not have much effect on the dating. At present the most probable date is a little earlier, about 1230 B.C., perhaps.

But the Greeks themselves failed to agree about the date of Homer. There are three beliefs about it.

Hecataeus and Eratosthenes thought Homer a contemporary of the heroes of whom he tells, about 1200 B.C.

Thucydides (I. 3, 3) says that Homer lived long after the

Trojan War, and Herodotus (II. 53, 2) that both Homer and
Hesiod lived four hundred years, not more, before himself,
which would be about 850 B.C.

Theopompus regards Homer and Archilochus of Paros as
contemporaries, so that Homer's date would be about 700 B.C.

By Homer it is hard to mean any one but the supreme poet
who created the harmony and revelation of Homeric poetry.
Hecataeus and Eratosthenes can only be right if they refer to
some poet who furnished Homer with sources, an epic poet
who made poems of the tale of Troy soon after the events.
Homer undoubtedly depends on at least one such predecessor,
because his poetry is very often in close touch with the original
facts. But the poems as we have them imply a long interval
between Homer and Trojan times, as Thucydides saw.

Some of the reasons for this are as follows. Homer often
contrasts the men of his day with the men of Trojan times in the
Iliad. 'Two such men, as men are now' could not lift into a
wagon a boulder which Hector lifted unaided, and threw at the
gate of the Achaean camp. Diomedes also threw a rock at
Aeneas, and Aeneas threw one, described in the same words,
at Achilles. (12. 445–9; 5. 302–4; 20. 285–7; also 1. 271–2;
12. 380–3.)

Twice in the *Odyssey* (16. 294; 19. 13) iron is mentioned in a
proverb, 'iron by its very self can lure a man to act'. That
shews that already iron had been well known for weapons long
enough for it to start a proverbial saying. Iron elsewhere in
Homer is used for tools, but seldom for weapons. Possibly it
was used for tools first, and bronze was kept for weapons because
it was better known, and trusted more for important purposes.
No iron weapons have been found at Mycenae. They occur
first about 1100 in Thessaly and Syria. Homer composed when
iron was used, and probably had been much used, for a long
time; and therefore he lived a considerable time after the
Trojan War.

In mentioning iron Homer represents his own Hellenic age
rather than the Mycenaean age of Trojan times. He appears to
do so also in describing Greek armour, helmet, shield, corslet,
greaves, instead of, and as well as, Mycenaean armour, the
large tower shield, without a metal helmet or other armour;
Greek cremation instead of Mycenaean embalming and

inhumation; Greek temples instead of Mycenaean chapels and altars and high places; Greek statues, instead of Mycenaean symbols; and indeed Greek religion, with a supreme god Zeus, at home on the northern Greek mountain Olympus, and surrounded by other gods and goddesses of varied functions and subject to him like a baron's retainers, instead of the Mycenaean religion, of a simpler, less organized sort, with a single supreme goddess and a younger male associate, not a large variety of departmental divinities. Some of these elements of culture may however prove to be considerably earlier than Homer himself. It is beginning to seem that his heroes are armed more or less as real warriors might have been armed, and were armed in eastern armies, about 1000 B.C.

These and other comparisons do not always prove as much as they are thought to prove.

The armour in Homer is sometimes apparently 'Hellenic' and sometimes Mycenaean. But the apparently 'Hellenic' armour need not be late. It is very like the armour shewn on the very late Mycenaean 'Warrior Vase' from Mycenae, on which are marching men carrying round shields and wearing greaves and plumed helmets. The date is about 1200 B.C. At this time similar equipment was used in Western Asia. Corslets, plumed headdresses, and round shields are worn by Philistines in Egyptian pictures just about the time of the Trojan War; and the round shields and plumes are even represented on the Phaistos Disk, a round plaque with a spiral inscription, not yet deciphered, found in southern Crete and dated 1600 B.C. It follows that 'Hellenic' armour, or something sufficiently like it, may have been worn by the heroes at Troy, as well as the Mycenaean. Homer mainly represents this, probably actual, kind of armour. But even so he sometimes altered inherited descriptions, bringing them into closer agreement with the armour universal in his own time. There are places where such adaptation, probably unconscious, has left discrepancies; for example (11. 15–46, 251–3), when Agamemnon is wounded, and the passage of the spear is described in detail, there are anomalies, as if originally he had been carrying a Mycenaean shield and not wearing full 'Hellenic' armour. But it remains true that differences of armour do not certainly prove that Homer lived long after the fall of Troy. The Warrior Vase shews us an armament actually in use at the time of the Trojan War, and extensively implied by Homer's descriptions, even when he seems to be thinking of the not very dissimilar equipment of full Hellenic times.

The Mycenaeans embalmed their dead and buried them in graves. The 'shaft graves' and 'beehive tombs' of princes at Mycenae are known. There is no cremation; signs of fire found in graves do not imply it, but rather something else, probably sacrifice. Homeric heroes would therefore be expected to practise inhumation. But in Homer cremation is universal. However, this proves nothing; for in the last excavations at Troy several cremation burials have been found. Perhaps Homer's accounts of cremation are true, or at most exaggerated, modernized and too exclusive; they need not necessarily be anachronisms.

Homeric religion certainly seems much nearer to Hellenic than to Mycenaean. The Olympian Family under Zeus and the Greek temples are quite different from anything Mycenaean. It is even barely possible that the Mycenaeans, unlike Homeric heroes and indeed unlike the Minoans also, disbelieved in a life after death, since the gold masks, laid on the faces of the dead, have their eyes tight shut. Other distinctions are less certain. In the *Iliad* (6. 264 *ff.*) Trojan women lay a robe on the knees of a seated statue of Athena, and in the *Odyssey* (7. 81) Athena goes to the 'solid house of Erechtheus' in Athens. That might look like an anachronism, as if Homer was thinking of Hellenic Athens. But there is evidence for large statues in Mycenaean times, though it is not very conclusive, and anyway there is no proof that large statues were unknown; they were universal in Egypt and usual in eastern lands; and after all the Homeric statue is not in Greece, but in Troy, which was an eastern city. No more can be argued from the reference to Athens. Athens was a Mycenaean centre, with a fortress on the Acropolis. The later Erechtheum or House of Erechtheus is on or near the site of the palace of Mycenaean princes; and it is known that the Hellenic goddess Athena herself is at least in part the descendant of the armed Mycenaean goddess of the home or palace or citadel. Moreover, we do not know how much Mycenaean life had grown to resemble later Hellenic life in the next generation or two after the fall of

Troy. The Hellenic outlook may have begun. The Olympian religion may have been known already. Many of its myths existed, and its feudal form is appropriate to heroic times. It is just possible, on this evidence, to suppose that Homer lived soon after the war.

Other internal evidence concerns objects and scenes described. Nestor in the *Iliad* (11. 632–7) uses a cup never understood until a real Mycenaean cup was found at Mycenae 'related in some degree', according to Miss H. L. Lorimer, to Homer's description. It is gold, and has two 'stalks' supporting its two handles, and two gold birds above them. The date is the fifteenth century B.C. Either the poetry, or the memory preserved, is very old; or a cup like this must have survived to be seen by the poet many centuries after it was made; and either supposition is credible. Again (11. 19–28), Agamemnon has a richly ornamented cuirass of various metals, which is called Phoenician work, a present from the Cypriote king, Cinyras. Its close parallels are in Cypriote work of the eighth and seventh centuries. But it is possible that there was work of Mycenaean date equally close to Homer's description. One of the most persuasive examples is the brooch clasping the dress of Odysseus described near the end of the *Odyssey* (19. 226–9). It is a relief of a dog pulling down a stag and eating it. There is no close parallel in any real object till the seventh century. Examples a little earlier could not have suggested the description. But though the motive could not have been fully executed in the depth of the dark age, between the Mycenaean and the early Hellenic cultures, it could easily be a Mycenaean memory; though there is no Mycenaean parallel, it is the kind of scene which Mycenaean art might easily have handled; and there is sufficient uncertainty about the dating of brooches, *fibulae*, as they are called, to leave open the possibility that the brooch of Odysseus represents a real brooch made before the fall of Troy. That any sort of brooch should be mentioned is significant within its limits for chronology. Brooches belong to Hellenic, northern dress, not southern; and Mycenaeans took over the southern, Cretan dress. But brooches, and therefore northern dress, begin well before the end of the Mycenaean age. Lastly, the description of the scene need not necessarily, according to Homer's words, apply to the brooch. It may, and so it was believed in antiquity, apply to the robe, and mean embroidery on it.

The Homeric poems, therefore, might conceivably have been created soon after the Trojan War, but the evidence so far suggests and practically proves, if it is taken all together, that several generations elapsed between the events of the poems and the poems themselves. This conclusion is positively confirmed by the nature of the poems and the history of their material. It is quite certain that the original versions of Trojan stories, though they might have become legendary, mythical, and artistic within one or two generations, could never have developed into the *Iliad* and the *Odyssey* nearly so soon. But that will be explained later in this book.

If the earliest date, chosen by Hecataeus and Eratosthenes, will not do, neither will the latest, given by Theopompus.

Homer has a different mental life and clearly belongs to a different age from Archilochus and the lyric and elegiac poets who soon followed him. Generations of experience must have been needed to change so much the focalization of man's address to the problems of his consciousness, and make him abandon the poetry of impersonally observed action for a poetry of inward-turning reflection.

There are more objective arguments. Later poetry presupposes Homer. The next extant poetry is poetry attributed to Hesiod, who was always supposed by the Greeks, with very few exceptions, to have been later than Homer.

Hesiod composed *The Works and Days*, in hexameter verse of the Homeric kind. Other poems went under his name, such as *The Origin of the Gods*. They seem to be the work of a school of poets going on for a long time. A passage seeming to be by Hesiod himself is astronomically dated to the ninth century B.C. by a remark that he makes about the time that Arcturus rose. This suggests that Hesiod lived not much later than 800 B.C. and would put Homer nearer 850 B.C.; which is to say that astronomy confirms Herodotus, the earliest and best literary authority.

The *Iliad* and *Odyssey* were followed by other epic poems about the tale of Troy, and they were carefully designed to describe events which belong to times before and after the Homeric poems. They vary in size and date and nature. All are after Homer, and not one seems to have had a spiritualized unity such as his poems have. The earliest are probably the *Aethiopis* and *The Sack of Troy*, attributed to Arctinus of Miletus, and both he and Lesches of Mitylene, said to have been the author of the *Little Iliad*, belong to the eighth century. The tradition says so; and, if it is wrong, there is no room for the other poets, who lived between then and the sixth century, when epic poetry was composed by Eugammon of Cyrene, that is, the place to which, of all Greek cities, Homer's poetry was last introduced.

Besides, the very early elegiac poet, Callinus, already in the eighth century mentions Homer, attributing to him an old epic, the *Thebais*. Homer soon begins clearly to influence other poets, such as Mimnermus of Colophon, who develops Homer's comparison of men to the leaves that perish.

These arguments shew that Theopompus' date of 700 B.C. is rather late. It may be safer to allow some margin of error, and to say that it need not be very much too late. Still later dates are surely wrong. Modern views that the Homeric poems were not finished till the sixth century are countered by the facts that Homer was certainly well known long before that, and had already exercised a wide influence for generations.

Homer lived and composed the *Iliad* and *Odyssey* about 800; he may have been born not long after 900, but he can hardly have been alive in 700 B.C.

There was a tradition about Homer himself. A guild called Homeridae lived in Chios, a large island towards the middle of the western coast of Asia Minor, one of the seven places which claimed to be Homer's birthplace—'Smyrna, Chios, Colophon, Salamis, Rhodos, Argos, Athenae'—they fit into a hexameter verse. Chios is the most likely to be right, and the Homeridae were a quite genuine institution. There were other institutions like them in Greece, claiming to be in the first place the descendants of a great man whose name they carry. For instance, there were the Eumolpidae at Eleusis, one of the two families which managed the Eleusinian Mysteries, and to whom Aeschylus belonged. Some of these guilds went by the name of a probably mythical ancestor, who never lived as a historical person; actually, though there are plenty of un-historical figures like Hellen, ancestor of the Hellenes, and

Dorus, of the Dorians, to whom tribes and nations are traced, it is doubtful if there is any instance in Greece in which the 'name father', the 'eponymous ancestor' of a family, can positively be proved to be unreal. Others carried the name of their calling, such as the other of the two families at Eleusis which managed the mysteries, the Kerykes, 'Heralds'. But there were many families named after a real founder, and discharging hereditary functions; and at first the Homeridae were one of them. Their function was poetic. They preserved some epic poetry inherited from Homer himself, and composed more of it. There is a parallel to their function in the work of the school of Hesiod in Boeotia, which preserved poems, or a poem, by Hesiod, and created other 'Hesiodic' poetry.

According to tradition, the earliest and most important 'Homeric' poems after Homer were the *Aethiopis*, *The Sack of Troy*, and the *Little Iliad* (p. 64, above). These poems were obviously meant to complete the *Iliad* of Homer, by the use, of course, of old material. Arctinus and Lesches, their reputed authors, came from places not far away from Chios, the most likely, and Smyrna, the second most likely, of Homer's reputed birthplaces. Both the poets were clearly connected with Homer's school. That at first was Homer's family; but afterwards it was joined by poets who were no relation to him. There are signs that Lesches composed a poem actually about Homer himself, traces of which remain.

There are eight documents ostensibly giving information about Homer's life (Allen). We meet them first in manuscripts of the *Iliad* and *Odyssey*.

One is called the *Herodotean Life* because the unknown writer pretends to be the historian Herodotus, though he must be centuries later. The *Life* says that Homer was born at Smyrna on the banks of the river Meles; his mother was Cretheis or Critheis; that he travelled about Ithaca and Leucas, the large island north of it; that he returned to Asia Minor; settled at Colophon and there became blind; and the date of Homer's birth is given as 168 years, or according to some manuscripts 160 years, after the Trojan War, that is 1102 B.C. or 1110 B.C. There are also in it twenty-eight verse quotations. Eight come from the *Iliad* or *Odyssey*, and five are epitaphs or otherwise intelligible, but fifteen, all clearly relating to Homer's life, and

E

shewing no sign that they are later than early epic, have only been satisfactorily explained as coming from a very early poem, probably by Lesches himself, about the life of Homer. Lines from this same poem have been identified in another document, *The Competition between Homer and Hesiod*, in the main part of which Hesiod recites apparently nonsensical verses to each of which Homer replies with another verse that turns the first into sense. Thus there may be very old and good material in the *Lives* of Homer. Most of the other seven *Lives* mainly go back to the same source, best represented in the *Life* which is numbered VI. The other *Lives* mainly dilute this one. The common source was a kind of article on Homer's place and time, quoting opinions of earlier writers on Homer and starting with Pindar. Behind this source are earlier writers, including writers of full classical times. The *Lives* suggest that information about Homer was preserved by the Homeridae; that Homer lived in Chios, or possibly Smyrna or another place not far away, late in the heroic or early in the Hellenic Age, that is in the tenth or ninth century B.C.; that he was a poor man; and that he travelled widely, visiting especially the realm of Odysseus.

The Alexandrians worked seriously at the problem of Homer from the historical point of view, and so did Aristotle and his school to some extent. Historians of the fourth and third centuries had already discussed Homer. Among them was Theopompus, who dated him at 700 B.C. or later. Ephorus of Cyme, in the northern or Aeolian part of Asia Minor, seems to have written at length on Homer, supplying local knowledge and other information which was eventually used in the *Lives*. Both Plato and Isocrates write of the Homeridae and their secret records about Homer which they preserved mainly in esoteric poetry.

Still earlier, Hellanicus in the fifth century offered a date for Homer, and traced Homer's descent to Orpheus. Pindar, Semonides, and Bacchylides mention Homer, saying respectively that he was born in Smyrna, Chios, and Ios, and Pindar adds a legend that Homer composed the poem called *Cypria*, and gave it away as his daughter's dowry. Solon about 600 B.C. referred to Homer; and about 700 B.C. or earlier Callinus mentioned Homer as the author of the *Thebais*. That is the earliest literary reference; but to about the same date belongs a piece of history, that Cynaethus of Chios, who probably composed part of the Homeric *Hymn to Apollo*, introduced the poems of Homer to Syracuse at some date wrongly given as 504 B.C. It is clear that this was about two centuries earlier, probably soon after the foundation of Syracuse.

The available tradition about Homer himself is partly genuine, going back to real information preserved by the Homeridae, but in the form in which it has reached us the fancies far outnumber the facts, and indeed the tradition is often considered worthless. It is worth something, however, and may be taken as satisfactory evidence for a few simple statements. They are these.

Homer lived on or near the west coast of Asia Minor before the earliest historical Greek poets, Hesiod, Arctinus, Lesches, Callinus and Archilochus, or as the earlier contemporary of the earliest of them. He was poor, and though he had some honour in his life, he had neither the honour nor the wealth that he deserved. He travelled over the Aegean, and to Ithaca. At some stage of his life he became blind. His ancestry was not well known; legend soon began to affect the accounts of it, and he is even called the son of a river. Perhaps it was some time after Homer's death, two or three generations, when facts had already been lost, that the biographical tradition became fixed in the poetry of the Homeridae. It is at least clear that there were Homeridae, genuinely preserving and continuing the work of Homer, and guarding the record of his life.

Living at about 800 B.C., Homer looked at a world surprisingly obscure to us. We have scarcely anything belonging to it left, except Homer's poems, and some vases and stone reliefs. The age is called the Dark Age of Greece; it extended from the coming of the Dorians about 1100 B.C. till the known poets begin. Possibly in Asia Minor where Homer lived it was not entirely a Dark Age. But anyhow Homer himself is on the borderline between light and dark.

This is bewildering to some extent because Homer is so civilized and perfect that it is hard to imagine him living in a Dark Age, which is easily supposed an age of barbarism. This supposition has led critics to bring Homer's date down to the seventh or even the sixth century, or to push it back to the tenth or eleventh. Neither is really necessary; though it is possible to argue sensibly for a very early date. The ninth century in Asia Minor need not have been at all barbaric, actually, and it is hard to see how it could have been as bad as that. In fact, if only poetry is remembered and everything else forgotten, the development is natural and credible. The date of Archilochus of Paros is roughly fixed by his own references both to Gyges, king of Lydia from about 687 to 651 B.C., and to an eclipse of the sun in either 711 B.C. or 648 B.C. (Blakeway; Jacoby). Archilochus wrote bitter personal poetry about politics, for he was a victim of political disturbances, and about the hardships of his adventurous life, especially in the invasion of the island of Thasos in the north Aegean, in which he took part. His bitterness is reflective and self-conscious, not in the least primitive; he is rather decadent, with the sort of mind which is met in overdeveloped and decaying civilizations. Callinus is self-conscious too, and he is earlier still; so is Mimnermus, not very long afterwards; but they are without the aggressive bitterness of Archilochus.

Homer came before them, with perhaps some epic poets of his school in between. His tone is just what would be expected of a poet, provided that he were great enough, of just a few generations before the decadence began. There are countless comparisons, none very exact, but many enlightening. The change from the French *Chansons de Geste* to the poetry of the Pléiade might be suggested; or from Shakespeare to Pope, in his later work; or from Goethe to Rilke; or from Shelley to Swinburne; the sort of change that is always happening within a space of time of more than a generation but not much more than a century or two.

Homer lived in an age of just enough hope for courage and effort and trust in God; not an age of failure and hopelessness, nor an age of placidity and secure luxury. He looks back to the past as a greater time than his own; that would be natural among the remnants of aristocratic families, who, driven from Greece by the Dorians, started new homes across the Aegean Sea. But he also catches the community of past and present. The Trojan War meant all the more to him because he could see in it the tensions and balances of his own contemporaries, the Greeks who were trying to make a life in Asia beside people who had long had Asia for their home. The wanderings and leadership of Odysseus meant all the more to him, because in his day there were more and more voyages to the west and east, voyages already in his life-time leading, or soon to lead, to the foundation, or refoundation, of Greek colonies on distant shores; and because, as there can be no doubt, problems of civil government, royal rights and duties, the constitutional balance, and risk of changing sovereignty as economic forces changed, were very near to his observation and thought. It is because Homer was caught by the likeness of the Mycenaean past to the Hellenic present, across generations or even centuries, and because his imagination had just this chance to do what the strong artistic imagination always likes to do, or even has to do, and to interpret the content of the individual present in the forms of a past experience of a wider world, that much of the Homeric question has arisen. It is in the question that the answer lies.

No age in Greek history is known in which poems as long as Homer's were certainly recited. Parts of the *Iliad* and *Odyssey* were recited at festivals in many places, a different part on each day. That meant that the performance did not quite provide the purpose for which Homer composed. The right occasions, probably in royal courts, seem to have stopped almost in Homer's life-time, since his successors composed much shorter poems, which would have served well for festivals historically known, as at Athens; though there Homeric poems might be finished in successive days. There, at the Panathenaea, performers took turns with parts of Homeric poetry, so much each day; there may have been time for the whole of a Homeric poem, but not certainly. It is clear that Homer planned his poems to be recited right through, on day after day at long festivals or perhaps still more likely each evening at ordinary times, when there was no festival. Of such occasions among Greeks it is hard to say that anything whatever is known, apart from the practice of the minstrels Phemius and Demodocus, and of Achilles himself and of the Muses, in Homer's own poems. But it is hard to doubt that such epic recitation, on occasions and on a scale which gave the *Iliad* and *Odyssey* a chance to be followed and understood in their grand and revealing architecture, happened somewhere and at some time. It must have been at a time and place of which little is known. It is safe to say that the place can only have been along the coast of Asia Minor, in rich, civilized cities there, where a refined and quick-witted aristocratic society survived; and the time was when Homer lived, between 900 and 750 B.C.

Of Homer himself the tradition and the poems tell us something. T. E. Lawrence, half bitterly, half in dissimulation, said that Homer was a townsman, a kind of book-worm, not thoroughly knowing the manly life of which he tells in any of its works and ways. I expect Lawrence meant what is the truth. Homer knew and saw and loved all these things, good and bad, as a poet, not as a soldier or sailor. A poet must foreshorten and eliminate, even in the very seeing and hearing, to be a poet at all. Without making mistakes you may make other things, but certainly not poetry of any length. Homer was not a traveller or fighter making poems in his spare time. He travelled; he saw Ithaca; probably he saw Troy. But he was a poet all the time, quite different from his own Achilles, who sang in his hut, but was first a fighter.

IV

TROJAN STORY

Homer tells, at great length, stories taken from a group or 'cycle' of stories, legendary and mythical, which had for the centre and focus a probably real event, the capture of the fortress of Troy or Ilion, now Hissarlik, at the north-west corner of Asia Minor, by 'Achaean' Greeks from the Greek mainland and islands. The date must be a little before or a little after 1200 B.C.; just before is now most probable.

The words 'legendary' and 'mythical' both need discussion, but they can wait for it till after the outline of the stories has been told. Countless variations in the stories exist. But one version has survived which is of special importance, because it claims to be the version followed by a large number of early Greek epic poems which were composed after Homer to make a complete sequence, comprising the whole group of stories. This version is quoted by Photius from Proclus, a grammarian of the second century A.D. He could have read the actual poems; it has been doubted that he did, but perhaps for insufficient reasons. Of these poems only Homer's *Iliad* and *Odyssey* survive. They deal with quite small parts of the whole group of stories. The other poems are lost. I give a still further shortened version, relying on Homer for his part, on Proclus for the rest, and inserting a few explanatory phrases of my own.

My account will necessarily be sketchy and pedestrian; the reading of it will be easy, though scarcely exciting. Nevertheless a knowledge of the full Cyclic story will bear directly on our appreciation of Homer.

The first poem in the sequence is the *Cypria*, whose author is given as Stasinus of Cyprus or Hegesias of Salamis in Cyprus, a poem in eleven books. The story is this. Zeus, the high god, plotted the Trojan War with Themis, an interesting goddess of nature and also of natural right among mankind. At this time the gods were enjoying the festivities at the wedding of Peleus, a mortal hero, and Thetis, a goddess or nymph of the sea. So, to carry out the plan, Eris, the goddess of strife, inspired three goddesses at the wedding to argue which of them was most beautiful. They were Hera, Athena, and Aphrodite—the goddesses, if their meanings can be safely represented in single words, of power, mind, and love. At the command of Zeus Hermes the messenger-god took them to Paris, otherwise Alexander, a prince of Troy who was shepherding sheep on Mount Ida near the city, to get him to decide between them. Persuaded by the offer of marriage with the lovely Greek queen Helen, Paris put Aphrodite first. At her suggestion ships were built to sail to Greece; she advised that Aeneas, another Trojan prince, should go too. Helenus a prophet and Cassandra a prophetess prophesied the future, but in vain. Paris reached Sparta, in the southern part of Greece where Helen was queen. He was entertained by her brothers, Castor and Polydeuces, and then by Menelaus, king of Sparta, Helen's husband. Paris gave Helen presents. Then Menelaus sailed off to Crete, giving orders to Helen to supply the needs of the guests till they went away. Aphrodite brought Paris and Helen together. After the union they put much royal property on board their ships and sailed away at night. But Hera brought a storm upon them. They were driven to the city of Sidon, and Paris captured it. In the end, having reached Troy, Paris married Helen.

Meanwhile her two brothers, Castor and Polydeuces, stole cattle belonging to Idas and Lynceus. Castor was killed by Idas, and Lynceus and Idas by Polydeuces. Zeus gave Castor and Polydeuces immortality in turn, to be enjoyed by each on alternate days. After this the divine messenger Iris told Menelaus what had happened in his house. He came back, and planned an expedition against Troy first with his brother, Agamemnon, king of Mycenae in the north of southern Greece, and the strongest of the Greek kings, and then with Nestor, the very aged and wise king of Pylos, on the coast to the west of Sparta. Nestor in a digression told Menelaus the stories of Epopeus, who raped the daughter of Lycus and was destroyed, of Oedipus king of Thebes, of Heracles and how he went mad, and of Theseus and Ariadne. After the talk they went round Greece collecting leaders for the expedition. Odysseus, king of a kingdom in the Ionian islands to the south of the Adriatic, with his capital in the island of Ithaca, did not want to go, and pretended to be mad. But at the suggestion of the cunning hero Palamedes they outwitted him by seizing his son Telemachus in return.

The Greeks now assembled at Aulis, on the south-east coast of northern Greece, on the sea-channel called Euripus dividing the mainland from the large island of Euboea. Here they sacrificed, and saw an omen, a snake eating nine small birds, according to Calchas their prophet a sign (as Homer makes clear) that they would take Troy in the tenth year. They put to sea, came to Teuthrania in Mysia, and mistaking it for Troy, sacked it. Telephus, resisting, killed Thersander the son of Polyneices, and was wounded in turn by Achilles. Next a storm scattered the fleet. Achilles, son of Peleus king of Phthia in north Greece with whose wedding the story began, put in to the island of Scyros and there married Deidameia the daughter of Lycomedes. Meanwhile Telephus, told by an oracle to go to Argos, was on his way and met Achilles. Achilles healed his wound, intending him to pilot them on their way to Troy.

The expedition assembled at Aulis a second time. Agamemnon went stag-hunting and boasted that he was better at it than Artemis the goddess of hunting. She was angry and sent a storm to stop them sailing. This Calchas explained, and added that they must sacrifice Agamemnon's daughter, Iphigeneia, to Artemis. This they tried to do, having sent for the girl pretending that she was to marry Achilles. But Artemis seized her away to the land of the Tauri in south Russia, making her immortal and putting a stag in her place at the altar.

They sailed at last. At Tenedos, an island near Troy, as they feasted, one of their number, Philoctetes, was bitten by a water-snake. The wound went septic, and smelt so unpleasantly that Philoctetes was left behind in Lemnos. Achilles was offended at receiving his invitation for the feast too late, and quarrelled with Agamemnon. They now made their landing near Troy, opposed by the Trojans, whose greatest fighter Hector killed Protesilaus, the first casualty of the war. Achilles then routed the Trojans, killing Cycnus, son of Poseidon, god of the sea. They gathered up the dead, and an embassy went to Troy to demand back Helen and the property of Menelaus. The Trojans refused and the siege began. The Greeks devastated the open country and neighbouring cities. Presently

Achilles wanted to look at Helen. So Aphrodite, protector of Helen, and Thetis, mother of Achilles, brought them to meet; and afterwards when the Greeks wanted to go home Achilles dissuaded them. Achilles drove off cattle belonging to Aeneas, devastated Lyrnessus, Pedasus and many other cities, and killed the Trojan prince Troilus. Patroclus, the great friend of Achilles, took the captive Lycaon to Lemnos and sold him. Out of the spoils a girl called Briseis was given as a prize to Achilles and another called Chryseis to Agamemnon. The next event is the death of Palamedes. Zeus now plans to relieve the Trojans by withdrawing Achilles from his alliance with the other Greeks. The *Cypria* ended with a list of all who fought as allies on the side of the Trojans.

Homer's *Iliad* in twenty-four books now begins. At the start, Apollo afflicted the Greeks with a plague in answer to the prayer of his priest Chryses, whose daughter Chryseis Agamemnon held in captivity and refused to ransom. In the end Agamemnon had to release her; but in a quarrel with Achilles he seized from him another captive girl, Briseis, to replace the one whom he had lost. Achilles was furious, and refused to fight any more for the Greeks. His mother Thetis begged Zeus to give success to the Trojans, that the Greeks might value Achilles the more; and, though that would anger Hera, he consented. There was in fact a quarrel, but Zeus frightened Hera and quelled her; and all the gods started to feast happily, laughing at the sight of the lame fire-god Hephaestus carrying round the drink for them.

In the night Zeus could not sleep, through planning destruction for many of the Greeks. Presently he sent a Dream to Agamemnon, ordering the Dream to tell him to arm the Greeks and attack, for there was a chance to take Troy. The Dream did so. Agamemnon paraded the army, but first tested them by saying they were all to go home. They acted on this all too readily. But order was restored by Odysseus, the most cunning, and Nestor, the most experienced, of the chiefs. Thersites, a vulgar man, continued mutinously, but Odysseus hit him. Eventually they began marching to battle, and a list is given of the contingents and leaders on the Greek and on the Trojan sides.

The two armies approached each other. Paris nearly met

Menelaus, but retired at sight of him. Hector taunted Paris, and suggested a single combat. All agreed. Oaths to accept the decision were taken; and Menelaus was already winning when Aphrodite magically rescued Paris, hid him in a cloud, and put him back in his house.

In Olympus, where the gods lived, Hera now quarrelled with Zeus again because other gods favoured the Trojans against her friends the Greeks, and she told him to make Athena persuade the Trojans to break the existing truce. This happened, with the help of the Trojan Pandarus, who just grazed Menelaus with an arrow. Agamemnon urged the Greeks to battle. His talk with individual leaders and their replies help to define their characters. There was a stirring fight, and some less important chiefs were killed.

Athena now inspired Diomedes, a great fighter but a modest man, to win great glory; and then left the fight, taking Ares with her, to return later to strengthen Diomedes when he was slightly wounded. He killed many, till Aeneas attacked him; he would have killed him too, if Aeneas' mother Aphrodite had not saved him. Diomedes then wounded the goddess herself, and she fled; then, pursuing Aeneas, he met Apollo, who three times thrust him back, and loudly warned him, so that he withdrew. Ares encouraged the Trojans, and stood by Hector. Seeing him Diomedes was afraid. But the fight went on furiously. Sarpedon, son of Zeus, was wounded and rescued by Hector. Hector, with Ares helping, began to win, till Hera and Athena went in Hera's chariot together to help the Greeks again. Encouraged by Athena, Diomedes wounded Ares, who went to Zeus with comical complaints. The two goddesses also then returned to Olympus.

The battle went fiercely on, and Troy would have fallen if Helenus, Hector's brother who was a prophet, had not warned Hector to go to Troy and ask Hecuba their mother to make offerings to Athena. As Hector went, Diomedes met Glaucus from Lycia, asked who he was, and in reply was told the story of his ancestor, Bellerophon. They exchanged armour, bronze for gold. Hector reached home and talked to Hecuba. A robe was offered to Athena, who rejected the offering. Hector rebuked Paris for cowardice, and talked to Helen without reproaching her, and to his wife Andromache in words of touching loveliness. His baby, Astyanax, was frightened at his great nodding plume.

Then Hector and Paris went back to the fight. By a plan of Athena and Apollo, Hector and Ajax, who was chosen by lot to fight him, met in a single combat; which was indecisive, and they parted friends. In the evening both sides held meetings. Nestor suggested an elaborate funeral of the dead, and the construction of a wall, gaining assent; and Antenor, the Trojan, proposed the surrender of Helen, but Paris refused, offering only to restore the stolen property, an offer which the Greeks rejected. When the Greeks built their wall, Poseidon was angry because they did it without sacrificing to him; Zeus told him to destroy it later. The Greeks feasted and slept.

Zeus, next day, told the gods not to join in the war, and himself drove to Ida, to watch the fighting. At midday he weighed the fortunes of both sides in his scales; destiny favoured the Trojans, and the only Greek who did not retire was Nestor; he had a wounded horse, and had to be saved by Diomedes, with Hector in such close pursuit that he nearly reached the Greek ships. Next, helped by Zeus and Hera, the Greeks counter-attacked. Hector prevailed again; and Zeus prevented Hera and Athena from resisting him. Hector arranged watch-fires in the plain to stop the Greeks sailing away unobserved.

The Greeks, including Agamemnon, had lost their nerve; and he himself wanted to go home. Diomedes and Nestor steadied him; and on Nestor's advice he sent an embassy to Achilles with generous offers to persuade him to rejoin the fighting. Achilles refused courteously but decidedly. There was great depression, which Diomedes again sought to dispel.

That night, Agamemnon was again restless. He woke Nestor, who woke others; he was very anxious about his outposts and about the enemy. So Odysseus and Diomedes went out on a reconnoitring patrol. They met and killed a Trojan, Dolon, who was engaged on a similar enterprise, sent by Hector. On information from Dolon, they killed Rhesus, a new ally of the Trojans, drove off his splendid white horses, and came safely back with them.

The next day's fighting began with great deeds by Agamemnon. But under the direction of Zeus the fortunes changed; the Greeks were driven back and most of their chief fighters were wounded. Nestor, with a long story, asked Patroclus to prevail on Achilles to rescue the army; but still Achilles did not fight.

Even the wall round the camp, built without sacrifices and destined to be swept away after the war by Poseidon and Apollo, was in danger, for Hector and the rest actually assailed it, Asius, son of Hyrtacus, even trying to drive his chariot to the ships. The defence was as vigorous. An omen appeared; an eagle carrying a snake in the air, but having to drop it. Hector was not discouraged. Sarpedon and Glaucus tried to storm a gate; Sarpedon in talk to Glaucus expressed the heroic rule, 'As we are noble, and must anyhow die, let us go forward'. The two Ajaxes, sons of Telamon and of Oileus, resisted, but Hector broke through the gate.

Poseidon inspired the two Ajaxes. They, Idomeneus, and others fought fiercely. Zeus wanted the Greeks to be pressed hard, but not to be destroyed. On the Greek side Idomeneus, and on the Trojan Deiphobus and Aeneas, were noticeable. Polydamas told Hector to improve his tactics. Hector found Paris and reproved him. An omen, an eagle on the right, cheered the Greeks.

Agamemnon, who again wanted to launch the ships, Nestor, and Odysseus now conferred. They took the advice of Diomedes to renew the fighting, putting in all the men they had. Poseidon helped; Hera was pleased, but not Zeus, and she planned to distract him by sleeping with him. With the help of Aphrodite and Sleep Zeus was beguiled, and Poseidon helped the Greeks. Ajax son of Telamon hurt Hector with a stone; then many Trojans were killed, especially by the other Ajax.

Zeus, waking, was very angry with Hera. She put the blame on Poseidon. They made it up. Zeus next explained the future course of the fighting, sent Poseidon away, and told Apollo to inspire Hector again. The Trojans charged back up to the Greek camp; Apollo knocked down the wall; Zeus fulfilled the prayer of Thetis; and Hector began to burn the ships.

Patroclus appealed to Achilles again, and got permission to wear the arms of Achilles, and fight, leading the men of Achilles, the Myrmidons. Zeus, sadly, had to sacrifice his own son Sarpedon to be killed by Patroclus. The fighting was fierce, especially round the dead Sarpedon; but, though he was despoiled, at the command of Zeus Apollo had him conveyed to his home in Lycia by Sleep and Death. Patroclus came right up to Troy. Apollo drove him back three times; then commanded him to retire; and he did. Then, helped by Apollo, Hector killed him.

There was more fierce fighting. Menelaus did great deeds. The Greeks, by the will of Zeus, were routed again, but managed to save the body of Patroclus from capture.

Achilles at last received the news of the death of Patroclus. Thetis went to him and reminded him that his prayer had been granted; but he replied that that was no use to him now that he had lost Patroclus. He must now take vengeance on Hector, though soon after he must himself die. He repented of his anger, and hated quarrels now. Thetis promised to get divine arms for him, made by Hephaestus. Iris, sent by Hera, told Achilles to rescue the body of Patroclus, not yet clear of the fighting; as he had no arms, he must appear, and shout. Athena made him look terrible, and he shouted; the Trojans withdrew, and the body of Patroclus was saved. The Myrmidons washed it and lamented all night. Thetis got Hephaestus to make the divine arms; they were wonderful, and especially the shield, pictured with scenes representing all the life of mankind.

At dawn Thetis brought the arms; and made the body of Patroclus safe from corruption. Achilles made friends with Agamemnon; who gave him recompense. Sustained and strengthened by Athena, Achilles armed. The chariot was ready; Achilles spoke to his horses. One, given human voice by Hera, replied, and prophesied the death of Achilles. He answered that he knew; and with a shout drove forward in the battle-front.

For fear that Achilles might take Troy before the time, Zeus gave the gods permission to join the fight; and they marched and took sides. Apollo inspired Aeneas to meet Achilles. Poseidon, with other gods, watched; and saved Aeneas when Achilles seemed about to kill him. Warned by Apollo, Hector withdrew; but, when his brother, Polydorus, was killed, he faced Achilles, and was only saved by Apollo's intervention. Achilles made havoc.

The river Xanthus, or Scamander, was filled with dead. Achilles captured twelve young fighters for a human sacrifice to the ghost of Patroclus. Achilles fought on pitilessly, making the river angry because he choked it with corpses; he killed a son of the river Axius, saying that Zeus is mightier than all rivers. The river Scamander now protested to Achilles; and nearly drowned him. Poseidon and Athena, however, saved him. The water spread more, till Hephaestus resisted it with fire. The gods fought together; and then returned to Olympus, except Apollo, who inspired Agenor to face Achilles and then saved him. Then he himself, disguised as Agenor, resisted Achilles. The Trojans crowded into the city.

Hector was compelled by fate to stay outside. Apollo rebuked Achilles; who replied angrily to him. Priam and Hecuba tried to make Hector come into Troy; he thought out for himself what he must do, and first faced Achilles; but then he fled. Achilles pursued him three times round Troy. Athena helped Achilles; but Apollo deserted Hector, when his destiny, weighed by Zeus in his scales, sank down. Achilles brutally killed Hector, despoiled him, and dragged him back to the ships, tied to his chariot. The Trojans lamented bitterly.

Achilles and his men lamented Patroclus. Then in the night the ghost of Patroclus appeared, and begged for burial, and burial with Achilles, both friends together at the last. At dawn the pyre for Patroclus was begun. Achilles sacrificed animals, and the twelve Trojans. The pyre would not burn; but Achilles prayed to the winds, and then it burned. Achilles with care and courtesy held splendid funeral games.

After them, Achilles dragged Hector daily three times round the grave of Patroclus, mutilating him; but Apollo miraculously preserved him, and then appealed to the gods for him. Hera argued for Achilles. Zeus decided on the restoration of Hector's body; sent Iris for Thetis; and made her persuade Achilles. Then Zeus sent Iris to Priam, to make him go to Achilles in the enemy camp. Achilles gave way; his arrogant soul was won at last. The body of Hector was taken back to Troy, and given splendid burial.

The *Iliad* is followed by the *Aethiopis*, in five books, attributed to Arctinus of Miletus. The story is this. Penthesilea, queen of the Amazons, a tribe of fighting women, a Thracian and a daughter of the war-god Ares, came to help the Trojans. After fighting valiantly she was killed by Achilles, and the Trojans buried her. Thersites then mocked Achilles, because he was supposed to have fallen in love with Penthesilea; and was killed by him in return. This was murder, and since the Greeks were disputing what should be done about it, Achilles sailed to the island of Lesbos, sacrificed to Apollo and Artemis and the goddess who was their mother, Leto, and was ritually purified from his guilt by Odysseus. Next Memnon, son of the Dawn, bearing a set of arms made by Hephaestus the god of fire and metal-work, came to help the Trojans. Thetis communicated predictions about him to Achilles. A fight began. Memnon killed Nestor's son Antilochus, and was killed in turn by Achilles. However his mother the Dawn, having asked permission from Zeus, conferred immortality on him. Then, having routed the Trojans, as he pursued them right into Troy, Achilles himself met his death, killed by Paris and Apollo at the gate. There was intense fighting where he fell; but Ajax carried the dead Achilles to the ships, while Odysseus held the Trojans off. Then the Greeks buried Antilochus, and laid out Achilles for burial. Thetis came with the Muses and her sister nymphs, and they sang laments for her son. Then, when he lay on the funeral pyre, she took him up, and took him to the White Island. The Greeks built a barrow tomb for him and initiated funeral games. Then Odysseus and Ajax fell into dispute, who should inherit the divine arms of Achilles.

The *Little Iliad*, in four books, supposed to be by Lesches of Mitylene, joined on to the *Aethiopis*. The story is this. The arms of Achilles were adjudged to Odysseus by the Greeks, because that was the wish of Athena. Bitterly indignant, Ajax became insane, slaughtered the cattle of the Greeks in mistake for the chieftains, and finally killed himself. After that Odysseus ambushed and captured Helenus, the Trojan prince who was a prophet; and heard from him predictions about the fall of Troy. With this guidance, Philoctetes was fetched from Lemnos by Diomedes, and cured by the physician Machaon; and then he killed Paris. Menelaus mutilated the body, but the Trojans recovered it and buried it; and Deiphobus married Helen. Odysseus next fetched Neoptolemus, the son of Achilles, from Scyros, and gave him his father's arms. The ghost of Achilles appeared to him. Eurypylus, son of Telephus, now came to help the Trojans, but was killed, fighting valiantly, by Neoptolemus. The Trojans were now closely besieged, and the Greeks

adopted the plan of entering the city by means of a Wooden
Horse. The plan was in some sense due to Athena; a Greek
called Epeus built the horse. Meanwhile Odysseus, having
mutilated himself, probably to make the Trojans believe that
he had become an enemy to the Greeks, as if they had mutilated
him, entered Troy as a spy. There he was recognized by Helen,
and made a compact with her for capturing the city. He then
escaped back to the ships, killing some Trojans on the way.
After this he went back into Troy, this time with Diomedes,
and together they stole the 'palladion', supposed to be a small
statue of Pallas Athena, a talisman on which the safety of Troy
was thought to depend. The Greeks then made their best
chieftains get into the Wooden Horse, and the rest of them,
having burnt their tents or huts, sailed off to Tenedos. The
Trojans, thinking themselves rid of their afflictions, pulled the
horse into the city, breaking down part of their wall to do so,
and celebrated their supposed victory with festivities.

The *Little Iliad* was followed by *The Sack of Troy* in two
books, supposed to be by Arctinus of Miletus. Its story, which
seems to have overlapped the story of the *Little Iliad*, was this.
The Trojans, finding the horse on the shore, gathered round it
suspiciously, debating what to do. Some wanted to throw it
over a cliff, and others to burn it; and still others thought that it
should be dedicated as an offering sacred to Athena. This third
opinion prevailed; and the Trojans began to celebrate the end
of the war with festivities. Meanwhile two snakes suddenly
appeared and killed the Trojan Laocoon and one of his sons.
Aeneas and his followers took this as a bad omen, and departed
to Mount Ida. After that, Sinon, a Greek who had entered
Troy by a trick, indicated to the Greeks at Tenedos by means
of fire-signals that it was time to return. They sailed back; the
Greeks in the horse came out, attacked the Trojans and
admitted their friends; and together they captured the city,
killing many of the Trojans, who were off their guard. Neoptolemus killed Priam, though he had taken sanctuary at the altar
of Zeus, Guardian of the House Enclosure. Menelaus found
Helen, and having killed Deiphobus, to whom she was now
married, took her to the ships. The surviving Ajax, son of
Ileus, or Oileus, forcibly tore Cassandra away from the large
temple-statue of Athena to which she was clinging, and pulled

F

the statue down also. Angry at this dangerous sacrilege, the other Greeks planned to stone Ajax, but he escaped by taking refuge at the altar of Athena. The Greeks burnt Troy and sacrificed Polyxena, a daughter of Priam, as an offering at the grave of Achilles. Odysseus killed Astyanax, the young son of Hector, and Andromache was given as a prize to Neoptolemus. The rest of the spoil was distributed also. Demophon and Acamas found Aethra, the mother of Theseus, who had been in Troy, and took her with them. The Greeks at last sailed for home; but Athena planned destruction for them on the high seas.

After the *Sack of Troy* came the *Homeward Journeys* in five books, believed to be composed by Agias of Troezen, and relating these events. Athena made Agamemnon and Menelaus quarrel about when to start, and Agamemnon waited to propitiate Athena. Diomedes and Nestor started and got home safe; but Menelaus, who started after them, lost all but five of his ships and was driven by a storm to Egypt. Calchas, Leonteus, Polypoetes and their followers travelled on foot to Colophon in Asia Minor, where Teiresias died, and they buried him. When finally Agamemnon and his contingent were starting, the ghost of Achilles appeared and tried to dissuade them by prophesying the future (for Agamemnon was to be murdered by his wife when he reached home). The surviving Ajax, the Locrian, met his end in a storm at the Capherid rocks. On the advice of Thetis Neoptolemus went home on foot; coming to Thrace he met Odysseus at Maroneia, and having quickly travelled the rest of the journey, and buried Phoenix who died on it, reached the country of the Molossi and was there recognized by his grandfather Peleus. Next comes the murder of Agamemnon by Aegisthus and Clytaemnestra, and the revenge taken on them by Orestes his son and his friend Pylades; and finally the return of Menelaus to Sparta.

Next begins Homer's *Odyssey*, in twenty-four books, like the *Iliad*.

At its beginning, all the Greeks who had escaped death in war or at sea were at home, except Odysseus, who was being kept by a goddess, Calypso, in a cave, for she wanted to marry him. All the gods pitied him except Poseidon, who hated him for blinding his son, the Cyclops. With the approval of Zeus,

Athena, disguised as Mentes, a human friend of the family of Odysseus, visited the son of Odysseus, Telemachus, in his house in the island of Ithaca, where many suitors were pestering the wife of Odysseus, Penelope. Athena told Telemachus a plan to get rid of the suitors and advised him to go to Pylos and Sparta for news of his father; and she departed. Telemachus now dealt more confidently with the suitors.

Next day Telemachus, having been guided by Athena, called a meeting. There he protested that the suitors should not go on using up the property of Odysseus and annoying Penelope but that she should marry whom she liked and have her wedding from her father's house. He added that he would himself go to get news of Odysseus. There was much friction with the suitors; but he had also much help from Athena, now disguised as Mentor, and he prosperously started his voyage.

Athena, still disguised as Mentor, accompanied him to Pylos, and there she advised him, and helped him to behave confidently, for he was young for his responsibility, and shy. Nestor entertained them delightfully, told long stories of the departure from Troy and the home-coming of himself, Menelaus, and Agamemnon; but had no news of Odysseus. Athena, taking the form of an eagle, vanished; and Nestor congratulated Telemachus on such divine favour, since Mentor must clearly be a divinity. Telemachus, accompanied by Peisistratus, Nestor's son, started for Sparta by carriage, overland.

They found Menelaus busy with a double wedding-feast, for both his daughter and his son were soon to be wed. Menelaus and Helen entertained them charmingly. Menelaus told of his adventures, especially in Egypt, and on the island of Pharos, where he received a prophecy from Proteus, the sea-god who changed himself to many shapes. Proteus had told him that Agamemnon had been killed by Aegisthus, and that Odysseus was being detained by Calypso. Telemachus and Peisistratus left Sparta. The suitors prepared an ambush. Penelope prayed to Athena, who sent a wraith, in the shape of a woman, Iphthime, to tell her that Telemachus was protected by herself, Athena.

Athena next day appealed to Zeus for Odysseus, and he sent Hermes to tell the goddess or nymph Calypso, who had kept Odysseus, being in love with him, on her island Ogygia for

seven years, to send him away. Unwillingly, she did so; having
helped him to make a raft and having given him clothes and
provisions. Presently his great enemy Poseidon noticed the raft
and wrecked it. A sea-goddess Leucothea saved him by giving
him a magic veil; helped by it he swam to the island of the
Phaeacians, Scheria, and landed at last, and slept, dead tired.

Athena now went in disguise to Nausicaa, daughter of
Alcinous, king of the Phaeacians, and made her ask her father
for a mule-wagon, to take clothes, and wash them at the mouth
of the river. When she and her maidens were there Odysseus
saw them, and asked them if they chanced to have any clothes
to lend him, and if they would shew him the city. Nausicaa
befriended him, and they started for the city. He prayed to
Athena for a kind reception. She heard him; but out of respect
for Poseidon would not appear to him openly.

Athena hid Odysseus in a mist as he went, and, disguised as
a maiden, herself directed him—for Nausicaa to avoid scandal
made him go alone—and told him to be bold. He entered a
splendid, magically adorned palace, and was very kindly
received by the king Alcinous and his queen Arete, who took
him for a god. He told them that he was an unfortunate human
wanderer, and very hungry and thirsty; then, when the others
had gone to bed, he told the king and queen how he had come
from Ogygia, but not his name. Alcinous consented to send
him to his home, explaining the supreme seamanship of his
people. Then they all retired for the night.

The next day Athena arranged for a meeting of the Phaeacians to be called, to settle the return of Odysseus. She made
Odysseus splendid to see. The plans for the return were made,
and a new ship prepared. Afterwards they feasted in the palace.
The blind minstrel Demodocus sang a poem about a quarrel,
long ago, between Odysseus and Achilles. Odysseus wept, but
concealed his tears from all but Alcinous. He saw, and made
the party leave the palace and go out for games and dancing.
They went, and sports were held. Euryalus told Odysseus that
he did not look like an athlete; but he proved best at throwing
the discus. There was then some incomparable dancing; and
Demodocus sang the tale of the love of Ares and Aphrodite,
and how Hephaestus, who was married to Aphrodite, caught
them. Odysseus now asked for the story of the Wooden Horse.

Again he wept; again only Alcinous saw him; and this time asked him for his story, and whether he had lost some friend at Troy.

Odysseus then said who he was, and told his story. On leaving Troy, they had pillaged and fought the Cicones in Thrace; then they had visited the Lotus Eaters in Africa, but had come away before their eating of the lotus had made them too contented and lethargic to return home; and then they had landed in the country of the Cyclopes, perhaps Sicily, where the giant Cyclops Polyphemus entrapped several, including Odysseus, in his cave, ate six of them, and was defeated in the end by Odysseus, who blinded him and contrived the escape of the survivors.

Next they came to the island Aeolia, where lived Aeolus king of the winds. He received them kindly, and tied up in a bag all but the west wind, giving the bag to Odysseus. They were in sight of Ithaca, when, while Odysseus slept, his men untied the bag in search of treasure. The winds, released, drove them back to Aeolia. They appealed to Aeolus again, but this time he would not help. They came to the land of the Laestrygonians, giants who devoured some of the men and smashed all the ships but the ship of Odysseus. He and his crew came to the island of the witch Circe. She turned some of his men into pigs, but helped by Hermes Odysseus prevailed over her; the men were restored, and after a stay of a year all but one of them, Elpenor, who was killed by accident, sailed away to the land of the Cimmerians, supposed to lie towards the north and west of Europe; for there Circe had told Odysseus to visit the land of the dead, to hear prophecy from the blind seer Teiresias.

Having come to that land of darkness, Odysseus, as Circe had instructed him, sacrificed victims and let the blood fall into a trench, with wine and barley; but with his sword kept off the ghosts, who wanted to drink the blood, till the ghost of Teiresias came, and gave him warning and prophecy about his return. Then Odysseus met the shade of his mother Anticleia, who told him news of his home; and then he saw the ghosts of many heroines. Odysseus now suggested stopping his tale, but, asked by Alcinous, he told of his meetings with the shades of his comrades who fell at Troy, especially Agamemnon, Achilles,

Patroclus, Antilochus, and Ajax the son of Telamon; and also with the shades of elder heroes, Minos, Tityos, Heracles, and others. At last, fearing to stay longer, he returned to the ship, and put to sea.

They landed on Aeaea again, Circe's island; and she directed Odysseus to escape the Sirens, singing maidens who would try to entrap them; the Planctae, rocks that clashed together; the monster Scylla which would seize men of the crew; the other monster Charybdis, which would try to engulf the ship in a whirlpool; and the danger of the land of Thrinacia, where the cattle of the Sun were kept, for if they killed the cattle the crew would perish. By strong and clever leadership Odysseus saved the ship till the end, though Scylla seized six of the crew; but in Thrinacia the men disobeyed their orders and ate some of the cattle of the Sun. The result was quick. Zeus wrecked the ship. Only Odysseus escaped; and floating on wreckage he at last came to Ogygia, Calypso's island.

The Phaeacians were bewitched by the narrative of Odysseus. They soon loaded more presents on the ship, and the voyage began with magical speed. Odysseus slept all the way, and woke up to find himself alone with his presents on land. But in revenge Poseidon turned the ship to stone, just as she was reaching harbour on the return. Now Athena appeared to Odysseus, disguised as a young prince, and told him he was in Ithaca. He replied by starting a fictitious account of himself, how he was a refugee from Crete. Athena smiled and declared herself, and at last he believed that he was in Ithaca, and learnt from Athena about the plight and danger of his house, and about Telemachus, at that time still in Sparta. Athena went off to find him there.

Odysseus, who had been made to look like a beggar, walked away to the cottage of his faithful pig-man Eumaeus, and was entertained with the greatest friendliness. He now gave another fictitious account of himself, how he was a Cretan who had fought at Troy, and afterwards had been captured raiding Egypt; how he had later sailed away with Phoenicians, had been shipwrecked, had escaped from the Phoenicians, and reached Ithaca in mistake for Dulichium, an island near. He tried to make Eumaeus believe that he had proof that Odysseus would return, but did not convince him. Night came, cold and rainy, and they slept, after Odysseus had found ways of testing Eumaeus.

At Sparta, Athena warned Telemachus that all was not well at his home, and that there was a plan to ambush him. With some slight encouragement from an omen, an eagle carrying off a goose, interpreted by Helen to mean that Odysseus would return and take vengeance, Telemachus and Peisistratus set off. As Telemachus was embarking, a stranger, Theoclymenus, a prophet escaping the consequence of a murder, asked to go with him. He was allowed to embark, and they started. Meanwhile Odysseus was having a meal with Eumaeus, and telling him that he meant to go to the city and beg, or work, for food; and also got from him an account of Laertes his own father, who was living in sad hardship, and with that the story of Eumaeus himself, who had been a prince, but had been kidnapped when young. Now the ship of Telemachus reached Ithaca, and he landed at once, to avoid the ambush, and set off on foot. The others, including Theoclymenus, sailed on to the city. Telemachus walked first to the cottage of Eumaeus.

There he met Odysseus; he did not at first recognize his father, but sent Eumaeus to the palace to tell Penelope of his own safe return. Athena now appeared to Odysseus; told him to plan victory with Telemachus; and for the time transformed him back to his own natural appearance, so that his son at last knew him. Odysseus, explaining that Athena and Zeus were helping them, made their plan; Telemachus was to go home, not to mind seeing Odysseus, who would be there as a beggar, ill-treated; but, at a sign from him, to remove all weapons from the hall and hide them away. At the palace a herald from the returning ship, and Eumaeus, brought their news at the same time. The suitors were angry, but made a new effort to catch Telemachus. Eumaeus returned to his cottage.

The next morning Telemachus started for home. Eumaeus and Odysseus followed. Telemachus told Penelope how he had fared, mentioning the prophecy which Menelaus had reported to him, that Odysseus would come home. Theoclymenus, who had now come to the palace, added his similar interpretation of the omen which had been seen. Meanwhile Odysseus and Eumaeus had trouble with the aggressive goatherd, Melanthius, on the way; but soon arrived. The old dog Argus recognized

Odysseus, and died for joy. In the hall, with permission from Telemachus, Odysseus started to beg. The rest gave him food, but not Antinous, a leading suitor, who threw a footstool at him. Eumaeus told Penelope that the stranger had news of Odysseus; it was agreed that he should give his account later. Telemachus sneezed—a happy omen.

Odysseus improved his reputation in the palace by defeating a real beggar in a fight. Guided by Athena, Penelope appeared, looking lovely, and rebuked the suitors for taking, instead of giving, presents. Odysseus was pleased. The suitors sent to their homes for rich presents. Later Odysseus reproved the serving maids and suitors; and Telemachus made an impression by his new boldness of speech. The suitors went home to bed.

Odysseus and Telemachus now hid the arms, Athena herself providing them with light. Then at last Penelope asked Odysseus who he was, and he told a false story how he was a Cretan, and in the course of his adventures had heard of Odysseus himself, among the Thesprotians in north Greece, where he had lately been; he had gone from there to ask the oracle of Zeus at Dodona what was his best plan for coming home. Then it happened that Odysseus had a bath, and was recognized by the old nurse Eurycleia from a scar. He hastily forced her to keep the secret. Penelope next told a dream, asking if it really meant that Odysseus would come home. He said that it did; and advised her to hurry on a plan which she had, to test the suitors by a competition of archery, in which they first had to string the bow of Odysseus.

As he lay anxious and doubtful in the entrance hall, Odysseus was once more encouraged by Athena, who assured him of victory. He prayed to Zeus; who, to his joy, thundered for good omen; and a woman grinding at a mill made a remark of good omen, too. The suitors were deterred by another omen, an eagle carrying a dove, from their plot to kill Telemachus. Telemachus boldly guaranteed the safety of the supposed beggar, annoying the suitors, whom Athena did not allow to stop their insults, so that Odysseus might be sufficiently angry to take full vengeance. She made them mock at Telemachus too, and at Theoclymenus the prophet, who, so impelled, told them his vision of their destruction.

Inspired by Athena, Penelope arranged the competition in archery. She fetched the bow of Odysseus, and Telemachus set up twelve axes in a row; only a strong bowman could shoot hard enough for an arrow to go straight through all the holes in the axes. The suitors could not even string the bow, and decided to sacrifice to Apollo for help. Then Odysseus secretly revealed himself to Eumaeus, and also to Philoetius, the cowman; and got them as allies. It was suggested that Odysseus should try the bow, and Eumaeus quickly brought it, by prearrangement. Odysseus lovingly handled it, and succeeded at once, and shot an arrow through all the axes. At his words of irony and triumph, Telemachus armed.

Now Odysseus flung off his rags, leapt to the threshold, and threw the arrows ready on the ground. Then he shot. Helped by Athena, the four had a hard but successful fight, and in the end all the suitors were killed. Phemius the minstrel and Medon a herald were spared. The hall was cleansed and purified, twelve faithless serving-women were executed, and Eurycleia was sent to tell the news to Penelope, who by the act of Athena had slept through it all.

Penelope was at first incredulous, but when the old nurse told of seeing the scar, she had second thoughts. She went down to meet Odysseus, and saw the slain suitors; but still she was doubtful. Meanwhile, Odysseus recalled that there might be trouble from the killing of so many important Ithacans, and he ordered music and dancing to allay suspicion among people outside the palace. Athena again made Odysseus splendid to see. As a final test Penelope now suggested taking their own bed to the entrance hall, where Odysseus had slept before; but in sudden anger he retorted that he knew well that the bed was immovable, as he had made it himself, one bedpost being a still growing olive tree. Penelope believed at last. In the talk that followed, Odysseus told Penelope his adventures, including a strange prophecy of Teiresias, how he must go inland with an oar till he met men who did not know the sea, one of whom should take the oar for a winnowing-fan; and there sacrifice to Poseidon, and end his troubles. They slept, and awoke; and Odysseus with his three allies went out to settle the kingdom.

Hermes led the souls of the dead suitors to Hades. They met

the souls of heroes of the Trojan War, and there was some talk. Meanwhile Odysseus visited his father Laertes on his little farm; he at first gave one of his fictitious accounts of himself, saying that he had news that Odysseus would come. Then he revealed himself, again referring to the scar. Meanwhile the Ithacans met in assembly, having heard the news, and planned revolt. Some repented, but others went to attack the palace. Athena appealed to Zeus, who ordained that Odysseus and his subjects should live in happiness, reconciliation, and forgetfulness of wrong. At the palace, Odysseus and his party, now reinforced, met the attack successfully; till Athena herself cried aloud that they must stop the fight, and in fear and obedience all swore to remain at peace.

The *Odyssey* was followed by the *Telegony* or story of Telegonus, said to be by Eugammon of Cyrene, a poem in two books, with these contents. The suitors, killed by Odysseus and Telemachus, were buried by their relatives. Then Odysseus sacrificed to the nymphs and sailed to Elis to look at the cattle there. He was entertained at the house of Polyxenus and given a mixing-bowl, decorated with representations of the stories of Trophonius, Agamedes, and Augeas. He then sailed back to Ithaca and performed the sacrifices which Teiresias had instructed. He visited the Thesprotians, married their queen Callidice, and led them in a war against the Brygi. But Ares routed Odysseus and his men, and Athena began to fight Ares, till Apollo parted them. At the death of Callidice, a son of Odysseus, Polypoetes, inherited the kingdom, while Odysseus returned to Ithaca. Meanwhile, Telegonus, son of Odysseus and Circe, came in search of his father, and also landed on Ithaca, and ravaged it, not knowing where he was. Odysseus came to repel him, and was killed by his son in ignorance. Telegonus then realized what he had done, and took his father's body, and Telemachus and Penelope, back to his mother Circe, who made them immortal. They settled down, Telegonus living with Penelope and Telemachus with Circe.

I might apologize for my bare and boring précis of Proclus' précis, and of Homer. But it has a merit. It is so bare and so boring that two things[1] are helped to emerge from it. One is

[1] It has yet another value, indicating the sources of so many Greek tragedies.—J.D.C.

the contrast between what appears to have been the Cyclic way of 'one thing after another,' and Homer's more meaningful tale. The other is the apocalyptic force of at least a few of the great moments in Homer's story, standing out all the more stark and grand from their context.

V

HOMERIC MYTH AND LEGEND

The poetry of Homer, according to the usual and natural supposition, tells myths. These 'myths' are stories about gods and men, who act with powers of physique, intellect, and emotion, and also by supernatural means and aid. They have characters of their own, and they have a special culture, more or less coherent and distinct from other cultures known to history.

Besides the gods and men there are other beings, less natural, and belonging to a sort of fairy-land. They have human and animal qualities, but do not agree in the combination of them with known types; and they often add to known qualities others which are imaginary.

It would be possible to consider the human parts of the stories, in which there is nothing to conflict with nature and possibility, literally true. No one, however, does so; and the Greeks themselves soon began to see reasons why this view is untenable.

Homer's myths are not simple stories made in a single act from similar parts. It would be possible to say that they are not pure myths at all. But it is anyhow necessary first to find out what a myth is.

The word is a Greek word, μῦθος, mythos, used by Homer himself to mean speech in conversation, including commands, persuasions, and ordinary exchanges of thought. About four hundred years later not only has its meaning been expanded to cover 'story', 'narrative', but Thucydides (I. 21) uses the word to imply a mythical quality, in the modern sense, that is, a quality of what is untrue, exaggerated, and fanciful. About a hundred years later, or less, Aristotle gives a scientific meaning to the word 'myth' (*Poetics*, 6. 8–13). He is talking about stage tragedies, and he says that the most important thing in them is the 'myth' or 'plan by which the actions are organized', which means almost exactly the plot of the play.

Aristotle characteristically concentrates on the finished thing and its use, rather than on origins. To him a myth is a story arranged for the stage in order to affect the minds and hearts of an audience. It has an emotive purpose. It does not have to be true literally, and it does not much matter how the myth started. But it has to be in a way true. Poetry describes, not what once happened, but the sort of thing which should be expected to happen. That is how Aristotle regards it, as something general or universal, and for that reason actually more profound, 'more philosophic' as he says, than history itself (*Poetics*, 9.3).

The theory of Aristotle could be illustrated from what his master Plato had already made his practice. After he has got as far as he can, in the search for the truth of any matter, by argument and inference, Plato very often writes what he calls a 'talk', or 'story', λόγος, logos. He does not often use the word 'myth' for his stories, but it is the most appropriate word. Plato's myths are communicative in a poetical way. They might almost be compared to Bible stories, and considered half-way between the narratives of the Old Testament, which are instructive but not entirely planned to be instructive in the way in which, principally, they are and have been, and the parables of the New Testament, which are invented on purpose for their persuasive value, and fined down to give just what is wanted for moral effect by poetry, and almost nothing more. Plato's myths are old stories of gods and heroes, shewing particularly the origin of the world and human society, and explaining in picture-language the nature and destiny of the spirit and the quality of moral and mental life.

The myths are of course mixed. As they stand they are the creation of Plato. His own feeling for life and truth impelled him to them. But the method, the characters, the actions, and the descriptions are owed to the suggestion of old tales, of very different kinds and purposes, of former poetic creations, and of current or previous scientific and philosophic theory also. Plato strongly held the opinion that myths should not be related just because they were, or might be, literally true. Their literal truth he did not consider seriously at all. To him the justification of a myth was its moral utility, or power of enlightening truth by suggestion. To him, when poets related myths, they might, certainly, be inspired, and so reach what is right. But it was at least equally likely that they would not be inspired, and would then be simply dangerous, since they irresponsibly told all sorts of untrue and unhealthy stories; the chief risks being that the poets were supposed to know more than other men though really they did not, and that even though they might be inspired sometimes, it was impossible for the hearer or reader to know when they were. To Plato, therefore, the proper kind of enlightening and valuable myth is not spontaneous or made by inspiration. It is constructed for a special purpose by means of reasoned thought. So at least we have to understand his myths, in the light of what they are and how they are used, and also in the light of what he himself says of similar artistic creation. But the fact remains that Plato's myths are often, if not always, used by him to achieve an effect which reasoned argument has failed to attain.

Plato's practice and Aristotle's theory regard myths as constructions, in the last resort simple and controlled by a single design, consciously planned to produce psychological effect. The authority is good, and such a description of the meaning of myth may well be accepted, provided that the classification is not made so narrow as that. For if, according to Aristotle's own common-sense method, we give reasonable attention to what sensible people usually mean in English by a 'myth', we have to admit that we have no right to exclude many far less premeditated and more spontaneous stories. Most often, a myth means to us a primitive-looking tale, one which was not so much planned or constructed, but just happened.

But the difference is not as big as it looks. However spontaneous the simple sort of myth may be, it is chosen to be told and perpetuated because it has some special interest. It satisfies a need, like the calculated, artistic kind. It may even be that the needs are not very different, except that they are apprehended and met less consciously in the one and more consciously in the other. Chesterton said that fairy-tales are the only true stories.

It would be possible now to say that Homer's poetry is built into large, premeditated, rationally planned myths, like the myths of drama according to Aristotle, out of small, spontaneous, instinctively generated and preserved myths, like the myths of savages. This would be to some extent incomplete and misleading. Firstly, not all of Homer's large myths are rationally planned. Some parts are as spontaneous as ever and do not obviously help the main design of the stories; something of that sort should be there, perhaps, but not necessarily exactly that; Homer, like all poets, lets his memory and his interests run away with him. In the middle of the *Iliad* there are long passages, some perhaps amounting almost to a whole book together, which positively conflict with the main design, and at the beginning incidents occur which obviously belong to an earlier part of the story. There are the discrepancies normal in long poems; the same man may be killed twice. All this is natural and to some extent inevitable; but, though apparent oversights are increasingly discovered to be part of the design after all, neither the *Iliad* nor the *Odyssey* has quite as much unity as a play of Sophocles, a myth of Plato, or a parable of Christ. The second objection to regarding Homeric poetry as large myths built out of small ones is this. The parts are not all strictly myths. It is best to distinguish more kinds of story than that.

There are fairy-tales, or *märchen*, the German name often used to describe them. Such are the tales of the Cyclops and the Laestrygones in the *Odyssey*. They represent the results of strong impressions of surprise, fear and hope upon simple and un-developed people.

Then there are romances, stories to some extent planned to satisfy the desire of an audience for thrills, love interest, hero worship and admiration, the satisfaction of imaginary revenge, and the relief of a happy ending. Such is the broken tale of Nausicaa in the *Odyssey*, which misses its right ending, for we expect her and him to marry and live happily ever after, and half-contradicts the main subject of the *Odyssey*, the faithful return to a faithful home. These motives have been classified under names, 'the unknown stranger', 'the faithful wife', and many more.

But probably most of Homer's work is what it claims to be, recorded memory, more or less distorted, of events which happened. This is called saga or legend; perhaps it is best to call it saga when the emphasis is on the record of fact, and legend when the distortions and falsifications, to which such tradition is liable, are being clearly considered. Homer's account of the Trojan War, the fighting in it, the kingdoms of the Achaean chieftains, much of their family relationships, and some of the voyages in the *Odyssey*, including piratical descents, are saga or legend.

The classification must be more or less arbitrary. Any amount of subdivisions could be made. But it is enough to add one class, and on the whole it is satisfactory to call that class myth. This is a very complicated affair. The other classes of story are often complicated too; obviously what seems a fairy-tale may have begun as saga, and still more obviously a hero of saga often goes through the experience of a fairy-tale, or romances may be blended together, and blended with historical memories too, as in Homer's Scheria, where the motives of 'the unknown stranger' and 'winning a bride' are set in a scene which is contrived from memories of an old and rich civilization, to a great extent, perhaps, Minoan. In hundreds or even thousands of years there are great opportunities for stories to affect, or combine with, each other. But the class of real myths is special. They are best considered as narratives with a strong emotional appeal concerned with supernatural beings whose actions are conceived to be of great importance to man. That is only a rough description, but it is enough to suggest that the early, simple, and apparently spontaneous stories about gods, and the calculatedly developed plots which Aristotle thought the most important things in tragedies, can both be reasonably called by the same name, myths.

The myths in tragedies tell us of the conditions of human life and the hope amid its dangers, and allay the storms in our minds. The more nearly primitive myths do something like that also; they too tell us, in symbolic terms, of the conditions of human life and the hope amid its dangers. Such thoughts are very near the origin of some of the myths, for originally many were accounts in narrative form of ritual designed to bring men release from danger. Primitive people live in terror of the extinction of themselves and of their world. They perform rituals to defeat, for example, the power of drought, and to restore fertility to the land. They will pour out water, and perform other rain-making charms, including many formulae of words, intended to coerce nature by sympathetic magic. Such rituals were practised in early Babylonia, and a pendant from them is found in a text from Ras Shamra in northern Syria. It belongs to the thirteenth or fourteenth century B.C., but it is quite closely in the same form as a strict Greek tragedy, and even the averting of drought and infertility in it is a clear antecedent of the infertility and pestilence which, in the most highly refined of all Greek tragedies, the *Oedipus Rex* of Sophocles, is a sign of the curse which conditions the play.

In this text from Ras Shamra, and in others from there and from elsewhere also, including those that come from Babylonia, the libretto of the ritual drama was intended to direct what was done, in order to prevent defective procedure. Stage directions, and copies of prayers and hymns if any, ought to have been enough. But what is found is a narrative, describing not so obviously a rite to be done now and often, as a sequence of events which happened once and for all in the past. A libretto of a rite, therefore, looks exactly like a recorded myth; all the more because officiants in a rite may even be described as divine beings, as when human women, performing a rain charm, are represented by the words, 'Then came the goddesses . . .' They remind us of the Greek Danaids, who were set to drawing water endlessly in Hades for killing their Egyptian husbands; a mistake of the myth-tellers, for on a vase-painting they are shewn drawing water usefully to help the crops by a rain charm, rather like the 'goddesses' in the Ras Shamra text.

Elsewhere the evidence is very precise. In India the *Satapatha-brahmana* clearly states the symbolic nature of rites. A tomb represents the universe, and the stones round it the waters of the surrounding ocean. The performer of a rite positively represents a god; two human partners in a sacred marriage are closely identified with a divine pair, such as the sky and the earth; or rather it may be actually more likely that the conception of the earth and the sky as deities with human qualities is made possible at least in some places by their previous identification with human beings officiating in rites, from whom the ideas of divinity were developed.

There is a slight indication of such a history in the *Iliad* (14. 153 *ff.*). Hera tricks Zeus into falling in love with her again, and they lie together. The plan of course is to make Zeus forget to enforce his order and prevent the gods from joining in the fight. But Homer says that as their marriage was renewed, the flowers grew beneath them—a memory of the old sacred

G

marriage between earth and sky, that is, between their human representatives, on which hope of reviving nature was based.

Some myths which began in ritual may have lost all trace of that beginning, and may look like invented stories. Obviously there cannot be any certain example of them; but it may be guessed that Poseidon's destruction in the *Iliad* of the Achaean wall near Troy goes back in idea to a ritual designed to secure walls by the help of some priestly power, identified at some time with the power of Poseidon, god of walls, as of other things besides. Another probable example is Odysseus' visit to Hades. Elsewhere a mythical descent to the world of the dead may be modelled on ritual designed to preserve the spirits of men after life is done.

Myths do not all come from ritual, and it is a mistake to assume either that they all come from it, or that none of them come from it, just because some do not.

The same primitive power of identifying objects in the outside world, or even gods, with human beings, shewn in ritual, may produce personifications of forces in nature, and make myth out of their humanized interactions. A Chinese sailor is recorded to have been quite unable to conceive a waterspout at sea as just a waterspout and not a dragon; and the ancient Egyptians, and modern Red Indians, regard the wind as an animal. There are a great number of examples.

Myth may therefore arise from the direct personification of natural phenomena. This is none the less true because the view came into great disrepute when, in the last century, exponents of the 'solar' theory of myth carried their claims much too far. They conceived that humanity passed through a stage of temporary insanity, in which it created mythology, according to some scholars, as a 'disease of thought', and, according to others, as a 'disease of language'. By the 'disease of language' was meant the error of attributing the behaviour of a natural force to a divinity because 'force' and 'divinity' had similar names, especially in their Sanskrit forms. By the 'disease of thought' was meant a similar confusion, without the excuse of similarity of name. On either view all mythology was supposed to be what has been called 'highly poetical talk about the weather'.

The mistake is not so much the theory in itself but the

exclusiveness and the exaggeration of it. There was no sudden temporary insanity which fell on humanity; but the tendency to personify objects, and to symbolize what is apprehended, is general until the human mind develops something like a power of abstraction. It is rather we, who have reached that power to some degree, who are exceptional. There was no disease of thought, but only thought operating in a way usual and necessary to it in early stages; nor was there a disease of language, except in the sense that language has always found it hard to help thought, and to avoid adding confusion to it, since perfect expression of thought is not any kind of normal and minimum requirement of language, but rather a supreme triumph of its utmost elaboration. Yet the fact remains that myths arise in great numbers from something like a personification of sky, earth, sun, moon, winds and other such phenomena.

That is much more intelligible now than it was when the solar theory was fully elaborated, since there is more information about the minds and habits of early and simple people. Their outlook on ritual helps a great deal to explain the nature myths. So does the proved, natural tendency to personification. There is also another tendency among them, called by its discoverer, Lévy-Bruhl, by the French phrase 'participation mystique'. Savages 'mystically participate' in their world; they are conscious of a whole situation and do not much distinguish the parts of it, until practical needs compel them to do so. Dawn is a whole situation, part of which is the human family in the hut; there may be quite a different word for the sun at dawn and the sun at midday.

All this helps the savage to confuse human individuals with natural objects such as the sun and earth, and start the process towards highly poetical talk about the weather. Now here there are two points. One is that a criticism of the solar theory on the grounds that it supposes a high poetical gift in savages, is not fair. There are numerous instances of savage myths, alike all over the world, which are most unpoetic; yet myths of the same class, found among the Greeks and Red Indians, are otherwise like the rest, but very poetic indeed. These two people simply had, for whatever reason, a power of turning grotesque myths into poetry.

The next point is that the confusion which belongs to the savage mind, a confusion better described as an undifferentiating condition, continues. A myth about the sun will be mixed up with family relationships from the start, because the savage at dawn is conscious of the sun and of the members of his family at the same time. Originally the sun itself was not much noticed; there are savages who do not know that light is due to it. But apart from this there are further confusions. A myth about the sun setting is very likely to be also a myth about the journey of a dead man below the earth at death, where the sun goes. Which symbolizes which, is a hard question; probably most often both meanings are symbolic of each other; and probably both originated in a consciousness in which the sun and the dead man were parts of a single mode of thought, undifferentiated, given together, without any conscious act of symbolization.

Ritual myths may be simple at the start. Very many others have certainly never been simple. All are liable to contaminations all the time. Myths affect each other, and other kinds of early stories affect myths and are affected by them, continually; sometimes through accidents, forgetfulness or misunderstanding, and sometimes through conscious attempts to adapt existing myths either to practical needs, as in the adaptation of the genealogy of Hellen to make room for Achaeus, or to an artistic design, as when Homer gave to Thetis and Patroclus the sublime importance which they have in the *Iliad*.

In particular, a myth and a saga will often combine, especially if they are in some way alike. A most remarkable instance is this. There were myths about the capture of Babylon in 2375 B.C. The city goddess defended the city; but she was lured away to the other side. The plague god helped in the war. Here are the Trojan Athena, whose help, in her image the 'palladion', the Achaeans stole away; and the Greek Apollo, who at the beginning of the *Iliad* shoots his arrows of plague. The tale of the capture of Babylon became mythical; the facts of the siege of Troy were like it; and the myth of Babylon was imposed on the saga of Troy to produce the Trojan Legend.

For the *Iliad*, Homer started with a large general repertory of myths and fairy-tales, with the suggestions available from some romances, and above all with a large number of sagas, some about life in Greece, and some, and in particular one, about the siege of Troy. This one was about Achilles. There is no reason to suppose it long or impressive or like our *Iliad*. But poets often get a great idea from a small and apparently insignificant hint. Homer retold the tale. Achilles is central, and what matters most is how, as a Christian would put it, 'his soul is saved', and what hope there is for him and his friends, in spite of all. To this end Homer makes his immense range of knowledge and memory help. What had been central in other poetry is now subordinate, giving balance, suspense, pattern, emotional intensity, and finally discernment.

So it is in the *Odyssey* with Odysseus, how he comes to his heart's desire through harmony within himself and with the heaven that is in and with man. Homer here had vast memories in verse; the saga, chiefly, of the homeward voyage; other sagas, especially of attacks by sea-raiders of Mediterranean lands; romantic tales of old love and of new love, of greatness proved by deeds, of reward for the good, and of vengeance on the wicked; fairy-tales and tales of monsters and wonders, tales gathered through hundreds of years of adventuring in eastern and western and perhaps even in northern seas; and behind all is the great myth of the journey through life and death and beyond, the journey of the spirit with the sun to the west, and coming to a home, a home in this world or an eternal home, but home at last.

There are two mighty instruments for a mighty poet's hand, tragedy of conflict, and the pilgrim's progress. Homer found them both and made them perfect; he need do no more.

The gods of Homer are fully like human beings in behaviour, thoughts, emotions, and appearance, except that they are larger and finer, and may have supernatural powers.

They are not always imagined with the same powers. Zeus and Poseidon move without visible means of movement over long distances. But Poseidon travels from Samothrace to Troy by means of a chariot, which however conveys him across the sea (*Il.* 13. 23–31). Hera and Athena come by a chariot from the home of the gods to Troy (5. 719 *ff.*). Elsewhere (*Od.* 1. 96–8), Athena travels magically, but with a pair of magic sandals to carry her. She has powers of appearing and vanishing suddenly, and can assume the form of a bird; but she carries a great spear, which she uses in warfare. Apollo fights with his bow, and Ares with his spear.

The gods are organized not as a political union of vassals under the supreme sovereignty of Zeus, but as a family and its associates, living together as if in a baron's hall, as his retainers, some of them having wives, but none young children. Zeus is the father, and head of the family, never the king and head of a state or confederacy. He is called βασιλεύς, basileus, 'King', by Hesiod; but not by Homer. Gods appear as his children sometimes, and sometimes as his feudal retainers. This organization on a small scale, as if in a household, looks earlier than the kind of organization found among human beings in Homer. Homer remembers the comparatively advanced conditions of human political organization which existed at the time of the Trojan War; but he conceives the gods in a simpler kind of association, which had existed, presumably, in human life at an earlier time.

The gods have various and complicated origins. Zeus has an Indo-European name, like the corresponding Sanskrit name Dyaus. He is a sky-god. Sky-gods are very common, and are found all over the world. At first they are not gods at all, but the sky itself, conceived as the source of fertility in the earth, and of danger, too, from drought, rain, lightning, and meteorites. There is a controversy whether all humanity originally believed in a Supreme Being. One theory is that it did but in many places the belief degenerated; there seem to be plenty of tribes in which such a belief is unknown, though it is still doubtful whether any early man was ever quite without what might be called religion in some sense. It is likely that the belief in a Supreme Being is widespread, but not universal. Sometimes it may have been lost through the decay of culture; but in general, if a tribe is found to be without it, it has not yet developed it. However, the religious or quasi-religious awe of the sky and of its blessings and dangers, is usual, if not universal, and it may be very strong without the formulation of any sky-god. Early man naturally personifies, and talks as if he conceived objects in human shape. It is hard to say how much this is a peculiarity of thought or only of language, and how long it can be expected to go on before a god emerges. Sky and earth too were in very ancient times personified sufficiently for the formation of a belief that they united in marriage to produce all that came from the earth.

In Homer Zeus is still a sky-god, though he is more; and much more, of course, than merely the sky. He retains traces of his origin. He uses as his weapon the 'thunderbolt', an imaginary object, widely supposed to exist from observation of lightning and meteorites in thunderstorms. When Zeus does damage or gives a warning and so affects human action, there is in this a more or less complete moralization of the action of the sky, originally conceived to be controlled by ritual practices, and to be dangerous if the ritual is mismanaged. We have noticed a trace of the older sky-religion in Homer in the renewal of the union of Zeus and Hera, his regular consort. Homer uses it as a device for distracting the attention of Zeus from the war; but he says that flowers grew at their union, and that is clearly a memory of the old idea that the union of sky and earth produced fertility. Centuries later the old idea was revived by the religious sect of the Orphics, who had to declare that they themselves were children of earth and starry heaven.

Zeus in Homer has undergone various and complicated processes. Political ideas have been attached to him, as they are always attached to gods in developed religion, and indeed right from the start of much that happens during its development. W. R. Inge remarks that it has been hard for Americans, since the reign of George III, to be emotionally affected by the conception of God as a King. It is also hard to evolve and imagine democratic attributes for God; and that may be a reason why democracy is hard to sustain. Now though Zeus is in Homer rather the head of a family than a king, in his dealings with men he is in a sense an overlord, because human kings derive their authority from Zeus. He 'rears' them; he gives them their sceptres; and they, holding the sceptres, maintain the rules made by Zeus. This moral and political modification was presumably helped because Zeus, being at first the sky, might be supposed very powerful, all-seeing, and retributory. A further help was the primitive confusion between disparate elements within a single perception (see pp. 99–100 above); especially changes in the sky perceived in conjunction with the regular behaviour of human beings.

Hera, like Zeus, has an Indo-European name, which seems

to mean something like 'strong', and to come from the same root which gives the first syllables of 'Heracles' or 'Hercules', and the word 'virile'. In historical times she was worshipped particularly by women. As the wife of Zeus she would be expected to be the earth; but she is not so clearly an earth-goddess as several others. She leads the opposition to Zeus in the *Iliad*, and is resolutely on the side of the Achaeans.

Poseidon's name may be Indo-European, meaning the possessor or husband of the earth; or it may not. His cults are in places important before the Dorian invasion, and he may belong originally to pre-Greek people. He was first an earth-god, and also god of water, including springs. As an earth-god he controlled the walls of cities, and also earthquakes. Afterwards he became god of the sea. In the *Iliad* he is probably second to Zeus in power, but he can be quelled by Zeus without much difficulty. In the *Odyssey* he protects Polyphemus the Cyclops, his son, and persecutes Odysseus for blinding him. He is clearly a sea-god, because he controls the sea and in particular raises storms. His association with the Cyclops may refer to volcanoes in the earth, or to the round ring-walls of cities, either of which may be signified by the Cyclopes.

Hades is a god of the world to which the dead go, a world partly imagined in the far west and partly below the earth. He is the brother of Zeus and Poseidon, and the three share supremacy; Zeus rules the earth and sky, Poseidon the sea, and Hades the world below. The name Hades is in Homer 'Aïdes' and seems to mean 'unseen', originally Ἀϝίδης, Awides. The word sometimes seems to mean the place rather than its ruler, and perhaps it only became a personal name later. Indeed, Homer has another name for the ruler of the world below, 'Aïdoneus', which could mean 'he of Aïdes'. Aïdoneus is rarely mentioned and seems to live in the east where the sun rises rather than the west.

Apollo is a god of mysterious origin. He has been thought to come from Arabia. Another opinion is that he came from the far north in the neighbourhood of Jutland, that his journey south is marked by 'Apollo towns', such as Jablonetz in Central Europe and several places called Apollonia in Greece, and that his name means 'apple'; so that he was a northern god of the apple-tree. There is an opinion that he was one of the gods projected from mass emotion, and then imagined as a real being receiving worship, though the worship was the only thing that was real, and did not at first involve any deity other than nature in general and the emotional force of a crowd. On this theory his name is connected with the word 'apella', which is the name of the assembly of citizens at Sparta. This would suggest, since 'apella' seems a Dorian word, that Apollo first came to Greece with the Dorians, after the Trojan War. A divine pair called Apulunas and Rutamis existed in Asia Minor at the time of the Trojan War, and they have been suggested as the origin of Apollo and his sister Artemis. Since Apollo is strongly on the side of the Trojans in the *Iliad*, and since his sacred island of Delos has very ancient sanctities, a grave respected by the Greeks and a cave temple, which seem to shew eastern influence, this is an attractive theory; but in no sense proved, any more than the others, though it offers the most probable origin of the name. Apollo's instruments, the bow and the lyre, are compatible with an eastern origin. But his importance at the oracle of Delphi in north Greece, where his worship is said by the Homeric *Hymn to Apollo* to have come from Crete, and some mysterious offerings sent annually to him at Delos from somewhere in the north, beyond Greece, suggest that the eastern origin is a mistake. On the other hand, Apollo may have come from the east to Crete first and then to Delphi; and the offerings may have come from Greek colonists in the area of the eastern Danube, not from any place of Apollo's origin in the north. Apollo was specially a god both of Dorians, and of Greeks in Asia Minor. He may well represent a fusion of divine figures from the east and from the north; or cognate invaders from the north may have brought Apollo with them, some to Greece and others to Asia Minor.

Athena also has a mysterious name. It is not Indo-European. It has a termination belonging to a pre-Greek language which left behind place-names such as Mycenae, Priene, and Mitylene. This language must have been imposed from the east on Greece not long after 2000 B.C., according to the correspondence of the place-names with sites occupied at such dates. Athena has much in common with Asiatic goddesses, especially Ishtar, who was, like her, peculiarly the defender of cities, and seems to have had as her attribute the owl; at least, a Babylonian relief shews an armed goddess flanked by owls, clearly, in a sense, a form of Ishtar, whatever her name may have been. Athena however has other antecedents. She is certainly a descendant of the Minoan armed goddess of the home or palace, known from plastic art. She has as her attribute a shield, and originally she may have been a shield, later personified. A shield belonging to her was ritually washed and carried round the city of Argos in historical times. From the armed goddess of the Mycenaean palace she became the armed goddess of the Greek citadel; it might happen as at Athens that her temple was built near or at the place where the old palace had been, and perhaps an old heroic king would be remembered, as Ajax was, not as the master of the house she guarded, but as her consort. Athena has been thought to have come to Greece from Crete and to Crete from Egypt or Libya. She has affinities with a goddess known there, and Homer calls her Tritonis or Tritogeneia, a name sometimes associated with the lake Tritonis on the coast of Libya where Herodotus (IV. 180) says that she was still worshipped.

In the *Iliad* Athena is strongly on the side of the Achaeans, and especially protects Achilles and Diomedes; in the *Odyssey* she guides Odysseus with unceasing care. She thus protects Homer's favourite heroes, and she is clearly his favourite goddess. In the *Iliad* she has a temple in Troy, where excavation shews that birds thought by some to be owls were represented; and the Trojans worship her, to gain her protection. In earlier versions of the story of Troy Athena very likely protected the city till the 'palladion', the sacred talisman carrying the luck of the city and to some extent representing her, was stolen by Odysseus and Diomedes. But either led by that hint, or for other reasons, Homer chose her to protect the Achaeans all the time, and especially his favourite heroes. There is an obscure sense in which Athena is goddess of the air, and the αἰγίς, aigis, or goatskin, which she carries represents storm clouds. But it is not very relevant. More relevant is her care of the civilized arts of the household, and the sensible, harmonious life which went on in the houses and cities which she protected. She was said to have been born motherless from the head of Zeus, a story which has been explained as meaning that she was born out of the earth, on a mountain, since Zeus is at home on mountains; perhaps the idea originated in some folk-lore like the modern Tibetan, in which it is believed that a living being, created by the intense mental concentration of an adept, first appears emanating from the adept's head.

Artemis has, like Apollo, a difficult name, and the only probable suggestion is that she is the eastern Rutamis. The transposition of the first vowel and consonant, and the change of the vowel, present no difficulty philologically. The name cannot be explained as meaning anything in any Indo-European dialect. She is perhaps the most important of the Greek goddesses who represent the earth-goddesses of eastern and Mediterranean lands. These earth-goddesses are old, and spread over the neolithic area from Western Asia, through Crete, towards Western Europe. They are known by the fat clay images of them found in many places from palaeolithic times onwards. In a sense it was the same goddess everywhere. Even in the highly developed Minoan and Mycenaean civilizations there seems to have been only one important goddess, though she may have had emanations or manifestations in a few various forms. She may have been what Aeschylus calls her, 'Earth, a single form, of many names'.

That is what she was afterwards. The Greeks had Gaia, which means 'earth', Rhea, possibly not originally a Greek name, Demeter, supposed to mean 'earth mother' or 'barley mother', Hera herself, possibly Themis, a mysterious goddess who may mean the laws of nature, Persephone, to some degree Aphrodite the love-goddess, Athena herself in some aspects, and Artemis, all goddesses important as representative to them of the universal goddess of the earth and nature, mother of all. Artemis like Athena came to be emphatically a maiden. But for early times that does not mean permanent maidenhood, but recurrent maidenhood, like the maidenhood of the earth in winter, before fertilization starts the spring. There was a Greek rite to renew the maidenhood of Hera. Both were often, certainly, married, especially Artemis. As nature-goddess, she is 'the queen of wild beasts' like the goddesses of Crete and Asia, and at Ephesus was pictured with a large number of beasts in association with her. In poetry Artemis is closely associated with the country and wild life. In Homer she is an archer, like Apollo her brother; their mother Leto bore them together on Delos. She is not very active in taking sides or protecting men; but she particularly looks after women, especially at childbirth, and she is mysteriously the cause of natural death, for she is often said to 'take' someone 'for her mark, and slay with gentle missiles'.

Hermes is unusually interesting. He has an Indo-European name, meaning something like 'fixture'. So far as his name goes, he is originally a monolith or pillar. Now in the ancient neolithic or early bronze-age culture which is at the base of the classical civilizations, Minoan and Palestinian included, standing stones were most important religious objects. They were centres of power for reasons that are not entirely clear. In general, stone was venerated for its qualities of strength and utility, just as metal was later venerated for its sharpness and hardness, and as, in general, weapons have commanded reverence everywhere. In Egypt the hieroglyphic sign for any god, 'neter', seems to depict an axe. But stones were revered for other reasons, at the same or at different times. They were thought to contain the spirits of ancestors. This is general in 'stone' cultures. Partly combined with the same conception there was a tendency to make standing stones phallic, symbols of the organ of life. From the standing stone comes the gravestone, in Greek στήλη, stēlē, which means something that stands. Stones, then, mean life in death; or they may be regarded as the way between life and death. Perhaps independent of this original conception is the conception of the boundary stone, dividing one man's land from another's; this use is certain to be later, because private ownership of land is later.

Hermes represents all these notions, with a mysterious multiplicity of identities. Lucian in one of his works (*D. Deor.* 24) makes Hermes complain about his manifold duties. It is clear that he is many things. All is intelligible, if he began as a standing stone, as his name suggests. That he did so is made certain by what are called herms, ἕρμαι, hermai. They are standing stones; and 'Hermes' is really only the common name applied to them. These standing stones are at first square blocks. Then the tops are roughly sculptured into heads. Eventually the blocks become graceful statue busts, such as the 'hermai' damaged by Alcibiades in 415 B.C. just before the

Athenian expedition to Sicily; but still square from the neck down. Their old nature, however, sometimes survives explicitly in a strongly marked phallic organ.

The Greek Hermes stands between life and death. He takes the souls of the dead to their home beyond the grave; and he is shewn doing this in the last book of the *Odyssey*. He can also call up the spirits of the dead into the world of men again, as in some famous vase-paintings. He uses a magic wand, called a caduceus, with two snakes twined round it. The snakes are presumably the snakes in which the dead are widely supposed to manifest themselves above the earth; but their development into a wand would take too long to discuss.

It is as a messenger between two worlds that Hermes appears chiefly in Homer, but they are especially the world of gods above and the world of men. Hermes takes a message from Zeus to Calypso, to tell her to let Odysseus go. In the *Iliad* he uses his function of guide to guide Priam to the Achaean camp, to meet Achilles and ask for the body of Hector. He is young and attractive, and never seems to have strong opinions of his own.

There is another messenger of the gods, Iris. She has nothing to do with the earth originally, but is mainly a personification of the rainbow, which stretches down from the sky. She seems to be far more important in Homer, where she takes several messages, than she is anywhere else, except in Vergil. She is a graceful symbol of divine intercourse with men; but she hardly has a personality.

Ares the war-god has an Indo-European name, which seems to mean something like 'strong'. He is always more at home in the North, and is really a Thracian, never quite acclimatized in Greece. This says much for the Greeks. In Homer his character is unpleasant; he is selfish, rude and cowardly; he is wounded by the mortal Diomedes, retreats to Olympus, howling with pain, and there, after some nursing, sits 'exulting in his glory'. He fights for the Trojans. He is never at all a sympathetic figure except when he is used for a comparison. A fighting man is sometimes praised by being compared to Ares.

There is another war-god, Enyalios, and a kind of war-goddess, Enyo, besides. Enyalios is used in comparisons, especially at the impressive moment (22. 132) when Achilles is advancing on Hector, 'a match for Enyalios, warrior god, with his darting plume'. Ares and Enyo are said to revel madly in the melée. But Enyalios and Enyo are vague in outline. Their names are not known as Indo-European; they presumably had an obscure origin in the Minoan or Mycenaean world.

Aphrodite is specially at home in Cyprus. She came from the south and east, not from the north. She is a form of the earthgoddess originally, and her name is apparently a local name for her in some unknown language. In Greek myth she 'rose from the sea', and the Greeks connected her name with ἀφρός, aphros, 'foam'. She is akin to the Minoan and Asiatic earthgoddesses, who have associated with them a young male god, partly son and partly lover, such as Tammuz and Adonis. In Homer she is a source of attractiveness. She makes Hera beautiful, so that Zeus may fall in love with her again. Paris is her special favourite, and she gave Helen to him. She has somehow become married to the lame craftsman-god Hephaestus in the *Odyssey*, where Ares commits adultery with her, reported in a lay of Demodocus clearly meant to be amusing. In the *Iliad* (18. 382–3) Hephaestus is married to a symbolic figure Charis, a name which means 'grace'.

Hephaestus has a name recalling Phaistos, a Minoan town in Southern Crete, but he is closely comparable in his functions to the northern god Weyland the Smith. He is specially at home in the island of Lemnos, where he fell, after Zeus threw him out of heaven in anger. He presumably to some extent represents a meteorite, worshipped as such; but to a greater extent the spirit of skill projected by some close guild of metal workers, in Lemnos or elsewhere.

Lastly, there is silver-footed Thetis of the sea, mother of Achilles by a mortal father Peleus. Her name seems Greek. She seems to have been not quite a full goddess, but one among many spirits of the sea, a sea-nymph. But she is more than a Homeric divinity; she is Homer's type of a mother, and she is all Greek, and all Homeric.

There are many less important deities, some not quite deities at all, but supernatural beings of narrower power and dignity.[1] There is Calypso, who is the remains of a kind of guardian ghost, who admits the dead into the cave of burial and the life beyond. Her name is Greek and means 'she who covers'. There is the witch Circe, whose name is like the Greek word for a hawk, κίρκος, kirkos. She bewitches the sailors of Odysseus with drugs and a magic wand. She seems to originate in some ritual of purification for a new stage of life, here or hereafter, and to have found a place in some ritual-myth of the soul's journey, like the guardian witch in the Babylonian *Epic of Gilgamish* called Sidurri Sabîtu. Then there are the Muses, who themselves sing at ceremonies for great heroes, at the marriage of Peleus and Thetis, and at the funeral of Patroclus; they were at first spirits of brooks and streams, and later represented especially the musical and poetic power which the flowing water seemed to possess. There is Leucothea or Ino, a mysterious but lovely sea-nymph who saves Odysseus; there are the Cyclopes, wild giants who live in caves, and seem to be partly real men who spread from Lycia to Greece about 2000 B.C. and later built ring-walls round cities, the 'Cyclopean walls' of old Greece, and may be the same as the race who left a series of place-names with special endings, like Parnassos, Korinthos (Corinth), and Mycenae; partly also gorillas or very savage human beings; and partly symbols of volcano craters; though they owe something also to a Babylonian fire-god. There are Scylla and Charybdis, the former a rock, perhaps from the root of our words 'Scilly' and 'Skerrig', and the latter a whirlpool, which has been compared for its name with the whirlpool Corrievreckan off the west coast of Scotland, but both developed into living monsters of dangerous powers. The Phaeacians who live in the land, probably an island, of Scheria are not entirely human. The gods visit them on equal terms. They have no war, and their ships steer of their own accord. Their land is a kind of fairy-land, where things grow with a strange luxuriance; and when Odysseus leaves Phaeacia, he travels home in a magical sleep, like the sleep which ends the ordeal of many a religious rite.

Proteus, the old sea-god who shepherds seals, is peculiarly

[1] The substance of pp. 111–12 receives an extended treatment in the author's *Cumaean Gates*, now reissued as part of a composite volume, *Vergil: Epic and Anthropology*, London, 1967.—J.D.C.

interesting. He prophesied to Menelaus, but first had to be caught, which was difficult since he changed to so many shapes. He is, in so far as he is one real person rather than another, an Egyptian pharaoh with magical powers. Even his name may represent Prouti, which was one of the indirect descriptions of the king of Egypt used by Egyptians, to whom the king was too sacred to mention directly. 'Pharaoh' itself is another. It means 'Big House', Per aah, reminding us of modern usages like 'The White House', 'Downing Street', and 'The Quai d'Orsay'. Herodotus (II. 112 *ff.*) may be representing 'Prouti' when he calls an Egyptian king 'Proteus'.

The gods who are gods in the fullest sense live together in separate houses. Where they live is not uniformly and clearly specified throughout Homer. In the *Iliad* it is apparently Mount Olympus. Mount Olympus is in northern Greece, to the north of Thessaly. The tradition about it must have been started by Greeks living within sight of it. It is usual to imagine gods living on mountains, especially sky-gods and weather-gods. The mountain-sign is known to describe a god in Egypt. There were 'high places', sanctuaries of a god of a mountain, of the sky, or of the weather, in Crete, as in Palestine. The Greeks who lived near Mount Olympus imagined their particular gods on this particular mountain; and apparently continued to do so when they were out of sight of it. There is nothing strange in this, all the less because Mount Olympus is far the most impressive mountain in Greece. There mountains often rise sharply to several thousand feet; on the little island of Thasos to about 3,500, and on the still smaller island of Samothrace, only about eight miles long by six wide, to more than 5,000. This is a not uncommon height. Pelion is not much more. There are higher mountains; Parnassus is more than 8,000. But Olympus is quite by itself, in its height of nearly 9,600 feet. Further, it is a wild and terrifying mountain, where thunderstorms are surprisingly frequent, and, further, meteorites often fall. It inevitably seemed to be the very home of the mightiest sky-god, and it was so remembered.

There were other mountains in Greece called Olympus, and there was the place Olympia in the north-west of the Peloponnese. Here there was an ancient worship; the oldest houses are of about 1500 B.C. Some Greeks came there from the north and established their Olympian Zeus. The place was called after him; there was no Mount Olympus there, but only a small hill, known as the Mount of Kronos, who was the father of Zeus and son of Οὐρανός, Uranos, 'sky', the first ruler of the universe according to tradition. The place became famous for the Olympic games, probably the survival or revival of something which had been there before the coming of Olympian Zeus.

In the *Iliad* the gods seem to live on Olympus, possibly at varying levels, but not far apart. They visit other mountains, Ida which overlooks Troy, and Samothrace which is in sight of it; and they move about on the earth. But Homer also regards the sky as in some sense the home of the gods. He often describes them as possessing, or living in, the wide sky; but there is no real confusion in imagining the gods both there and on the mountain.

In the *Odyssey* the sky is in a clearer sense their home, rather than Mount Olympus. Apparently a process, started when the worshippers of Olympian Zeus left the neighbourhood of Mount Olympus, had reached its natural result. It is really a return to an older conception, in which Zeus *was* the sky. After that he came down to live on Olympus, when he became more personal; then he attracted the other gods to live there near him; and lastly they all went into the sky together.

The result is to some extent artificial, as all the gods except Zeus may be said to belong to the earth or sea. In fact, many have local homes. Athena when she goes to her home in the *Odyssey* (7. 81), goes to the 'solid house of Erechtheus' in Athens. Apollo is especially attached to Delos. Homer calls Hera 'Argive'; 'argos' in Homer means 'plain', and the Argives are 'people of the plain', a general Homeric name for Achaeans; and so Hera is the goddess of the Argives and at home in some 'plain', probably near the northern coast of the Peloponnese, or some less mountainous area in north Greece.

The Olympian family is thus a very peculiar creation, the result of many different processes, going on at different places and times. There is no unitary Greek mythology. Herodotus (II. 53) says that Homer and Hesiod defined the names and functions of the gods. There is some truth in this. The unification of the pantheon is artificial, however natural the development of many local cults may have been. And even Homer's pantheon is not unitary, less unitary than Milton's, for example, which it resembles in its artificiality. For Homer uses gods for different purposes. They give him delightful old tales, which he brings up to date in his own way and makes as comic as they are naturally qualified to become. To him, joking about the Olympians was like joking about Jonah and the whale is to us. It was all so remote from his feelings of sanctity. He joked not about the Divine but about what foolish people said about the gods. That is not the whole story. Homer lived in a sophisticated age, but he was nearer to early conditions of society than we are. And in such conditions reverence is not so insistently claimed by a divine being as are many other tributes of various kinds such as ritual purity and accuracy of observances. Besides some acts which we should call positively sinful, merriment was enjoined in Greek worship, as in the procession from Athens to Eleusis before the celebration of the Eleusinian Mysteries. In Attic comedy, and elsewhere—it happened in Japanese drama—the gods were mocked. You either had to laugh, or might laugh; but there was much else which you were peremptorily ordered or forbidden to do.

There is another side, however. The great Greek poets and philosophers add something always. They have their personal moral convictions and spiritual apprehensions. It has been said that all Greek literature is highly moral. Each great writer transcends the mythology which he inherits from a predecessor. The mythology is not great enough to carry the message. A successor creates a sufficient mythology; but one sufficient only for his predecessor's message, not for his own.

Homer is like that, but in one way peculiar. He composes epic, a peculiarly complete kind of literature, with very many moods and meanings and kinds of adventure. There must be the comic side of life, and Homer chooses an old-fashioned framework for it. But he has his own majestic religious convictions, awe, and hope; and for them there was no mythology or symbolism which was quite new. So Homer worked on two levels. He selected from the old mythology what might serve to carry his own personal meaning. Without caring that the nursery-rhyme Zeus had been used for comic amusement, Homer could suddenly introduce apparently the same Zeus, and then make him the supreme and awful sovereign of all the universe. It works well. We are quite content to accept the moment (*Il.* 1. 528–30) when Zeus nods consent, his dark hair swinging forward, and all Olympus shaking, or (22. 209–13) when he weighs the souls of Achilles and Hector in the scales, and 'down went for Hector his day of destiny'. Homer is so great that he can put any character back on his pedestal, whatever has happened before.

He nevertheless distinguishes between the deities. Some he rarely if ever takes seriously, as if they meant little to his religious sense, and seemed unnecessary. Perhaps he did not think a god of war, for example, necessary, or a proper object of worship. But three deities meant so much to him that he always respects their dignity. They fit his own sense of awe, of right, and of hope. They are his gods; by coincidence forms created by other minds very nearly fit his needs.

One of these deities is Poseidon. Like all Greeks, Homer found it hard to laugh at the power of the sea. He thrilled to its peril, and to its loveliness. But he did not laugh. Nor could he laugh at Apollo, god of the silver bow and wondrous lyre, for Apollo was in his own song, and he knew Apollo's might on him; and of Apollo was his song, Apollo who hit from afar, the lovely, the masterful, the dangerous, Apollo who could not save Hector, but who thrust Patroclus back from Troy wall. Then, lastly, Athena was not for Homer's laughter; Athena, the power in the world which answers man out of the impossible, if man can do for himself the possible, and a little more; Athena, the brave clear wisdom and will and restraint in man, when he stands on his own feet and holds to the knowledge that it is the living and the way of it that count; Athena, again and again in the verse 'own daughter of the Father', the active force for good and bright living, which yet is the strongest thing that ever came from behind the darkness of that dark hair which clusters over the will and purpose of all the world.

VI

HOMERIC MYTH AND LEGEND
(*continued*)

The heroes of Homer, who are represented as certainly human, with nothing supernatural about them except sometimes divine descent, do not raise the same problem as Homer's gods. The gods have very various and composite origins. Euhemerus, who lived in Sicily in the fourth century B.C., thought that all the gods were originally men. This is not wholly false; few theories about mythology are. Some gods were originally in some degree men. Zeus, at first the sky regarded with fear and hope, became, without much doubt, a human rainmaker, representing the sky and later the god of the sky living on Mount Olympus, and in the end a god of all the world, living in the sky. Some of the earth-goddesses certainly were to some extent, in early stages of their development, priestesses or other human officiants taking part in sacred marriages, to promote fertility by sympathetic magic. Hermes was partly a dead ancestor, and in part also the monolith in which the dead ancestor was supposed to live on. But many other influences went towards making gods. Trees had a part. For example, Zeus includes in him the spirit of the oak tree, in close touch with the sky because oaks are so often hit by lightning; the oldest oracle in Greece is said to be the oracle of Zeus at Dodona, where oracles were given by priestesses from the movement of oak trees. Animals too have a part; it is not entirely false to say that Hera was once a cow and Athena an owl.

Heroes also have complex origins. A great man is at the base of many or most heroic personalities, but not all, though in Homer they are all so well characterized that it is hard to believe that they have not all equal right to their humanity. That they have not all an equal right is certain; but just how much right each has, it is rarely if ever possible to decide exactly, since there is no kind of irresistible proof available.

There are plenty of proved historical personalities long before the Trojan War. In Mesopotamia and Egypt there are contemporary records of real men before 3000 B.C.; Hittite names are reliable from about the eighteenth century B.C. But in

Europe there are no contemporary historical documents which can be read till the eighth century, and very little until the fifth.

There are foreign records about Greeks. Egyptian monuments mention Greek tribes attacking Egypt or serving as mercenary troops in the Egyptian army in the thirteenth century; and before that, as early as the fifteenth, correspondence in Hittite on clay tablets exchanged between Hittite kings and Achaean leaders gives names not only of peoples and places, but of individuals also. There are however difficulties. There are uncertainties in the reading of the records. But some names are certain or nearly certain.

The Egyptian and Hittite documents prove that Homer is at least approximately accurate in saying that Achaeans and other Greeks had active power in the east Mediterranean between about 1500 and 1150 B.C. It is, therefore, extremely likely that many of his characters are historical, but not one certainly is.

In the reign of Mursilis II, king of the Hittites from about 1336 B.C., a ritual text invokes the gods of the Hittite king and of the countries Ahhiyawā and Lazpa and mentions Antarawas a king of Ahhiyawā. A royal letter of about the same date calls the king of Ahhiyawā 'brother', implying that he is a great king also; a people in southern Asia Minor had asked help against invasion both from the Hittite king and from Tawagalawas, a relative of the king of Ahhiyawā, and himself an 'Ayavalash' king. In another letter the kings of Ahhiyawā, Egypt, Babylonia, Assyria and the Hittites are all regarded as equal in dignity. Then there are later documents of the reign of Tudhaliyas IV, dated soon after 1250 B.C. They say that Attarissiyas, a king of Ahhiyawā, attacked Caria, in the south of Asia Minor, several times unsuccessfully but later, about 1225 B.C., ravaged Cyprus. In the earlier period a country Assuwa, in north-western Asia Minor, is mentioned, and in it, and near to Lazpa, a city called Taroisa, which might be Troy. About 1300 B.C. King Muwatallis made an agreement with Alaksandus, king of Wilusiya in Arzawa; Wilusiya was a city in southern Asia Minor, so that it cannot be Ilion or Troy, and it had had relations with the Hittite King Labarnas, several generations before Mursilis.

Early in the fourteenth century Akhenaton, king of Egypt,

exchanged letters with the Hittite king, and the correspondence survives on clay tablets found where Akhenaton's capital was, Tell el-Amarna. A tribe called Danuna is mentioned as settled on the coast of Palestine. When Ramesses II fought his great battle at Kadesh in 1286 B.C., among his enemies on the Hittite side were tribes called Lukka, Pidasa, Karkisa, Dardanya, Masa, and another tribe called perhaps Yawan or Arawanna.

Later in this century there were attacks on Egypt from the north, east and west; Merneptah, the Egyptian king, had to fight a great battle, both by land and by sea, in the Egyptian delta in 1221 B.C. to repel them. According to an Egyptian inscription at Medinet Habu, they came from all directions and from 'the islands in the great green', and 'fought daily in order to fill their stomachs'. Some came with their families, carried on ox-waggons. There were Libyans from the west, and also Luka, Aqiwasa, and Turusa or Tursha.

A generation afterwards, in 1190 B.C., there was another attack. This time the king of Egypt, Ramesses III, had Shardina and Tursha on his side as mercenaries. The tribes mentioned are Shardina, Pulusatha, Uashasha, Tshakaray, and Danau or Danuna.

This amounts to contemporary, literary evidence for the peoples who are the subject of the Homeric poems, and for others who belonged to their world. The evidence is at first much earlier than the Trojan War.

Some of the peoples mentioned by the Hittites and Egyptians can be identified with greater or less assurance. It is not often possible to be quite sure because in languages written in syllabic or hieroglyphic script words cannot always be transliterated exactly; a sign may convey more or less than the original sound. There are also doubts about how to read the names; for example in Egyptian the same sign stands for 'l' and for 'r', so that a tribe called 'Iliunna' has been thought by some to come from Oroanda, and by others to be Ilians from Ilion, the other name of Troy.

There are, however, some names which can be thought certainly identified. There is no need to doubt that Greek Achaeans, men of Mycenaean culture, are mentioned in contemporary Hittite and Egyptian records under the names of Ahhiyawā and Aqiwasa. A king of Achaeans, therefore,

reigned over a political unit comparable in power and dignity
to the great empires of the east before 1300 B.C. Some of these
Achaeans lived somewhere in southern Asia Minor. Between
1250 and 1200 B.C. the men of Ahhiyawā attacked Caria
repeatedly but unsuccessfully, and then succeeded in ravaging
Cyprus. In 1221, with other tribes, they were defeated by the
Egyptians as they attempted to invade Egypt.

If that was all, it would be important enough. And perhaps
the identification of the Achaeans might be considered the only
one that is quite certain. There are however others which are
probable or possible.

Of the names in the Hittite documents, Lazpa may be
Lesbos. It was occupied by Agamemnon according to the *Iliad*
(9. 128–30); but more archaeological confirmation is needed,
if the equation is to be trusted. Tawagalawas and Antarawas
were at first thought to be Eteocles, or Eteoklewes, and
Andreus; princes of Boeotia, according to the legends, have
these names, but they are too remote, and the identification is
not probable. Attarissiyas was supposed to be Atreus, father of
Agamemnon. There are philological arguments against that,
but he may well be Perseus, who according to Josephus was
operating with a large fleet on the south coast of Asia Minor
about that time, and founded Tarsus, a city possibly called
after his name. Alaksandus, king of Wilusiya in Arzawa, was
believed to be Alexander, king of Ilios. Wilusiya turns out
to be too far to the south in the context, but Alexander may
well represent the name represented as Alaksandus, even if a
different Alexander is meant.

Of the tribes mentioned by the Egyptians, the Danuna or
Danau are almost or quite certainly Danaans, Danaoi; that is
in Homer apparently a rather old name for Greeks or a Greek
tribe, which was already going out of use in favour of Achaeans,
Achaioi, and Argives, Argeioi. The Lukka are clearly Lycians.
The Pidasa may be from near Pedasus, but are less certain.
There is little doubt that Karkisa, Dardanya, and Masa are
Cilicians, Dardanians, in Homer close kin to Trojans, and
Mysians. The Yawan, or whatever the spelling ought to be,
used to be supposed Ionians, but that was wrong, and they are
admitted now to be unknown. The Lycians and Achaeans occur
again among tribes defeated by Merneptah in 1221 B.C. There

are also Turusa or Tursha, who are probably Tyrseni, Tyrsenoi, the people from Lydia in western Asia Minor who sailed to Italy and became known as the Etruscans. In the attack of 1190 B.C. they appear on the side of Egypt, with Shardina, who are possibly Sardinians on their way from Sardis in Asia Minor to Sardinia in the west Mediterranean. The Pulusatha are Philistines, the Uashasha are uncertain, the Tshakaray may be Teucri, close kin of the Trojans, and the Danau or Danuna are Danaans as before.

The Homeric idea of an Achaean confederacy occupying lands and fortresses and sailing the seas is fully confirmed by the records of the Egyptians and Hittites, and by the remains. The individuals in Homer have names in general probable enough, and behave often in a probable way. But some have religious associations. Agamemnon was worshipped as Zeus Agamemnon. Menelaus had a shrine at Sparta called the Menelaeion in which Helen was worshipped; and a 'Helenē dendritis', 'Helen spirit of the tree', was worshipped in Rhodes. In many parts of Greece heroes were worshipped who have the names of Homeric heroes. Aias, Ajax, appears as the divine consort of Athena, forming with her a divine pair sharing temples. A Hector, taken to be the Trojan Hector, was worshipped in Greek Thebes.

The status of all these heroes is not the same. Agamemnon's name is scarcely Greek; the names of the others vary. This suggests that the Greeks at any rate did not invent him as a human being. In other epic, elsewhere, the leading prince is usually historical, as for example Theodoric in Teutonic epic, and Charlemagne in the *Chansons de Geste*. That Agamemnon is called Zeus proves little. The process is apparently this. Herodotus (II. 52) says that the 'Pelasgians', who lived in Greece before the Greeks, worshipped nameless spirits to whom the Greeks gave names. It is unlikely that the tribe called Pelasgians occupied all the places later occupied by Greeks, but otherwise the statement is credible. The names given by the Greeks to the nameless spirits might be names of gods or names of heroes, probably often ancestors. What happened to Agamemnon was this. His name was given to some power already worshipped. The name of Zeus was given too, either before or after. Agamemnon was treated as an epithet of Zeus,

who is found with many epithets, such as Zeus Horkios, Zeus
god of oaths, Zeus Labrayndos, Zeus god of the double axe,
and Zeus Xenios, Zeus god of strangers. Zeus is not alike
everywhere; in Crete he actually had a tomb, as if he were not
a god at all, but a hero.

Menelaus and Helen are different. Menelaus has a Greek
name; he may well be quite historical. He was worshipped like
many other heroes, and the worship proves nothing. Helen's
name is obscure. It has been traced to a Teutonic root meaning
'light', but without certainty. It is possibly enough a human
name; but the occurrence of Helenus as the name of a Trojan
prince suggests that it was a divine name first, adopted by some
one as a human name. Then there was the tree-spirit called
Helen. A heroine's name might easily be given to a spirit that
was nameless. But then Helen was in some myths rescued
from the world below. She was rescued by Theseus. So she is
like Persephone, also rescued from the world below, or Ariadne,
certainly a kind of goddess, who was rescued by Theseus. On
the whole Helen looks like a human princess with a divine
name. A human princess was stolen from Sparta, probably
because the throne depended on marriage with an heiress.
Then the name of the princess was forgotten; and her adventures and personality became attached to the name of a
goddess who was like her in beauty, and in having to be
rescued. Perhaps this comes to seem still more likely when it is
remembered that Paris, who stole her, has a name that is not
Greek, and is probably enough Trojan, and has also another
name, Alexander, which is the name of a robber in Greek
story. So then a historical event concerning Paris and a nameless princess has been attached to the names of a goddess from
myth, and a robber from legend or folk-tale. It is an example
of similar myth and fact combining to form what might be
called a mythical legend.

The claim of Aias, Ajax, to be human is less. He is the
ancestor of a clan, giving his name to it, the Aiantidae; it is not
agreed whether this is an argument for or against his humanity,
but by analogy it should probably count for it. Ajax has
become attached to Athena as her consort, possibly in the way
in which the divine personality Helen has become attached in
cult to the more probably human personality Menelaus, but

possibly because Ajax is originally a sort of shadow of Athena. She is the armed Mycenaean goddess of the fort or home; her symbol is a shield. Now Ajax is remarkable for his tower shield in Homer, a shield of the Minoan or Mycenaean pattern, meant to cover the whole of a man and to be used without armour. Further, Ajax was said to have a father called Telamon, which means a shield-strap. Also, he was said to have been buried in a sarcophagus, like the Minoans and Mycenaeans of archaeology, and not cremated, like other heroes in Homer, and like Trojans who really died at Troy, according to the latest discovery of cremation burials there. Ajax, then, looks less human than other heroes in origin. Ultimately, he may even be the male attendant on the goddess, shewn on a Minoan gem, coming down, with his shield, from the sky to join her. If so, he could naturally have become detached from his religious setting, and might then have developed a human personality, like the Olympian gods themselves.

Other heroes have been thought to have started as divinities. There is Nestor, who has been regarded as a god of death, his name meaning something like 'to whom all come'. Laomedon, father of Priam, has also been regarded as a death-god; he is notable for his horses, and horses are symbols of death; and his name means something like 'ruler of the people', a description possibly applicable to a god of death. But neither theory is sufficiently proved.

Achilles has even been supposed to be really the sun, and his career the daily passage of the sun, its conflict with darkness, and its setting. This old-fashioned, and apparently grotesque and fantastic, opinion is on the one hand a dangerous fallacy, and on the other contains or implies a certain degree of truth. The fallacy is obvious. An immense number of heroes have been regarded as the sun, and to go on this way is to ruin mythological science. Plenty of legendary heroes are real men. Even if nature-myths are important, myths of the sun are not nearly the most important. The earth and even the moon are much more noticed by early men, who indeed do not at first realize that the sun is the cause of light; only a few years ago a native of Egypt shewed by an answer that he gave that he did not realize it fully. Further, the solar theory is inclined to say that Achilles and others are nothing but the sun. This is the most dangerous part, since fully developed mythological beings are nearly always many things at once. The truth implied in the theory is this. In Babylonia and Egypt the journey of the sun below the earth, from sunset to sunrise, came to symbolize the journey of dead men, who passed at burial into the earth, and so returned to the mother who bore them. The sun came to be noticed as doing something like this, and it and the soul of the departed were either confused, or at least thought to go the same way. As far away as New Zealand and North America such a conception is found. If it is natural to identify a man with the sun for one purpose, the identification may be made again for others. The mind follows the old mythological pattern; as when the Phoenician 'Heracles' travels on his labours, twelve in number like the months of the year, in the cup of the sun, recalling the boat of the sun in Egyptian myth. Such myths, from Egypt or elsewhere, certainly affected Greece. But there is no reliable sign that Achilles and the sun have any sort of identity.

Tithonus, who married the Dawn, and Memnon, their son who fought for Troy after the place in the story where the *Iliad* ends, obviously have something to do with the sun. It is hard to say what; both may be developed out of officiants at some forgotten ceremony connected with the dawn. In Egypt divine or partly divine beings, the 'monkey gods', are represented as welcoming the sun at its rising.

Odysseus, in spite of the mythological antecedents of his name as Olysseus, is quite possibly the most human in origin of all the heroes. His kingdom is a natural dominion over real places, clearly according to a reliable tradition. He fought at Troy and was remembered. There is a view that he was a much greater king than Homer says, and ruled far into the western lands and seas; but that in a manner characteristic of epic, especially in the European dark ages, the scale of his public importance has been reduced to increase, by concentration, his human appeal. This is possible but unproved. But it is hard not to think that the pilgrim's progress on which Odysseus goes is partly modelled on the imaginative plan of the journey of the dead man to the life beyond the grave, a journey itself blended with the journey of the sun. It is a westward journey, to a journey's end of heart's desire and of life; it passes through the cave of Calypso, 'She who hides', to the shades, by the stream of Oceanus, that is, the 'waters of death'; and it ends in a western island. All this and more is characteristic of the mythical journey of the dead which survives in many lands. Homer, and other poets, found themselves telling the tale according to a familiar, mythical sequence. Fact, and myth that was like it, coalesced again, to form a legend. This is one of the 'myths' which evoke our sympathy. A westward journey in Homer means more to us, just because it meant so very much to our far distant ancestors.

It seems to be true that a real person not only can, but usually does, develop mythical attributes, if he does at all, within about two generations of his death. Many of Homer's heroes may have been real men and nothing more about 1200 B.C., and have reached a mythical aspect by the time the Dorians came, about 1100. But the mythical attributes which they acquired may have been far more ancient than they; a man might acquire quite quickly nearly all the attributes and even the name of a personality which had existed as something quite mythical and imaginary, for centuries.

The myths of Homer are true myths, in the sense that they have meaning; they are myths in the sense in which there are valuable myths today; and also in the sense in which some Christian people can talk about Christian mythology. They are not merely untrue statements, often about beings that never existed; they are useful to Homer in telling his tale, and useful too in helping his audience to win his world-view. They reveal Homer's wisdom.

Now how they do this has always been a question for controversy. The myths do not state what happened with literal truth, and so present definite and possibly useful knowledge. That might have been one excuse for them. Neither do they state something which, though it never happened, yet serves as a model of behaviour, and so imparts moral lessons by example.

There was much talk in ancient times about allegory, whether, and why, the myths and symbols of Homer should be, or should have been, taken to mean something that they do not say. The controversy is very enlightening by its uncertainties. Everything is allegory; and nothing is.

Greek science and philosophy grew out of myth and observation combined. The Greek thinkers at first used mythological thought and language to express their conclusions. Myth gave them a scheme to follow, and they used it to develop their rational structures, by substituting abstract conceptions for the concrete personalities in the myths.

Greek thinkers must soon have started imputing hidden meanings to Homer's myths. They had sharp intellects, and believing in reason could not be content with the plain meaning of the myths. The only other escape was to say that Homer's myths, being neither informative nor edifying, were bad. This many did not like to do, partly because they had the good judgment not to reject the general testimony of ordinary Greeks that Homer's poems, which were strongly mythical, were useful and good. So here was another motive why they should think that Homer used myths as they themselves did. But the defensive purpose of allegory was later than its earliest natural development.

Mythological language and patterns of thought were used more and more consciously and rationally to express scientific, philosophical, and religious theories. This seems to have had a reaction on Homer: the poems were interpreted allegorically, and the myths in them were understood to have hidden meanings not unlike the meanings which rational speculation had come to put into the mythological schemes, developed from old myths.

But allegorical interpretation, however much some writers, from Heraclitus onwards, must have trusted it as a defence of Homer, did not succeed when Plato shewed that, because the myths were neither exact truth nor morally edifying by the example which they set, Homer and other poets must be dangerous to society. So they must be, but they were not abandoned on account of that; mainly because they were enjoyable, and partly, perhaps, also because the ancients instinctively realized that, even if they were dangerous, it would be more dangerous still to abolish them.

Allegory is not taken seriously now, but, in various senses, some reasonable and others less reasonable, symbolism is. Symbolism, in the common-sense meaning which is sufficient for this argument, can reasonably be supposed to involve a process by which a sight seen or a sound heard, or combinations of them, or any of these imagined, suggest to the mind feelings and thoughts, simple or in combinations, which go far beyond the simplest meanings of the original apprehensions. Symbolism varies in its effect according to the history and condition of the receiving mind. It is not concerned with such fixed equations as allegory.

Further, it is found that symbolism does not depend originally on the conscious design of its apparent author. Shelley describes what poets do. They know not what they inspire. They are like a relay on a telegraph system. Current actuates the relay; it cannot itself read the message; but it reacts by releasing a new, stronger, current, with the same dots and dashes, to replace the current which has grown weak with distance. So a poet passes on a message with new strength; but unlike the telegraphic relay he alters and enriches the message with new meanings. The old superstitions of a distant past have a special power on poets, and awake their activity. They catch their imagination not entirely because they are intelligible and naturally acceptable to their thought, but even partly because they are mysterious, and hard to understand. They work with the attraction of the strange and unfamiliar; but only in part, and perhaps chiefly to conscious thinking. They also act by a mysterious familiarity, this time, probably, on the unconscious kind of mental receptivity. They enliven what survives in the unconscious mind, which wakes, and supplies power of itself in answer and in turn actuates consciousness.

In some way like this, myths appeal to an instinctive acceptance in a sympathy general to a class, a city, a nation, a culture, or even all humanity. They are more than untrue stories chosen at random, and just invented, if such a thing is possible. 'The oldest things last longest', and what is wholly new is wholly mad. You can put old content into a new form or new content into an old form; but if you put old content into an old form, that is death, and if you put new content into a new form, that is madness.

In so far as 'allegory', or at least something like new or secondary meanings given to old stories, is naturally late rather than early, it would belong to the more literary, reflective, and consciously planned kind of poetry rather than to spontaneous and simple-minded poetic performances, if such things exist.

In the beginning myths were formed by simple representation in narrative of the interaction of objects and forces made personal by the natural tendency of primitive apprehension, with or without the intervention of ritual performed by human beings who in some sense signified objects and forces.

This representation need carry little or no moral meaning. The mythic personalities which emerge may be feared or liked, but at first they are hardly considered bad or good. Later, goodness and badness are attributed to them naturally enough. The myths are told for centuries, and the mythic manner is applied more widely. Imperceptibly, moral ideas begin to be expressed mythically. A defeated god becomes a bad god, and then becomes a subject of compositions in which his badness is emphasized. Next an allegorical outlook nearly or quite intervenes. The good man protected by the good god is meant to be, and is understood as, some sort of statement about the place of goodness in the world. Odysseus protected by Athena is at least a little allegorical. The story makes some statement of the class 'Fortune favours the brave' or 'Those who deserve luck generally get it' or 'It is a good rule to trust in God and also to keep your powder dry'. Then the process may go the other way, and allegory may be turned back into myth. Hesiod has been cleverly said to do this. He strongly personifies moral states and forces and they come alive, like mythical figures that act first and are moralized and made informative after. The distinction is between what is meant to be that, and what is not. Of course, the best myths are often inevitably moral and informative, even if they are not meant to be.

The myths in Homer are at various stages of intentional and unintentional moralization. The gods, when they quarrel and are undignified, are often just fun and perhaps unmoral satire on humanity, like Chinese gods who in plays behave just like thoroughly human bureaucrats. But quite a different condition is found also. Abstract things are assimilated to the mythic form, and Homer himself writes intentional allegory. Phoenix begs Achilles to hear prayers (9. 502–14). He explains that prayers are the daughters of Zeus, that a wicked man may go much faster, but that the prayers, lame, wrinkled, and squint-eyed though they are, in the end bring the vengeance of Zeus on the sinner. The prayers can do great good to one who hears them, but great harm to one who does not. Again, something like a combination of myth and allegory is easily possible. When Hera sleeps with Zeus it is myth; but she enlists the aid of Aphrodite and Sleep, and that is a kind of allegorical personification (*Il.* 14. 188–221, 231–91). Sleep and Death together carry Sarpedon, after he is killed, to Lycia, again a kind of allegorical personification trying to become myth; and succeeding, too (16. 681–3).

Homer is a very long way from the time when most of his myths were new or even in an early stage of their growth. They had had much opportunity of being changed, combined, reorganized, and moralized, or even replaced by new and consciously created myths, since the time when they were statements of natural forces or ritual in personification and narrative, or something else as simple as that. Homer's myths are not in their original forms; it was noticed even in antiquity that he had broken up the old myths, reproducing them in fragmentary condition, and adding 'fictions' of his own. Such things are going on all the time; it is hardly sensible to carry the distinction between what is natural and what is artificial very far.

Homer and history have not quite made final terms. Ostensibly, he must be telling about a time in the last centuries before 1000 B.C. We have noticed that the facts of that time are known to some extent archaeologically; and the archaeological evidence is of two kinds, material remains and written documents.

The written documents are again of two classes, those which can be read and those which cannot. Documents from Greek lands cannot all be read. There are as yet undeciphered the two kinds of hieroglyphic script and one of the two kinds of linear script from Crete; the other, 'Linear B', found also in mainland Greece, has now been deciphered by Michael Ventris. The other documents that can be read are Asiatic, especially Babylonian, Hittite, and Syrian, including the Bible, and Egyptian. Here again there are two classes, documents directly referring to people in, or in contact with, Greek lands, and others which do not mention such people, but give an idea of the stage of culture already reached elsewhere in the world.

The documents assure us that civilization, including some

refinement of thought and moral consciousness, had advanced far before Homer's heroes lived. They were in contact with high cultures; for, as we have seen, Hittites and Egyptians contemporary with them explicitly mention them and know them well. The documents explain the probability and to some extent the actuality of a heroic age of adventure and violent movement in and near Aegean lands, an age of Viking raids, but also of advanced political organization, of the kind that Homer may well remember in this poetically simplified picture of Agamemnon's loose, but active and extensive, confederacy.

Apart from written documents, the material finds give a fairly clear picture of life in Greece and a less clear picture of life in Troyland between the rise and fall of the Mycenaean culture, about 1700 to 1100 B.C. They tell us a few facts definitely relevant to Homer.

There was a city or fortress at a place now called Hissarlik, where Troy seems, according to Homer, to have been. It started about 2500 B.C. and went on to Roman times, though the site was slightly changed by then. The sixth settlement on the site was destroyed in the thirteenth century. This has usually been thought Homer's 'city'. It begins to appear now, however, that the earlier stage of the seventh settlement, called VIIa, is Homer's.

Hissarlik may be admitted to be Troy. Other sites near have been supposed to have a better claim, chiefly because Hissarlik is so small. You can walk round it in eleven minutes, and it could not have held all the troops Homer imagines within it. Hissarlik, which was not a Mycenaean fortress, is much smaller than nearly all the contemporary Mycenaean fortresses known. But it is much better to suppose that Homer employed a little reasonable exaggeration than that the great walls of Hissarlik are not the walls of Troy, or that other places, which agree less well with Homer's geographical picture, have a better claim. Troy was there and Troy fell. There is no archaeological proof that Troy even fell to Achaean Greeks from Greece; and attempts have been made to shew that it fell to Thracians from the north, or later to colonizing Greeks of the historic age, after 900 B.C. Pottery, however, shews that it was in contact with the Mycenaean world. Troy fell to an invader. The Greek tradition, in and outside Homer, that Achaeans sacked it is so strong that it almost amounts to history. For once a guess is likely enough to be considered quite safe—the guess that Achaeans took Troy, the modern Hissarlik, about 1200 B.C.

Homer either went to Troy or followed an authority who had been there. He gives quite small details of the topography which are right. He understands the gates and walls and the country round. He even knows (*Il.* 22. 147–52) that the sources of the river Scamander were one hot spring and one cold, but he placed them too near the city. He is not always easy to follow on the actual ground; there is doubt about a hill and a hollow and a ford which he mentions, and there is still controversy whether the Achaean camp on the shore was at a place to the west or to the north-west of Troy. A change in the river system may account for some of the difficulties. It is hard to say how much of the disagreement is Homer's fault, and how much is ours; or, if Homer misrepresented the topography, exactly how, when, and why he did so.

All this is of only technical interest. Of more general interest is the certainty that Homer has or implies a knowledge of the ground and often a detailed fidelity to the knowledge which is altogether surprising, perhaps unique, in the work of a great creative artist. The wonder is, not that Homer did not give a picture of the ground which we can immediately see to be in exact agreement with the actual ground as it is now, but that he managed in his Greek way to put in so much literal fact without spoiling his work of art. Almost any artist who was not a Greek would have failed.

It is the same story with Ithaca and the kingdom of Odysseus. There have been attempts to shew that the modern Thiaki is not Ithaca because a nearby island is not big enough to be the island near Ithaca behind which Homer says the suitors hid; because Thiaki does not shew signs of habitation where and as it should; and because Homer describes it as lying in a slightly wrong position relative to the other islands. The suggestion is that Ithaca was really Leucas further to the north. But discussion has shewn that Thiaki is Ithaca. The only real difficulty is that Homer imagines Ithaca to lie rather more to the west than it does, and that difficulty is very slight. Without maps, Homer has very naturally forgotten some of the complicated landscape, especially as the *Odyssey* is written less factually than the *Iliad*, and imagination—as in the later work of Shakespeare, for example—is given freer rein. Again it is surprising how much local detail Homer accurately reproduces without spoiling his poem. Either he went to Ithaca, as the ancient *Lives* of Homer say that he did, or he used the information, conveyed by poetry or otherwise, of someone who had been there.

Excavation has made less progress in Ithaca than in Troy. The palace of Odysseus has not been found, and pottery of exactly the right date is still missing. But the island is well enough investigated to make it easy to admit that it is Homer's island, and fits his story well. One find deserves mention—an inscription of the third century B.C. which proves that people then were convinced that Ithaca was the Ithaca of Odysseus.

The finds support the rest of Homer's geography. They agree well with the Catalogue of Ships in the second *Iliad*, which gives a distribution of occupation and of power which fits the Mycenaean world, but definitely does not fit the world of later Greece.

Agamemnon's Mycenae, the Tiryns of Eurystheus and Heracles, the Argos of Diomedes, Therapne, the old Sparta of Menelaus, which is across the river from later, Dorian, Sparta, the Pylos of Nestor, some way from the later Pylos, and Thebes, and Orchomenos, and Mycenaean Athens, are known to us, almost as well as they are from the epic, from the spade.

The finds in these places, above all the brilliant metal-work from the shaft-graves at Mycenae, shew a life different from the life of Crete whence culture came, and a little more different still from the life shewn in Homer's poems. We can see the remains of the Homeric house, and pictures of the large Homeric shield, and the Homeric chariot, and actual swords like Homer's. We can guess contentedly at barons in their halls with their retainers, loosely serving an overlord who ruled the country with the help of Homeric ships, and of the Mycenaean roads still to be seen. But there is no sign so early in Greece of the usual Homeric dress and Homeric worship of Olympian gods in temples. In Greece there is no cremation so soon; but cremation is known at Troy at least as early as the Trojan War.

Homer's people are perhaps more like the people of the Icelandic and Celtic epic than Mycenaeans. They seem like the people of the Bohemian bronze age, known from excavation. And they have some affinity with the culture shewn by a few unusual sites, of the late bronze age or very early iron age, especially Halos in Thessaly. But they are Mycenaean too, and reigned in Mycenaean palaces. Homer pictures them as they were in 1100 B.C. and colours them with memories of their ancestors, natural and spiritual, two centuries and more before them.

VII

THE SOURCES OF HOMER

The eighteenth-century belief that Homer is in some sense primaeval or primitive, singing artlessly in the childhood of the world, seems strange to us now. We can hardly believe that Dr Johnson could have meant to say that Homer started all the stories that ever existed, and that all that later story-tellers had done had been to change names and make new combinations. It is almost harder to understand how Gladstone himself, rather a good Homeric scholar, could have suspected that when works of art or craftsmanship are found which are like objects described by Homer, this is because Homer imagined them out of nothing, and started the artists and craftsmen doing what otherwise they could not have done at all.

As usual, there is some truth in all this. Homer was in some senses nearer to the simple outlook of early people. He concentrates on a single thought at a time, and even seems to forget what he has just said and what he means to say. He starts sentences without finishing them, and, in a way, temporarily loses the thread. His style is co-ordinated like the Bible, not subordinated like classical Latin oratory, or Milton's verse.

Again, it really seems to be true that there is only a small, fixed number of possible plots. It is said that a story may have one of five, or perhaps seven, plots; for a film twenty-one possibilities have been claimed, but there the method of classification must be different. Homer tells the stories, in some or all of their possible forms, so impressively that he has had an immense influence. But though the stories have never been quite the same since he left his impress on them, their forms are not his invention; they had already been developing in various places, some perhaps for thousands of years, and were partly fixed, before he made old tales new.

Something like that, but not so much, can be said of the objects. Homer (*Il.* 11. 632–7) describes exactly what he sees, or what another poet saw, as the cup of Nestor, with two 'stalks' below its handles and two doves above them, which is the more easily understood since Schliemann found the cup from the fifteenth century B.C. at Mycenae (p. 62, above). But

Homer does much more. He takes a geometric Cypriote style of the ninth or eighth century, and using its technical powers and its balanced schematism he creates the shield of Achilles, a thing far greater than any work of the hand that had ever been. Later, Greek vase-painting took not style but subjects from Homer; and Greek vases of the eighth and seventh centuries suggest that the *Iliad* and *Odyssey* existed then in much the same form in which we have them now.

As Coleridge depended on Purchas, Captain Cook, and other travellers, Shakespeare on Holinshed and Plutarch, Dante on the Vergil legend and the mediaeval collection of folk-tales called the *Dolopathos*, and Vergil on Theocritus, Sophocles, and hundreds of others, so Homer depended on his predecessors. This is now known so well that Homer's dependences have been used to defend Vergil's, on the ground that as Homer is supremely great in spite of derivations, so Vergil's derivations need not prevent him, too, from being supremely great. It used to be thought a great contrast between them, that Homer invented everything, and Vergil copied. But such questions are now almost out of date. Great poets regularly use the work of predecessors, even to tiny details, and sometimes the work of many for a single line.

While the debt we owe to Greece and Rome is perhaps not nearly so great as that which Greece and Rome owed to the civilizations anterior to them, it is only within the past few decades that classical historians have been able to break down one venerable tabu after another, and occupy themselves increasingly with Egypt and the ancient Near East.

It is hard to say in detail what was happening in the Greek world between about 1300 and 750 B.C. But one thing is very clear, that there must have been a great cultural impulse on Greece from the East.

Phoenicians sailed Greek seas and reached Carthage and probably Spain before 1000 B.C., bringing eastern influence. They were active, too, later, in the ninth and eighth centuries, until the rising activity of Greeks limited them to waters which they had made their own in the east and west. Greek geometric art depended very greatly on eastern suggestion, especially in the east of the Mediterranean about the ninth century.

At some time, perhaps then, perhaps earlier, the East became in many matters almost dominant in Greek thinking. Homer and Hesiod were strongly influenced.

A people of Asia Minor, the Hurri, developed at some time after 2000 B.C. a theology of a number of different gods. They told the stories of them in popular epic history, in which the deeds of the gods and the deeds of men are parallel; and, in the introduction to their legend of Kumarbi, there is an account of a divine succession, in which three pairs, each of a god and goddess, are in power, and the predecessors are dethroned. That is just like Hesiod's succession of Uranos and Gaia, Kronos and Rhea, and Zeus and Hera. There are parallels among the Hurri to the 'winged words' spoken by characters in Greek epic, to the archery competition in the *Odyssey*, and to the Greek spirits of vengeance, the Erinyes. Hesiod (*Theogony*, 319–22) has a description of a mythical, composite beast, the Chimaera, which has a clear origin in the plastic art of the East.

The new documents, principally of about the fourteenth century B.C., found at Ras Shamra (Ugarit) in north Syria, where influences from Mesopotamia, Asia Minor and Egypt met and confronted the Aegean world, are rapidly emphasizing more and more the debt of Greece to the East.

At Ras Shamra, the eagle has an importance like the Greek eagle of Zeus; and indeed Assyrian and Hittite seal-cylinders shew attendants on a god having eagles' heads, and the eagle is the emissary of the High God in the Hittite myth of Telipinu. The name of 'bees' is given to sacred officiants, as at Dodona in Greece. Goddesses corresponding to the Greek Graces were called 'swallows'; swallows have mythic importance in the Greek tale of Tereus and elsewhere.

The myth of Prometheus, chained to a mountain of the Caucasus by Zeus for bringing the gift of fire to men and so advancing civilization, is closely affiliated to eastern myths; and one form of it comes close to the Babylonian creation myth in which men are first created from the blood of a slain god.

To some extent it can be said that gods were communicated to Greece from the east. Kybele (Cybele) is the Hittite Kybaba; and in north Asia Minor, as we have seen, a divine pair is known with the names Apulunas and Rutamis, to which the names of Apollo and Artemis may be equated without offence to philology. Homer, on several occasions, gives different

names to things, one name in the language of men and another
in the language of gods (above, p. 37). This strange notion looks
like an inheritance from the Hittites, whose gods were not
introduced by the ruling element, speakers of Indo-European,
but were indigenous, and addressed in a special language, the
language of the conquered population.

One of the most surprising affiliations is a recent discovery
at Ras Shamra. There a text of a 'catalogue of ships' has been
found, and it uses a formula just like Homer's, in the Second
Iliad. It gives the identity of the commander of a ship, and of
the city from which his men came, and their numbers, and
ends each entry by a repeated statement that 'they went on
this expedition'. The number of men in each ship is ninety,
the number mentioned by the Babylonian king Hammurabi,
seven or eight centuries before, in a letter. The Homeric ships
carry about that number of men, or rather more. The document
seems to have been meant as a statement to be given to some
harbour-master, and it is clear that the Homeric catalogue,
which cannot now be regarded as any kind of late compilation,
is based on some genuine and quite probably contemporary
list, drafted on a hitherto unknown but in fact once common
and regular scheme.

The Greek underworld is incontestably indebted to the
underworld of Assyria and Babylonia. A late creation myth,
not earlier than Ashurbanipal, derived all things from the deep
and the chaos of the sea, and gave a starting point to scientific
theories of the Greek philosophers, Thales and Anaximander.
An earlier Akkadian legend tells a similar story, and agrees
further with the Greek physicist Anaximander in describing
the origin of life, first in experimental, hybrid forms, from the
sea.

The geographical experience of Mesopotamia, with its
recession of the sea and frequent floods, suggested the creation
legends, and myths of the underworld also. It is a dreary underworld. The heroes are there, crowned, and on thrones, and in
the middle is the fortress-palace of the goddess of death, Nin-
Sun or Allat. The oriental Hades has seven gates with seven
warders; and it may have affected the Greek mental picture
of the seven-gated city of Thebes. There was a spring of the
waters of life, as in Greek Orphic myth; and whoever could

drink some of it, might return to live again. Descents to the Greek underworld, such as the descent of Aphrodite to find Adonis, can be traced to oriental descents, such as the descent of Ishtar to find Tammuz.

At Ras Shamra a comparable underworld is described, with the added detail that it, like Homer's underworld, was over-grown with asphodel flowers; and there is described also a garden of the Hesperides, maidens of the west, well known to Greeks and a part of their dreams of a world beyond the grave, a garden where streams run together. Earlier still in Babylonia the apples of the Hesperides are represented; and there, among much besides, including the adventures of Heracles, Homer's Oceanus itself, partly a real sea channel, but still more 'waters of death' to be crossed on the way from life to death, has its counterpart.

The debt of early Greece to the East can be proved by facts long known, but the new facts which are being found put it in a much more significant light. Among them we have already noted (pp. 96–7, above) a north Syrian ritual drama of the thirteenth century, designed to overcome a god of drought, and restore fertility to the land. It is impressively like a Greek play in its structure, even to its five acts; it is hard to realize that the curse of infertility powerfully described for a very different purpose in the *Oedipus Rex* of Sophocles, belongs to a tradition a thousand years old, and originating far away in Asia.

Ras Shamra has explained something else, nearer to Homer. The other name of Homer's Troy, Ilion, earlier Wilion, has occurred as a general name for 'city', 'Wili', prefixed to a city's name.

Eastern influence, then, certainly helped much in Homer to grow. There was also Egyptian influence, but apart from rare finds in Greece it was, so far as our positive knowledge goes, in-direct; Crete was influenced from Egypt, and the Mycenaean world from Crete. There is also a mysterious part of Homer's background which seems to be reflected in the sea voyages. There are very many tales of wonders and adventures in the Mediterranean, or even beyond it, which have been traced to Phoenicians, partly because Homer has many words which seem Phoenician or at least Semitic in origin.

Among these words is Erebos, in Homer the name for a part of Hades, which looks like the Semitic *Ereb*, 'west', and the name of Circe's island, Aiaia, which strangely suggests the Semitic *aia*, 'hawk', while the Greek word for 'hawk' is κίρκος, kirkos, the very word from which Circe's name comes.

There may have been Phoenician tales of the west and central Mediterranean which Homer used. One is supposed to have been about the fabulously wealthy Spanish town of Tartessos, and known most generally from the 'ships of Tarshish' in the Bible. Homer is supposed to have used this tale for Scheria, the island of the Phaeacians. He certainly talks circumstantially about the Phoenicians, and treats them as the ordinary sea-merchants of the time, bringing beautiful things to Greece and selling them, with perhaps some piracy in their spare time. To Homer a Phoenician origin for beautiful things seems normal.

But it must be remembered that Minoans also sailed the seas, and must have brought home tales. It is just as easy to make it seem that Scheria is a memory of Crete. The Minoans were in communication with Troy in the east and Sicily in the west, as finds such as weapons prove. Stories like the story of Theseus and Ariadne assert contact between Greece and Crete in its powerful age; and anyhow Homer's Achaeans are now quite certainly Mycenaean in culture, and Mycenaean culture is almost, but not quite, a result of the Minoan. Minos himself is well known in Greek legend. The Minoan stories of travel must have reached some of Homer's heroes.

The main question is date. The Minoans sustained their greatest disaster in about 1440 B.C. and after that grew weaker and weaker till the twelfth century and then ceased to count. There may have been effective Minoans at the time of the Trojan War, but the main memory of them is earlier. The Phoenicians may have been active in the fifteenth century B.C. or soon after; but their real historical importance belongs to the time from about 1100 to 700 B.C.

Apparently the stories originally drawn from Minoans have been recoloured with Phoenician references. It is thought that 'Phoenician' may even mean 'Minoan'; Phoenix in Greek means 'red', and Minoan pictures shew Minoan men with red skins. There is however another derivation, from the Egyptian 'poni', which would make the word mean 'men of the coast'.

Some parts of the *Iliad* and *Odyssey* look as if they belong to the heroic age about 1300 to 1100 B.C., and some as if they belong to the Homeric, 900 to 700, or 850 to 750 B.C. It was once usual to talk about the older and the newer parts of the poems. It is more natural and more accurate now to talk about the poems, created in the Homeric age by Homer, and their sources, some older than others. Homer uses his sources as other great poets use theirs. But he is more like Shakespeare, who will take a story, and perhaps a large part of a page almost verbally reproduced, from a source, than Coleridge, who uses more than one source for almost every line of his best work. Whatever the sources provide is in any case accepted, blended, and reproduced by a process of reorganization, partly unconscious.

Homer sometimes remembered long passages of earlier poetry without rejecting them just because he found them ready made. These long passages were from older poems, often dealing with other subjects than Homer chose. They were equally useful to him, but needed different treatment. If the subject was different, large alterations might be necessary. People and places would be changed, but the subject and form of the story might remain otherwise unaltered. The quarrel between Achilles and Agamemnon has had much help from quarrels between Achilles and Odysseus, and between Ajax and Odysseus, and perhaps from the legend of Meleager too, all as told in earlier poetry. The secret entry of Odysseus into Troy as a spy in Homer (*Od.* 4. 242–58) is a combination of his own entry to steal the 'palladion', the city's talisman, and Sinon's entry into Troy to help the success of the wooden horse, both incidents from other poems. The destruction of the Achaean wall in Troyland by Poseidon (*Il.* 7. 459–63; 12. 13–33) looks like the destruction of the wall of Troy, by Poseidon also, but outside the scope of the *Iliad*.

Sometimes the long passages came from poems about Homer's subject but in a different treatment. The *Iliad* begins with the quarrel between Agamemnon and Achilles. Then in the second book lists of the opposing contingents are given. It is in the tenth year of the war. The story ought, in a sense, to go straight on. Homer has to provide an excuse for the lists by making Nestor advise Agamemnon to reorganize the army to fight by territorial units. It is hard to see what had been happening before; and there is no doubt that the 'catalogues', as they are called, belong to another place in the story. The Greek catalogue should come at the beginning of the war, either in Troyland, or better still when the army was assembling at Aulis, in Greece, the point at which the Cyclic poem called the *Cypria* had a catalogue. The Trojan catalogue may also belong at the beginning of the war, perhaps where fighting begins; or it may come from some place in the story at which reinforcements came to the Trojans.

There is plenty more in the *Iliad* which has been displaced. The duel between Menelaus and Paris (Book 3) also ought to be near the beginning; so should the discussion in Troy about whether to send back Helen or keep her (7. 345–64), all the more because after a ten years' siege the Trojans could hardly have continued to think it worth while for Paris to have his way, and he and they would surely have known that the offer of the stolen property, but not Helen, would be useless.

When Hector says goodbye to Andromache and Astyanax (6. 390 *ff.*), it is quite obviously a last goodbye. But it is not till we have read through sixteen more books that the death of Hector comes. The first half of the *Iliad* ends with Hector on the point of breaking into the Achaean camp, with nothing to stop him. Then follows much fighting, not inside the camp. In the next book (13. 723–53), quite late, Polydamas advises Hector, who is still outside, to improve his tactics. It is only after nearly three books have intervened from the time when Hector was practically through the gate, that the inevitably next minute comes, and he begins to burn the ships. Homer has split the narrative to make room for long passages about fighting. They are all good in their place, and necessary both for the 'pattern' of the *Iliad* and its strange organization by balancing themes, and also for action by the gods, especially the deception of Zeus by Hera (14. 159 *ff.*), its consequences in the Greek rally, and the reversal when Zeus awakes (15. 4 *ff.*), and allows success to Hector in order to bring honour to Achilles.

There is another use in the *Iliad* of lengthy source-material, by means of a more direct inclusion. Stories, clearly from older poems, are told by characters. Nestor (7. 123–60) tells a long tale of his youth, about fighting in the West Peloponnese, near his home. This is a detached saga, not originally worked up into an artistic and systematic whole, which related wars that happened when one wave of Acheans made this piece of country their own. Yet the tale is told at an urgent council. That is largely the idea of it; it shews how even serious things cannot stop Nestor's ill-restrained and self-centred reminiscences. In the middle of a battle (6. 119 *ff.*), Diomedes meets Glaucus, from Lycia. They are on different sides, but know of each other, and talk and in the end exchange armour. In the talk Glaucus tells Diomedes a long story of how his ancestor Bellerophon had been sent from Greece to Lycia to be killed, but how he had prevailed, and killed the Chimaera, a mythical monster developed out of oriental art, with the help of the winged horse, Pegasus. This is also saga, and it clearly is a version of the fighting and intrigues which led to the occupation of southwestern Asia Minor by Greeks in the fourteenth century B.C. But the saga has become mythical. It has acquired participants outside nature altogether, themselves the result of complex development, apparently through the vitalization of abstract plastic monsters in old soldiers' tales. But Homer's purpose succeeds; he delays the action as he wishes, he shews the generosity of Diomedes' character, and he reveals a little more of the folly and heartlessness of war.

Homer sometimes finds a motive in a source, and uses it in two ways, both for its original purpose, probably in a new part of the story, and also with a change of relevance. In this way he adopts the motive of a suggested retreat of the Achaeans from Troy, and uses it three times. Twice (9. 26–8; 14. 75–81) Agamemnon really wants to go. Once (2. 139–41) he only pretends that he does, and orders embarkation, but only to test the fighting spirit of the troops. They, quite ridiculously, for such humour is characteristic of Homer, do not hesitate a moment. They never think of wanting to stay. It is only with difficulty that Odysseus and Diomedes and others restore order. Here a motive has been used three times, and in two ways. This triple use of one motive is also characteristic of Homer, and will be met again.

The sources of the *Odyssey* are more complicated still. There may be much in it from earlier poetry about Odysseus himself. There was a saga of Odysseus; it seems obvious that he was a great leader, who won admiration by his qualities shewn in war and adventure. Possibly the stories about him suggested to some poet the moral qualities which Homer has developed so greatly in him, and the real man Odysseus may have been of small significance; but it is hard to believe. It is more likely that Odysseus was important as a far greater monarch than he appears in Homer, and that he has had his importance narrowed by tradition, so that his intrinsic and more universally human value has become focalized, and made stronger in its appeal.

The saga of Odysseus told of wanderings, but some of the wanderings in the *Odyssey* may have belonged to other stories first. Odysseus himself returned from Troy to Ithaca, almost certainly diverging by way of Sicily or at least somewhere towards the west. There must have been an immense volume of saga referring to the sea-raids and land-raids delivered by Achaeans and their allies against Egypt and Asia. The Trojan war is part of these activities. As the epic art developed, good pieces of material were bound to be adapted to new places in the whole cycle of stories, where they would be more effective still.

Pieces of saga so adapted can be found. When Telemachus goes to see Menelaus, Menelaus tells him of his voyage home (4. 351 *ff.*); how he had been to Egypt, and on the way back had heard from Proteus, the divine prophet who looked after seals and changed his shape (as Thetis did when Peleus sought to marry her), that Aegisthus had killed Agamemnon and that Calypso was detaining Odysseus on her island. This is saga of a sea-raid, probably with memories of the big raid repelled by the pharaoh Merneptah in 1221 B.C. But it has already acquired the mythical accretion of Proteus, who is only in part, if at all, a king of Egypt. He and Thetis are both divinities of the sea; both change quickly and elusively, and both may have begun as mythical personifications of the changeful southern sea itself.

When Odysseus reached Ithaca, and was met by Athena, he began to give a fictitious account of himself, how he was a refugee from Crete (13. 256 *ff.*). This might well have turned out to be an old saga, originally about someone else, if Athena had not stopped Odysseus short by declaring herself. But he succeeded in telling a Cretan story to the pig-man Eumaeus (14. 199 *ff.*); how he was a Cretan who had fought at Troy, and afterwards had been captured attempting a raid on Egypt; how he had managed to escape with some Phoenicians, and after a shipwreck had made another escape, and had found his way to Ithaca instead of the neighbouring island of Dulichium, which he pretended that he was trying to reach. He attempted, without success, to make Eumaeus believe that he had news of Odysseus himself. Later (19. 170 *ff.*) he pretended to Penelope that he was a Cretan and had entertained Odysseus on his way to Troy.

It seems that Homer has done here what he did in the *Iliad*, and taken a motive, not originally part of his story, or of his story as he told it, and used it, or something like it, three times. It is certain that he found saga about sea-raids and land-raids very useful. But they may not have reached him in anything very like their original form. It is probable that the Phoenicians did not belong to the story at the beginning, unless we believe that they were active on the sea about 1200 B.C. or sooner, which is, however, not impossible. Perhaps the Egyptian story was retold, with Phoenicians added for the first time, in the ninth century, either by Homer himself, or by another poet before him.

A large part of the *Odyssey* is remote from saga or anything very like an account of real events. The visits to the Laestrygonians and Lotus Eaters may represent adventures with real tribes of low culture. The lotus plant may well have been growing in north Africa, within reach of wanderers, and it may have had a sleepy effect; of the two varieties of the plant which are known one agrees roughly with Homer's account.

The Phaeacians are not quite half-way to fairy-land. Their ships steer themselves; there is no war; the gardens grow all the year, with a fertility and a precision more than natural; there are living statues of metal, of men and dogs; the harmony and discipline is ideal rather than real; and the gods associate as friends with the Phaeacians. There is, however, plenty of reality, and that part looks like Homer's own treatment of a theme which was itself remote from ordinary things. How a story came to be formed round 'Scheria' and 'the Phaeacians' is not known. Their similarities to Minoans, Phoenicians, and Spaniards have been noticed; and they are also compared with people and lands of the golden age, in the past, or in the far west, or both; and they have even been imagined to represent a memory of Atlantis and the Atlanteans, of whom Plato, not quite out of agreement with Homer, tells.

It is tempting to believe that the caves of the Cyclops and Calypso, the descent to the land of the dead among the Cimmerians, and also Circe, with her magic, against which Hermes, guide of the dead, can give, by magic of his own, a defence, all belong to a myth of the soul's journey through the grave. Many analogies are almost sufficient to prove it. But the myth has been imposed on facts, and the parts of it have even found a kind of vague geography of their own, plotting themselves here or there along coasts of the western seas. There is no certainty where any are; all are partly in fairy-land, anyway.

A different myth appears in the *Odyssey* (12. 260 *ff.*) when the sailors eat the cattle of the Sun. According to the old discredited solar theory they are clouds in the sky; and this is actually a very possible origin for them, as analogy shews. But much had happened to the myth, whatever its origin, before it came into an adventure story of real men.

Scylla and Charybdis are old sailors' tales, descriptions of a rock and a whirlpool. Homer's sources for deep-sea wonders must have been some sort of adventure stories, a kind of saga, developed at an early stage of culture when personification was natural and spontaneous, and mystified terror of the sea most sincere.

It is possible that all started very early indeed, perhaps a thousand years or more before Homer, when the first Greeks, or even perhaps Minoans, sailed, in daring and fright, to Sicily, Gibraltar, and perhaps beyond.

But in Ithaca, Pylos, Sparta and partly in Scheria also, it is quite different. This is a real world, and the people are people whom Homer knew, and we can know. Here it is very hard to distinguish the layers of the poetry.

The system of the narrative clearly has several plots which belong to folk-tale or romance, apparently an advanced, cultured, and rather subtle kind of story, not known in later Greece until after the end of fully classical literature.

These romances or developed folk-tales appear more than once. There is the tale of the faithful wife, who refuses to give up hope of her husband's return. Homer has joined this on to the story of the adventurous return of Odysseus. There may also be a different tale involved, a tale of the wicked subjects or servants surprised by the return of their lord. A similar but again a different tale is about the unknown prince, or stranger knight, who proves by success at games or fighting that he is no ordinary man. This Homer used in Scheria, at the games of the Phaeacians, where Odysseus is challenged and shews his powers; and he used it too for the climax in Ithaca. But Homer used another tale for Scheria too, the tale of the unknown prince who wins his princess. Now Homer has not finished the tale; he could not, because Penelope's tale was in conflict with it, so that Odysseus could not marry Nausicaa, and she just disappears from the story.

VIII

THE UNITY OF HOMER

The Greeks themselves began by attributing most of the Cyclic poems and all the Homeric Hymns, to Homer himself. Homer is first mentioned, by Callinus, as author of the *Thebais*. That is in the seventh century. In the fifth, Pindar (frag. 280: O.C.T.) tells the story of how Homer composed the *Cypria* but gave it away, and a few years later Herodotus (II. 117) gives it as his private opinion, rather as if everyone would not agree, that internal evidence proves that the *Cypria* is not by Homer.

Gradually criticism and research in classical times restored the Cyclic poems to their true, or probably true, authors, leaving to Homer the *Iliad* and the *Odyssey*, and, on the whole, though no one seems to have worried much about them, the Hymns. A theory was started that the *Odyssey* was by someone else, but it was a freak, and not taken very seriously. There was no suggestion that the *Iliad* or the *Odyssey* had multiple authors.

The first hint of that came from Giambattista Vico, who lived in the sixteenth and early seventeenth centuries, but it was only a hint. In the seventeenth century d'Aubignac developed the theory, making out that our Homer consists of lays originally independent and by different authors. Wolf at the end of the eighteenth century developed this theory still further with great care. He, however, fully recognized that the poems look like artistic wholes, and moreover confined his theory to the *Iliad* and accepted the unity of the *Odyssey*. In the nineteenth century the dissection continued. Extreme views were reached by Lachmann, Kirchhoff, and Wilamowitz, who is notable for the view that the *Iliad* is a bad and careless piece of work. In the twentieth century Bethe, followed by Gilbert Murray, reached an even more extreme view. More balanced but also extreme, was the second opinion held by Leaf, and published in 1902. Before, and after, for example in 1892 and 1912, he had more belief in the unity of Homer.

These are the 'separatists'. They started in France, but are mainly German. Towards the end of the nineteenth century 'unitarianism' revived again, partly by the influence of W. E. Gladstone. Drerup in Germany is an extreme unitarian;

Bérard in France is a unitarian of moderate views, like Myres, Allen, and Bowra in England, and Nilsson in Sweden. The strongest influence for reviving unitarianism was Andrew Lang, who died in 1934, after many years of vigorous attack on separatism, while maintaining the view that Homer composed, and probably wrote, in Europe, very soon after the age he describes. An extreme unitarian of the period is J. A. Scott, in America. Today the unitarian view is widely held.

Separatists lay stress on a strange story, to which Cicero, Pausanias and Aelian lightly refer, that Peisistratus, despot of Athens in the middle of the sixth century, 'collected' and 'arranged' the poems of Homer. There is no doubt that this, in so far as it is trustworthy, means little more than a task of copying out and editing the poems and getting for the first time a reliable text; and, as Megara was jealous of Athens and Athens based a territorial claim to the island of Salamis on Homer, it is more than likely that Dieuchidas of Megara, to whom the story is traced, coloured the facts to discredit Athenian policy.

Unitarians usually put Homer early, about 800 B.C. or earlier. That means that they have to face the difficulty of proving that certain things in Homer that look late do not upset their date. So most of them agree that there are interpolations in Homer. Scott is, or nearly is, an exception. There are in Homer a few passages which are supposed almost universally to be interpolated. One is the end of the *Odyssey*; another (19. 33–4) the scene where Athena shews a light while Odysseus, Telemachus, and Eumaeus remove the arms from the hall; a third is the reference to Athens in the Catalogue of Ships in the Second Iliad (546 *ff.*).

Internal evidence for the multiple authorship of the *Iliad* and *Odyssey* is sought in discrepancies, in the distinction between ideas that must be late and ideas that must be early, and in language. The question is not finally settled. The ordinary discrepancies count for very little. But some things seem of different date, and that may be due to the known habit of epic poetry to develop for centuries, admitting different things and ideas as time passes. The question is, how much of that happened before Homer and was taken over by him, and how much is due to adventures sustained by the text after Homer.

Very little of it indeed, some people would say none, is worse than what might easily happen to a fairly definitive text if Homer lived about 900 to 800. Many of the arguments depend on mistakes. The same may be said of arguments from language, which have failed to prove that Homer's poems include serious linguistic contradictions only to be resolved by assuming different dates. Of course the language has forms from many different times and many different places, but that proves little for the poems. It had come to be a very mixed language by Homer's time, rather like the language of the *Chanson de Roland* or the *Canterbury Tales*. We even have two dialects represented in one word, Ionic in stem, and Aeolic in ending, and even then not quite in accordance with either grammar.

The *Iliad* and *Odyssey* are as unlike as *Macbeth* and *Julius Caesar*, but not nearly as unlike as *Hamlet* and *The Tempest*. Homer's own authentic hand and feeling, in the words and thoughts, and equally in the message and vision of the two great schemes, are hard to miss. In both his poems he fights for love against death; only he fights not quite in the same way. It looks as if in the *Odyssey* he has found a wider and perhaps a more optimistic view, like a large number of great artists, who have faced the terrors in their earlier work and through them reached serenity and even optimism before the end of their lives.

Many attempts have been made to prove by internal evidence that the *Iliad* and *Odyssey* belong to very different dates. The evidence concerns mainly language and ideas.

It is often possible to say what forms in the Homeric dialect are old and what are later. The use of one word as the definite article 'the' is later than the use of the same word as the demonstrative 'this' or personal pronoun 'he'. Particles to give a potential meaning to verbs are two, older and later. The dative plural has an old long form, and a newer shorter form. There are forms of tenses which can be dated comparatively. Also, there are long, derivative abstract nouns, which are a late thing in language.

Another linguistic test is the old letter, the Digamma or Wau, *F*. Passages which imply it, by shewing in the metre that a word which now has no consonant in a certain place used to have one once, ought to be older than passages in which the Digamma is assumed never to have existed. The Greeks had no idea that the Digamma had been in Homeric language once but had disappeared, and the fact was only discovered by Bentley in the eighteenth century.

Such criteria have been thought to prove that some books of Homer are later than others, and that the *Odyssey* is later than the *Iliad*. There is so far no reliable and considerable result. Statistics have been found to be wrong; early and late forms are found together; and different critics reach contradictory results. Some language tests might even be thought to prove the *Odyssey* older than the *Iliad*.

There are various tests according to ideas. The purity and sanctity of marriage in the *Odyssey* is considered late; but in fact that is a sign rather of an early than of a late kind of society, and sometimes very primitive people are very accurate and faultless in this morality, far more than the highly civilized. Further, the marriage of Hector and Andromache in the *Iliad* is just as sacred. Then come the gods. In the *Iliad* they are treated humorously, but in the *Odyssey*, except for the inset 'Song of Demodocus', they are not; in the *Iliad* they seem to live on Olympus and in the *Odyssey* they appear to be in the sky. There are other differences. The gods are used differently; fewer are used in the *Odyssey* than in the *Iliad*, and those more regularly in direct relation to the human action. They are almost symbols of human powers, or attributes of a philosophically seen divinity, so that god and man act together, not, as in the *Iliad*, with some contrast and detachment, and some limitation of what we should call truly divine functions to a small number of divine figures. But none of this proves a different date for the poems. It might prove that some of the sources of the *Iliad* are older than some of the sources of the *Odyssey*, or that Homer's interests and views had changed between the times at which he finished the two epics. These two possibilities would anyhow be likely, if not certain. Homer presumably spent many years of his life on the poems, perhaps twenty on each, reciting them in changing forms until they were as perfect as they could be. He probably kept both going at once for some of the time; but the *Iliad* may have attained its final form almost a generation before the perfecting of the *Odyssey*.

One discrepancy is interesting. In the *Iliad*, Charis, a

'Grace', is wife of Hephaestus, the fire-god and smith-god, but in the *Odyssey* his wife is Aphrodite. This is no evidence for different authorship; but it shows how myths are symbolic in Homer, and their variants are chosen for their significance to the poem. Of course 'loveliness' was wanted to help the craft of metal-working in making the arms of Achilles; and of course the Love-goddess fits most easily into Demodocus' tale of illicit love.

The *Iliad* furnished a surprise in 1922, when the discovery that it had an apparently unique kind of organization was first published (Sheppard). Since then the original discovery has been enlarged and elaborated (Myres, Owen, Howald, Webster, Whitman), and already it is beginning to appear not so unique as it seemed at first. Recent investigation has shewn that the *Odyssey* too reveals a high degree of symmetrical organization formerly unsuspected (Myres, 1952).

The 'pattern' of the *Iliad* is immensely important not only for its own interest, but because of two consequences, also. It shews the unity of the poem, because symmetry so exact and convincing makes it very hard for reason to accept the many suggestions which have been made that some parts of the poem do not, in some sense, really belong to it. The pattern also shews something more valuable even than that. It will often declare and emphasize the very meaning of what Homer has to say; for by the balance of different characters and incidents with each other, their force and nature and eternal truth for all mankind are illuminated and revealed.

Some balances and contrasts are simple and obvious, as in the comparison of the treatment which the Achaean embassy and Priam received from Achilles, a comparison seen many years ago to belong to Homer's plan. Scarcely less obvious is the contrast of the treatment of Chryses in *Iliad* 1 with the treatment of Priam in *Iliad* 24; or again, in a narrower span, the balance of motives in the 'Shield of Achilles', city with country, peace with war, proportionately spaced. But the symmetry goes very much farther than that.

The shortest proof of the larger symmetry is in the chronology. The embassy to Achilles is clearly central in the story. There are twenty-six days before it and twenty-six after it. Each side there are one day, a nine-day interval, one day, a twelve-day interval, and then three days, symmetrically arranged about the embassy in the middle—

1—9—1—12—3— Embassy—3—12—1—9—1.

The first four are in Book 1: 1—9—1—12—; and the last in Book 24: —12—1—9—1. Obviously, then, these two books especially belong to the pattern.

But most of the symmetry concerns not length of time but similarity of incident, with the balance contained principally within two dimensions of span.

An incident within a single book has balances within itself; as when the 'Interrupted Fight' in Book 8 begins with Nestor's chariot, goes on with Agamemnon, then with Zeus on Ida, then with Agamemnon again, and ends with Hera's chariot; and when the 'Deception of Zeus' in Book 14 begins with an Achaean rally, goes on with Zeus on Ida, and ends with a rally of the Trojans; each of these two large incidents having many smaller symmetries of detail within it.

Then, too, the whole *Iliad* balances about its moral and chronological centre at the 'Embassy' in Book 9. The burning of the Achaeans in Book 1 is balanced by the burning of Hector in Book 24; the restoration of Chryseis in Book 1 by the restoration of Hector in Book 24; the meeting of Menelaus and Paris in Book 3 by the meeting of Hector and Achilles in Book 22, the right and the wrong way to end the war; the arming of Paris in Book 6 by the arming of Patroclus in Book 16; the building of the Achaean wall in Book 7 by its destruction in Book 15; and the night-watch of the Trojans in Book 8 by the watch of the Achaeans in Book 10.

Symmetrical design on the wider scale is less striking in the *Odyssey*, but it exists. Appropriately, the whole poem is enframed by two scenes in Olympus; in Book 1 the conversation about the hero's fate between Zeus and Athena, and in Book 24 their final intervention. On a smaller scale the Telemachus story, Books 1 to 4, has an 'enframing' structure; the journeys of Telemachus stand before and after insets that recount the 'Returns' of Nestor, Agamemnon, and Menelaus, with references to the fates of other heroes too.

Sir John Myres has shewn that events in the *Odyssey* constantly fall into groups of three, sometimes arranged A—B—A.

Of this pattern a specially interesting type has come to be known as 'ring composition', a term borrowed from vase-painting; it is a feature of both poems but particularly common in the *Odyssey*. Here an inset episode or digression is preceded by a passage, often formulaic, arising naturally from the main stream of narrative; then at the end of the digression, which may be of some length, the poet returns us to the main tale by a simple repetition of all or part of the transitional passage. A good instance is the scene where the nurse recognizes Odysseus by the scar: between her recognition and her exclamation of amazement, instantly stifled by Odysseus, comes an inset of over seventy lines describing the boar-hunt when Odysseus received the wound that formed the scar. The return to the main narrative is smoothly achieved by the simple statement that this was the very scar that the nurse now recognized; and so the tale can progress.

Myres remarked too that in the *Odyssey* speeches notably occur in groups of five, sometimes with an A—B—A—B—A arrangement. Yet it could be said that composition in 'triplets' and 'quintets', as these groupings have been called, is hardly unexpected. The presence of such groupings by threes and fives may be the mark of a natural, perhaps hardly conscious, narrative skill: their absence might have been even more significant, indicating poor artistry or even haphazard composition by several hands.

A more conscious artistry, governing a wider span, may be claimed for certain sections of the poem. For example it has been shewn that Book 8, the scene in the Phaeacian land, has a specific design. It opens with speculation about Odysseus' identity and discussion of his escort home: it ends with renewed promise of escort and again the question of his identity. Between are set the three Songs of Demodocus; the outside pair are about Trojan War incidents involving Odysseus himself, his quarrel with Achilles, and the Wooden Horse; and after each Odysseus weeps. The other Song is set at the heart of the book and is quite different; for it is the purely amusing tale of Ares and Aphrodite. Framing this central Song are two scenes of lively activity: in the first, the Games with the taunting challenge to Odysseus and his triumph, followed by dancing; in the second, dancing again, and then the giving of the gifts to

Odysseus, his bathing, and his farewell to Nausicaa. The symmetry is coherent, and surely under a single control.

Such control has been demonstrated, too, for the long series of adventures recounted by Odysseus in Books 9 to 12. Central is the Visit to the Underworld, enframed by the story of Elpenor's fate. Enframing this 'triplet' in turn are the two visits to Circe. Before the first of these, we have five adventures: the Cyclops encounter that roused Poseidon's wrath against the hero, told at length within a frame of two pairs of briefer episodes, the Ciconians and the Lotus Eaters on one side and Aeolus and the Laestrygonians on the other. The second Circe visit is followed by a similar 'quintet'; the crucial incident of the eating of the cattle of the Sun, framed on one side by the Sirens and the first encounter with Scylla and Charybdis, and on the other by the second encounter with Scylla and Charybdis and Odysseus' arrival, alone, at Ogygia, Calypso's isle.

Despite the patterned structure indicated for the *Odyssey*, it it still possible to argue that the symmetry of the *Odyssey* is less periodic, less interlocking, less subordinated in sub-classifications than the symmetry of the *Iliad*. The *Odyssey* has been compared to a frieze, or early Ionic art; whereas the *Iliad* is like a pediment, or the geometric art of the islands. There is more narrative in the one and more drama in the other; perhaps that is just the precision of Homer's genius, to fix in this way and handle the only two themes possible to highest poetry, the dramatic, tragic, theme of 'Wrath', and the narrative theme with its tales and happy ending, the theme of the 'Homecoming'.

Clearly, this balance and symmetry are a part of Homer's art. When the discovery was first made, it was so surprising that it was hard to believe. Such 'patterns' are never mentioned by ancient writers; and there was no known literary parallel, except on a very small scale, in the metre of elegiac couplets and verses constructed to be read forwards and backwards with the same result in words and meaning.

The only real illustration was found in the plastic arts, where of course there are frequent symmetries and balances. Pedimental sculpture is grouped about a centre like the *Iliad*, and like single incidents in the *Iliad*. Better still, geometric pottery, quite likely to be contemporary or nearly contemporary with the creation of the Homeric poems, is close to them in the arrangement of the balancing motives in its decoration.

Similar patterns have been discovered in other poetic works, both classical and modern, notably the Hesiodic *Shield of Heracles*, Catullus's Poem 64 'The Marriage of Peleus and Thetis', Vergil's *Eclogues*, *Georgics*, and *Aeneid*, and Lucan's *Pharsalia*; as well as the old English *Beowulf* and the poetry of Edmund Spenser.[1]

The Homeric patterns are therefore far from unique, and in fact seem to represent a strong tendency among certain poets, who are not even all epic poets, and certainly not all dependent for this method on a single original. There is no hint that the method was taught or transmitted; but it is very likely to have been traditional among some Greek and some Anglo-Saxon poets at least; if so, presumably there were two independent traditions.

Homer and perhaps Hesiod may have found the method to some extent natural and instinctive. The evidence of contemporary plastic art suggests that in their times there was a general mental habit of seeing and representing things in such symmetrical shapes. Whatever may have been the nature of the process, there is at least little doubt that the discovery of such intricate symmetries must go far to demonstrate the coherence and therefore unity of any work in which they are found. They could hardly have come together by chance.

---

[1] For some of the relevant discussion and references, see W. F. Jackson Knight, *Roman Vergil* (Peregrine Edition, 1966) Index s.v. 'Symmetry'.—J.D.C.

IX

THE GREATNESS OF HOMER

Pleasure may not be the best thing to be got out of poetry, and it may not be the purpose for which poetry ought to be created. But there is no doubt that Homeric poetry was meant to give pleasure and did give pleasure; or that it can give keen pleasure still.

There are however plenty of different ways in which poetry can give pleasure, and it is a mistake to expect single poems to give pleasure in only one way. It would be a particularly bad mistake with Homer.

Perhaps Greek epic lays were originally performed to please the actual chiefs whose deeds they celebrated. That is likely, and the minstrelsy mentioned in Homer, the minstrelsy of Achilles, Demodocus and Phemius, might suggest that a keen personal interest could be taken by audiences in the heroes of the poems. A great motive of action for Homer's heroes is the desire to 'become a song for men yet to be'. Epic poetry carried personal fame, and almost certainly gave pleasure by satisfying the pride of heroes who were represented, and of their relatives, friends, descendants, and compatriots.

That after the earlier stages of epic this was one of the main sources of pleasure is much less likely. Homer's poetry almost all the time sacrifices advertisement to art. Like the Anglo-Saxon poem *Beowulf* which was imported into England and greatly enjoyed by audiences in no way connected with the characters, Homer was liked by Greeks independently of their peculiar interest in heroes related to themselves. There was, however, such interest. The Megarians thought that the Athenians interpolated two lines into Homer's Greek Catalogue in the *Iliad* to gain a mention for themselves and their leader Menestheus. That is possibly but not certainly true. The Athenians seem to have used the lines in order to base a claim to the island of Salamis on them. Such a use of Homer, to support claims, is not unusual, and may well be a survival of a general use of traditional poetry as the repository of title deeds to land, a use made of it in Iceland and New Zealand, and perhaps partly accountable for the quantity of genealogical material which survives in the Homeric poems. Poets were used to relating genealogies for practical purposes. Cleisthenes of Sicyon, who led a kind of nationalist movement against the influence of the city of Argos, stopped Homeric recitation because there was too much about 'Argives' in Homer. In 480 before the battle of Salamis an argument from Homer was used by Greeks in Sicily to support a policy (Herodotus, VII. 153 *ff.*).

But few Greek audiences could have listened to Homer without finding far the greater part not personally relevant to themselves. There are reports of the introduction of Homeric poetry or recitation into Sparta, Athens, Syracuse, and Cyrene at definite dates; at these places, a demand for Homer is known or may be inferred to have existed, but in none of them was it particularly easy for audiences to consider that Homer's poetry contained much compliment to themselves. Athens and Athenians have a few passing mentions. The other places were Dorian; Dorians came into Greece after the times of which Homer tells, and Homer only mentions Dorians once, in a mysterious passage (*Od.* 19. 172–7) where he says that the inhabitants of Crete were Achaeans, 'True Cretans', Cydonians, Dorians, and Pelasgians.

The Spartans, it is true, might have appropriated to themselves Menelaus and Helen, who in historic times had a shrine and worship near Sparta. But Sparta's enemies were as fond, or still more fond, of Homer; and Menelaus and Helen are not unreservedly admired in Homeric poetry. They are treated poetically, like every one else in a poetry that is poetry and not the mere material out of which poetry might be made.

For Homer is an advanced and finished poet, who goes far beyond direct and simple participation in the conflict. He has sympathy for all and unqualified admiration for none. His best admiration may be qualified by an ability to laugh at his heroes. He even shews, especially in the *Iliad*, the unfavourable view of Odysseus, first in Agamemnon's disparaging reference to his cunning, and later when he runs away in a battle and refuses to stop; and he certainly laughs at him when he describes (*Il.* 3. 209 *ff.*) how he looks short when he stands up and tall when he is sitting down, and again when he has three large meals in quick succession (*Il.* 9 and 10). No one is quite perfect, least of all Agamemnon, who is always weak; twice he seriously suggests retreat from Troyland, even his victories in battle are all spoilt in some way and not as heroic as they might have been, and he always has to have his mind made up for him in important decisions. Hector is nearly perfect; he is noted as a leader, and not as a selfish fighter, like Achilles; but he is once (13. 723–53) reproved for neglecting his duty of commanding and organizing defence; and just before his death it is part of his tragedy that he runs away. The Achaeans regard all the sons of Priam as arrogant. Diomedes is the most perfect of the important heroes; perhaps he has to be, to shew how Achilles might have succeeded just where he fails. Achilles himself makes the *Iliad* to be the *Iliad* by his imperfection.

There is disagreement about Achilles' exact fault, and in particular his exact violation of the heroic knightly code. Apparently, he was within his rights as a man of chivalry to defy Agamemnon at the start, to retire from fighting, and to despoil and even to mutilate Hector's body. His religion was a religion of honour, and it was his right or even his duty to protect his honour in these ways. When he accepted conflict with the river god, he did much the same as Diomedes did when he wounded Aphrodite and then Ares. His real fault was less what he did than what he allowed himself to be. He lost balance, restraint, and thought for others. It was the usual sin of ὕβρις, hybris, a word hard to translate except as 'un-Christian behaviour'. In the end, he allowed Agamemnon to make amends, and he accepted reconciliation. But he refused reasonable and right redress, offered earlier by the embassy to him; and waited for the utter humiliation and desperate entreaties of his enemies. He went too far, and though he was naturally expected to guard his honour, he guarded it, even when he guarded it in the right way, in the wrong spirit. He thought more of it than of the lives of many comrades; even, in the terrible moment of their last parting, than the life of Patroclus himself, for he warned him to refrain from trying to take Troy, not to preserve the life of Patroclus, but in order to reserve that honour for himself.

The joy of the *Iliad*, then, is not, and never was, just pride in the praise of ancestors, or great compatriots, for the praise is always subordinated by Homer to universal poetic truth;

for the characters are universal, drawn without favour or fear. Nor, indeed, is it any one kind of joy only.

First there is the grand scheme of the whole poem to enjoy, and especially the recognition of the power of goodness at the end, how some law of god stands sure, in spite of battle-horror and Achilles' brutal, irresistible will; not quite irresistible, though, for a mother's love and its soft power are stronger, and Achilles becomes again at the last his own divine mother's son once more. We like finding that the ruthless, shameless tyranny of might does not have the last word, and that it prevails only for a time. There is an excitement, part ethical, part vindictive, in watching the process developing through suspense and delays. We like looking back from the end, and seeing how all of it has grown out of its beginnings, by unsuspected necessities, and the ready intervention of unknown powers at each turn.

But the victory of gentleness does not come quite as a surprise, for gentleness is never long forgotten. All the way, it balances in part the rough fear and pain and grief, at first over-balanced, and then overbalancing in the end; and it is there in two ways, in the home life, precarious in Troy, contrasted with the war, and in the similes of peace and nature, giving momentary relief, and reminders, amidst the fighting.

Yet there is a joy in the fighting itself, a savage thrill at casting restraint of fear and pity away, and letting go, the kind of joy we had as children in reading adventure stories, and which the Greeks, younger as a race than we are now, must have enjoyed more than we when they were individually grown up. And there is too the more respectable thrill of danger, and of escape delayed that comes at last, with its relief and rest.

The gods in Homer can be enjoyed by us as by the Greeks, not less because they belong to a quite inconsistent pair of worlds. As there is a contrast of softness and hardness, so there is a contrast of the serious and the comical. Achilles is never funny; but Odysseus is sometimes, Agamemnon often, and Nestor nearly always, though in spite of it Homer brilliantly makes his advice wise and good. Meanwhile the gods can be funny almost at any time, being less controlled in general than the men by the needs of the plot. Homer can make us laugh at them at one moment, and in the next subject us to their tremendous awe. Whatever theory we hold about divinity ought not to prevent us from enjoying the divine world of Homer in either mood, grave or gay, without any disturbance from what has been said or thought of the divine a few lines before, or may be soon again.

Then there is the mighty torrent of Homer's verse, a pleasure in itself, alike when its splendour is a decoration and when it expresses a splendour of vision. Homer is content to know that a long poem cannot be a poetical entirety, if each small part of it is poetic; a long poem must have many lines that are almost prosaic, to release the strain, and let the emotions rest in more rational attention, or even in attention that is less rational, even thoughtless, and governed by little more than rhythm alone.

For poetry supposed to have been created within an oral tradition, and poetry on which the best scholars in the world have found it necessary to say some of the world's most complicated things, the *Iliad* and the *Odyssey* have fared surprisingly well when read as ordinary written books, exceptionally good books no doubt but still ordinary books, which allow their readers to forget any odd secrets about them which there may be. The *Iliad* and *Odyssey* have been famous for their truth to human nature and their supremacy in sensitive characterization, for their unique vitality in picturing a world everywhere alive with movement, for their own smooth rapidity, dignity, and direct simple honesty, and for their rare success in momentous symbolic statement. Even on an assumption that the Homeric verses were in fact composed by many different poets at very different times, the Greeks have been praised for the sensitive precision with which they adhered to the traditional manner and traditional taste.

Yet there is still the Homeric 'formalism', and the more attention we give to it the more important it seems, until we stop giving it any attention at all, when it becomes unimportant again. Indeed, the formalism is most important of all to us when we are reading not Homer but statistics about the epic formulae. The formulae usually consist of two to four words, and about a third of the verses contain one or more. That is, the unit of composition, instead of being the single word, is sometimes the single phrase. It need not make much difference.

The best writing regularly uses older phrases and sometimes even clichés; but usually they are altered, sometimes very subtly, whereas Homer's are mainly not altered.

In all writing words and phrases carry their history with them, and in the best writing that history is often exploited for greater eloquence. How much Homer meant to use old associations for new individual effect is debated, but at least very often the formulae keep their old associations without being adjusted for new significances. They rather provide a certain permanent background or base for the rapid movement of the narrative.

But neither the formulae nor anything else prevents variety in Homer, and variety of many kinds. Some verses are smoother than others. In them the conventional restrictions of style and language are often dominated by a most complete mastery of expression. The older forms of phrase in Homer have been compared to stones in a river-bed, some rough and angular, but others worn round and smooth by the friction of countless years; so that Homer himself could scarcely have known for sure whether he or a predecessor was the original author of the words which he set in their place.

Homeric verses therefore may be more or may be less fluent, flexible, effortless in appearance at least, and happy with the verbal forms available to be used for full expression. At one extreme, words and meanings and syntax may fuse as well as any modern reader, accustomed to the verse of Pope and Tennyson, could wish. At the other extreme there are signs of less happy, less fluent, less inspired composition, perhaps even 'mere head-work'. Goethe said of some passage of his own that it was all done by thinking, '*es ist alles gedacht*', the opposite to what the same Goethe said about a good kind of style, the style which does the thinking and composes the poetry by itself without leaving anything for the poet to do.

Here perhaps are two kinds of style which ought to be detectable in Homer, as in other poets, but all the more on account of the formulary tradition. Homer himself seems to have admired spontaneous fluency. The minstrels he describes seem to be very positively inspired. Alcinous compared the fluent story of Odysseus to a minstrel's performance, saying

that it was just as entertaining, and implying fluency in both
(*Od.* 11. 367–9).

But this is only part of the question, for these two possible
styles are not exactly styles in the most interesting sense of the
word. They are rather methods of composition, each of which
could be used for composing in several different styles. No
doubt the fluent spontaneous method is likely to be the most
versatile.

To us the poetically intense and sublime passages of Homer
come much more frequently in some books than others. That
does not mean that books in which they are less frequent are
necessarily worse or less important for the greater plans of the
whole poem. A passage may be great in itself, or in reference
to other passages, or to a whole poem, or to both. A very
great proportion of the First *Iliad* is great in both ways.

'The Wrath, goddess of poetry, sing, the wrath of Achilles who
was Peleus' son; and it was a curse, that laid on Achaeans
agonies that were countless, sending many a valiant spirit to
Hades, and making the dying a prey for dogs and all the birds
that are; yet all the time a plan of Zeus was being fulfilled;
from the hour that first those two had their quarrel and
parted, the son of Atreus, sovereign of men, and Achilles the
brilliant.'

Agamemnon had a captive girl, Chryseis, whose father Chryses
by his prayers brought vengeance, for her sake, on the
Achaeans. Agamemnon had rejected his appeal:

'Cruelly he sent him away, and masterful was the reproof he
laid on him: "Let me not find you, old man, beside our
hollow ships, either lingering now or coming later again, for
fear, I tell you, that the god's staff and wreath may be no help
to you. Your daughter I shall not release, not ever till old age
come to her . . ." '

But prayer was stronger than anger. The old priest prayed to
his god Apollo:

' "May the Danai pay for these my tears in shafts that you
shall send." So he prayed. And he heard him, did Phoebus
Apollo, and down from the heights of Olympus he came, with a

L

heart of fury, having on shoulders his bow, and quiver of double lid. The arrows rattled on his shoulders, so angry was he, and so fast he moved; down like black night he came. Then taking his seat away from the ships, he released an arrow; and appalling was that silver bowstring's twang. First they were mules that were his mark, and brisk dogs only; but next it was upon the men that he sped an arrow with a load of pain; and smote. So all the time the pyres of the dead were in their plenty kindled.'

Here all works together, and the give and elasticity and tremendous strength and sound of the verse combine and work up together through all the quick story to the one word starting the last line, and its pause—'and smote'. And the rest is omitted; except that the pyres were burning soon.

Achilles calls a meeting. Calchas the prophet gets a guarantee of protection from Achilles:

' "Never, I swear by Apollo the dear to Zeus, to whom you, Calchas, pray when you reveal your prophecies to the Danai; never while I live, while I on the earth have still my seeing, shall any lay on you beside our hollow ships his heavy hands." '

So Calchas can prophesy the truth, and start the curse of the wrath, wrath of Achilles taking the place of wrath of Apollo. Agamemnon must give up Chryseis. But he is furious, and threatens to take someone else's captive, perhaps Achilles'.

'Achilles the swift of foot glared at him under his brows, and he said to him this—"Man dressed in shamelessness, with a heart all cunning for gain, how shall a single Achaean obey readily your commands, either to go a march or fight manfully with a foe? Certainly, I never came here to fight with any thought of those spearmen of Troy. They have done me no harm at all. Never once have they driven off my cows, nor yet my mares, nor have they either, in Phthia where soil is rich and men grow strong, ever ravaged my crops, for many and many the things between, both shadowed mountains and the ringing sea." '

In Greek the last line is:

οὔρεά τε σκιόεντα θάλασσά τε ἠχήεσσα.

It is tempting, if only for a moment, to think this line the loveliest in Homer.

Achilles says that he will go home, and Agamemnon tells him that he may. Achilles, angrier still, lays his hand on his hilt, and is drawing—when there behind him is Athena, appearing to him only and catching him by his golden hair, so that round he swings, and looks—and we can see him. He recognizes her: 'terrible shone her eyes'. He asks her if she has come 'to see the wickedness of the son of Atreus, Agamemnon'. Agamemnon, he says, will die for it. But she tells him to refrain, and obey; there would be three times the value in recompense to come. He agreed to her words; 'and on that silver hilt he stayed his heavy hand.'

But what Heaven let him do he did, and abused Agamemnon to the extreme:

' "Man heavy with drink, with the shameless eyes of a dog but coward heart of a deer, you have never had spirit to dare to put corslet on for warfare with your men, or march to the ambush with Achaea's chieftains. You know too well it would be death for you. Oh, far better is it to steal gifts away all down the wide array of Achaea, if ever one of us speaks up to you— just a king who devours his folk; for they must be weaklings over whom you rule, otherwise, O son of Atreus, this most surely would be the very last insult from you. But I shall say it to you right out, and add to it a terrible oath that I shall swear. Surely, by this sceptre, which can never again grow leaves and shoots since the day when first it left its stump in the mountains, nor ever flourish again, for in truth the bronze has stripped off around it its leaves and bark; so now the time has come that sons of Achaea in jurisdiction, who uphold the ordinances that are from Zeus, carry it in their palms; yes, be sure, a powerful oath this shall be—I swear that one day a yearning for Achilles shall touch Achaea's sons very near, each one of them; and on that day for all your pain you shall have power to do no good at all, when many shall be falling and dying under hand of Hector the man-slayer, while you within you rend your spirit for rage, that to Achaea's greatest you shewed no honour at all." So Peleus' son; and he banged on the earth that sceptre, pierced with its rivets of gold. Then down he sat. On his side meanwhile Atreus' son was furious too. But before them up leapt Nestor, charming of talk, the Pylians' fluent speaker.'

The fierce decision and deep swift tone of the quarrelling turns suddenly into softness, when Nestor, like Shakespeare's Polonius a statesman past his prime, garrulous and comical, but nearly always right in prudence if not in honesty, speaks to the princes and smooths them down. Heralds sent to fetch Briseis from Achilles need not have been frightened; he is courteous to them, knowing that it is not their fault. He tells Patroclus to bring her; and she goes, unwillingly.

'But Achilles started crying, and went off alone to sit down away from all his companions, to the margin of the salt grey sea, looking out over the limitless deep. He stretched out his hands and prayed long to his own dear mother: "Mother, you did bear me, your son, to live for a little, and no more; so the Thunderer on high, Olympian Zeus, gave me honour in compensation, to guarantee it into my hand. Yet now he has shewn me not even the tiniest honour; for I tell you Atreus' son, Agamemnon prince of wide sway, has disgraced me, by stealing my prize from me and taking it for himself."

So he said, the tears running, and his goddess mother heard him; she was sitting in the salt sea depths beside her old father, but quickly she came up out of the grey sea, just like a mist; then she sat down right in front of him as he wept, and reached to hold him with her hand, spoke to him, and said what she had to say: "Son, why are you crying, what is the sorrow that has touched your thoughts? Say it right out, do not hide it in your mind, so that we may both of us know." '

They talked; Thetis promised to persuade Zeus; and she did; he has now to make the Achaeans suffer. Then, quite soon, all is comedy, and in Heaven Zeus all too rightly fears that Hera will be most annoyed if he makes such a compact to harm her favourites, the Achaeans. Good temper is restored, however, when the lame god Hephaestus limps round comically, pouring out drink; after reminding all the gods how he had suffered from Zeus' anger, when he was thrown out of Heaven, and took nine days to fall.

Thus the First *Iliad* ends, with divine merriment, feasting and the music of Apollo and the Muses; then sunset, and sleep for all the gods but Zeus.

Homer's similes deserve, and have had, more extended treatment than can be given them here. Their poetic power has especial freedom and the technical mastery is high. Many of the similes can be felt to stand out from their more 'traditional' contexts; they seem to come from a single mind, the mind of a civilized person who is used to ordinary life, and loves ordinary and domestic things: perhaps even, in some sense, as Giambattista Vico said, 'a man of the people', however much we must for ever call our Homer an aristocrat of all the earth.

Generally the similes act to relieve pressure, and in the *Iliad* especially they do this by offering, for mind and eye, contrast and the reminder that there is another world beyond the bitter quarrelling and the strife by the walls of Troy; another world of the familiar, quieter things of home. Yet at times too the similes bring pictures from wilder nature, to match the violence of the onset of warring men and gods.

Pandarus the Trojan archer, breaking the truce, has wounded Menelaus. The Greek leaders are roused to renew furious battle:

'Now as when on a sea beach, always sounding, the sea's swell is driven ever faster by the west wind when it sets it moving there; and first on the deep ocean it rises crested, and next is breaking on the dry land, and roaring, loud; while, either side the headlands, it arches and lifts its crest, spewing away the froth of the salt sea; so then faster and faster the ranks of the Danai were moving resistlessly to war.'   (4. 422–8)

Later, Diomedes wounded Ares, the war-god, and he went up to the sky like a thundercloud and roaring like nine or ten thousand men:

'As that blackest mist appears out of clouds, after heat, when a foul hot wind starts to blow its blast, so bronzen Ares appeared to Diomedes, Tydeus' son, as he passed with the clouds into the wide heaven.'   (5. 864–7)

But the widening of view to embrace the world of nature

beyond the battlefield does not come in the similes only. The
gods move freely in the world at large; we see them on the
mountain-tops and moving across the wide seas. Poseidon from
the crest of the tiny, towering island of Samothrace sees the
Achaeans being defeated, and is furious, and comes to help:

'At once he came down from the rocky mountain, walking
with quick steps forward. Atremble were the mountain's
length and its forest beneath those immortal feet, as Poseidon
passed. Three strides he made and at the fourth he came to
his destination, Aegae, just where is his renowned palace, in
the depths of the mere, all built of glittering gold, destructible
never. Then he went and harnessed at his chariot his bronze-
foot pair of horses, quick flyers, with long manes of gold, and
gold too the garment their master put over his skin. He gripped
his whip, and it too was gold, beautifully made; then stepping
on to his chariot started to drive over the waves. From all their
hidden depths the sea-monsters frisked beneath him, well
knowing their lord, and for joy the sea stood parted. On those
horses flew most swiftly, without ever the bronze axle being
wet beneath, till, bounding, they brought him to the Achaean
ships.'   (13. 17–31)

Very near the middle of the whole *Iliad* (12. 310–28), when
things are near their worst for the Achaeans, and the two
Lycian allies of Troy, Sarpedon, own son of Zeus, and Glaucus,
are just going to break through the Achaean defensive wall
into their camp, Homer includes a passage which is often
thought his very best, and which seems to be his answer to his
question, *why* all the pain and the tears, and the force to wreak
them, and endure, and not go back? The Lycians talk, and
Sarpedon says:

' "Glaucus, just why have we two greatest honour, with chief
place at banquets and most meat and full cups, in Lycia,
where all look at us as if we were gods, and where we have as
our share by the banks of Xanthus a large estate and lovely, for
its orchard-land and its wheat-growing soil? Well, therefore,
it is our duty now, here where we are among the Lycian
foremost, to stand, and go to front the searing scorch of
battle, that any of the tight-cuirassed Lycians well may say,

"Oh no, they have their rightful fame, our princes who rule sovereign in Lycia, and deserve to feast on fat sheep and wine sweet as honey, chosen out for them; for just as noble proves their force of valour too—they fight among the Lycian foremost." Dear boy, think, if we two, escaping, and surviving from this war, were destined for ever and ever to be ageless and deathless also, then I should never fight in the foremost, nor should I send you on into the battle where the glory is for men to win. But it is not so. Everywhere in countless number flit over us the angels of death. No mortal man can ever evade them and escape. So, let us go forward, whether we shall hand to another his pride, or another to us." '

There is nothing more musical than the Greek here, more perfect in the rise and fall, with the meaning, of the loveliest tones, with all the notes and colours of sound.

Great poets have an eye and an ear and a mind to discern a chance, and use it; a chance to let and make the pressure of experience in the secret places of their brain come out to fit and to organize and shed light on all the world of men, now and to come. Homer had a memory full of tales, charged with hopes and fears strengthened by sharp pictorial and symphonic life, in the lines of chieftain facing chieftain, poising 'the long-shadowing spear', or 'staying on silver hilt a heavy hand'; and in the swell and heave, and recession and heave again, of a verse that matches the swell of empty seas, the same old swell of Homeric measure and tone, as each time we push off from peril to peril, 'piercing our way through wars with men, and over the sea swell and all its pain.'

And we hear and see with Homer. We see into Achilles' bitter heart when at the outset he turns on Agamemnon: we are with him in his fierce will, before Athena comes. And we see into Hector's mind too when at the crisis of the action of the poem (22. 90 *ff.*) he awaits the deadly advance of Achilles. In extremity he sees clear. He must meet the hopeless fight. It has come to him:

' "There cannot anyhow be any way to talk to *him* in country talk, resting on oak stock or on stone, love-talk like a boy and girl together, boy and girl talking love together." '

The cadence carries us within his thoughts, fainting in reminiscence away into sweetness. No, he must fight.

'So he thought, and he stayed. Meanwhile Achilles drew near him, looking like the war-god when his helmet dazzles and he is set for war; and he held shaking on his right shoulder that frightful lance of Pelian ash, as all over him the bright bronze glared like the blaze of fire or the sun at its rising.'

The contrast; and all that has been and all that is to come; and our own moods, our terrors, our awes, our loves.

Once, for a moment, we are given the sight and thought of the Great Bear in the sky, seen from the open sea:

'Now in its own place it stays, turning, and fixes its watch on Orion, alone of them all without part in the Ocean bathing of stars.   (*Od.* 5. 273–5)

Between Scylla and Charybdis the course is set, the sea has control and we have to go. We are with Odysseus in the bow sheets. He is armed, though Circe had told him that arms would be of no use:

'I saw smoke and a great wave, and I heard a noise. Sudden, the oars just flew from the hands of my friends in their terror. It was just one roar of sound down that mill-race.'[1]
                                                    (12. 202–4)

Odysseus looked for Scylla:

'But I could see her nowhere, though my eyes got tired as I peered all over that mist-clad rock.'   (232–3)

This is how at moments the eye and the ear take perfect note, and the mind allows perfect fitness of thought and suggestion to join. And all the tremendous, mysterious engines of rhythm turn, with energy's swift strength and always, if only in one vowel-sound, when it is wanted, some lovely surprise. The little things, if they are little, are ready to serve the big.

The big things in Homer are hard to explain. In great poems,

---

[1] This phrase, βόμβησαν δ'ἄρα πάντα κατὰ ῥόον, is however usually taken to describe the noise made by all the oar-blades smacking down on the water.—J.D.C.

all works together and seems automatically to fit in and make a great revelation, leaving us different, and leaving us either knowing, or ready and fit to know, what was beyond us before. 'It is not the poet's business', said James Elroy Flecker, 'to save man's soul, but to make it fit for saving.' Homer shews pictures of people in the human situation, which compel us to have thoughts, charged with emotion and will. The *Iliad* must make us want to forgive and be kind; the *Odyssey* must make us less ready to give way to the moment's fear or joy, less ready to despair, and stop the quest. They do infinitely more; but even on this level you can see how the Greeks were somehow right to think that poets, apprehended poetically, are or should be instructive, and you can see too how they were right to use Homer for education, and would have faced a grave risk if they had taken Plato's advice in the *Republic*, and banned him.

The larger effects come by character working itself out to consequences of itself and of other things in action. That again is much too simple. But Aristotle is right to say that in a tragedy —and Homer is the most dramatic of poets—it is the 'myth', or organization of incidents, that is, the plot, which matters most. In Homer, the plots matter most, made as they are of characters who mean something and actions which also mean something, all of course supported by the little things, of sight and sound, which win us, and put us in a mood in which we are ready to be won. The only danger is that the loveliness and power of the little things may make us overlook the big.

In the *Iliad* Achilles lives for glory, and is as terrible in council and in war as he is magnificent to see. But his heart is all the time tender and young, and longs to be released for kindness and love. His only peace is in telling all to his mother, Thetis of the sea, rising, silver-foot, like a mist from the mere. There is hardly even glory to madden him while he talks to her, or even the early death, with which he has bought the glory that he now seems to be losing after all. But, right from the beginning of the great first book, the counsel of Zeus started to be fulfilled. A mystery it is, but somehow all the fountains of blood and tears, like the furious bloody rivers that Achilles has to fight near the end, are doing divine work, making, creating something that has to be; and in all the *Iliad* it is a new Achilles who is being made, an Achilles who is led down strange dark ways, back to his mother's knee, and to a glory that he never guessed, a glory that the great Alexander envied.

Homeric poetry shews, majestically, the forces arrayed when in defiance or submission man confronts the Divine; with exquisite subtlety reveals the relations between men themselves, humane and civilized, or violent and wild; and turns the brightest intuition to birds and animals, and to inanimate things. The verse may be of velvet or of resilient steel; it may have thunderous, electric force; but the great structural architecture, more intricate and elaborate than any other poet has contrived, tells secrets too. Perhaps it is in what we have still to learn from Homer that his greatness principally lies.

EPILOGUE

(*First published as 'Many-Minded Homer' in* Orpheus,
Vol. I, 1954)

Two very great Homeric scholars, Paul Mazon and Albert
Severyns, have both lately said that it is hardly possible to write
one single sentence about Homer and to be quite sure that it
is the truth. To make a list of reasons why this should be so is
easy. But the main reason is the difficulty of being sure what
sort of poets or poet composed the Homeric poems, and what
sort of poems he composed; and sometimes the most obvious
assumptions about the poems and the poets may turn out to be
based on guesswork which overlooked some of the complications. For the complications are very many. Yet on the other
hand the poetry, or much of it, is very great; it is hard to
believe that all those who have thought so are wrong. But the
uncertainty remains, and it is depressing. Sometimes it seems
hardly worth while to think about the subject, when there is
so little chance of a sure result. It is not, however, really so bad
as that. A way out is suggested by a brilliant phrase of W. B.
Yeats. He called Homer 'many-minded Homer'.

To treat any great poem as a product of a single individual
poet's conscious mind is always unsafe. Poets themselves are
often very unwilling to treat their poetry so. 'It does not seem
to go through my head at all', said one, Noel Essex. 'The poems
just had to be like that' said T. S. Eliot himself. John Keats, if
he went into a room with many people in it, felt himself to
become each of them in turn and cease to be himself. There is
regularly interplay or even interpenetration of minds or parts
of minds to make poetry. Old poetry lives on in new poetry and
helps to make it. There is often a noticeable debate in a single
poet's mind or minds when he seems to be choosing and recon-
ciling poetic elements from different sources all retained within
himself.

Usually one single poet actually writes down the resulting
poem. A single poet may have written down the *Iliad* and the
Odyssey almost in their present form. But, if so, he hardly set
his own stamp on almost every verse or even every phrase as
Sophocles, Vergil, Dante and Milton probably did. For the

Iliad and the *Odyssey* grew in the manner of oral and traditional poems for much or most of their time of growing. The formulae, as treated by Milman Parry, are sufficient proof; and much has been made clearer concerning the method of oral composition, with its rigidities and also opportunities for flexibility, by Parry again, and among others by H. M. Chadwick, M. P. Nilsson and Sir Maurice Bowra, all of them giving many comparisons and descriptions, some proving that oral poetry can be written down at a late stage of a long oral life without losing its oral aspect. It is reasonably certain that the Homeric poems fit into the class of traditional, oral poems, developed continuously for many centuries by minstrels of a single tradition or of similar traditions. This is something, and it is sufficiently certain. What is now wanted is more light on the changes made by poets in the inherited poetry and on the meaning to be drawn from them. That is, attempts should be made to penetrate the minds of the poets and to learn progressively better how to read Homer without deceptive distraction by the sometimes rather remote and mysterious aspect of Homeric verse. For example, it is natural to wonder how much personal feeling or indeed topical allusion can legitimately be extracted from a formal, archaic language not fully understood by the poets who composed in it, and containing many assumptions and allusions which had long been obsolete when the tradition was mature. Much help in such uncertainties is offered by Bowra's collection of 'heroic' poetry from many parts of the world, principally in Europe and Asia, but also elsewhere. Heroic poetry can be considered as a class of traditional oral poetry, and many later poems and other literature have in some sense evolved from it. The *Iliad* and the *Odyssey* are not strictly, in this sense, heroic poems, but there is clearly heroic poetry in them, and they certainly must have a heroic ancestry. There is a phase of oral heroic poetry in, or behind, the literary history of many peoples.

The minstrels of oral, heroic poetry tell stories about well-known characters and their adventures in a formal and conventional style. But many heroic poems have been recorded and exist in different versions. Many minstrels have improvized extempore as they recited; but apparently some have most often, or even always, recited poetry which they have learnt as accurately as possible without attempting to change it. The same or similar adventures and situations recur widely diffused, and the characters are rather grand than subtle, and not very various. Historical events and people are regularly recalled, sometimes during many centuries of recitation in which more recent history might have been, but has not been, introduced. The historical attachment is regularly loose; little can be learnt with any confidence from heroic poetry about what did in fact happen. The impulse of minstrels and hearers is for presentation of courage, strength, wit and intelligence, of reverence for personal honour, and of great crimes, fierce battles, terrible dangers and fearful sufferings. There are two stages. At first heroes are magicians prevailing by strength of magic. Then they are humanized, and they prevail rather by human virtues, sometimes with aid from the divine. There may even be a third stage, in which the assumptions and ideals, at first aristocratic, have become, or are becoming, popular, or even democratic through a change from aristocratic to popular conditions in society. Obviously, heroic poems are very valuable indeed as documents for social and mental changes contemporary with the poems. Indeed heroic poetry seems to trace for posterity a sequence of human development at periods when that development reached stages of great and permanent importance.

Rhys Carpenter and Émile Mireaux have argued with brilliance that the *Iliad* and *Odyssey*, in small allusions and also large matters of organic structure, refer pointedly to the contemporary history of the periods between 750 B.C. and 700 B.C.; Mireaux even continues his identifications down to the restoration of Peisistratus, and argues that there are many references of about 650 B.C. and after. Their arguments are perhaps not quite sufficient for proof, in spite of their brilliance. Neither are they easy to disprove. Time will be needed to decide.

Meanwhile there are other considerations. Homer is 'many-minded'. Perhaps all great poets are; but possibly he is the most many-minded of them all. In any case there is a kind of timelessness in great poems. The topical allusions to some contemporary world in them are not what is most important. This has been very strongly expressed by G. Wilson Knight: '. . . the reading of works of genius in the light of their age nearly always in practice, unless very carefully watched, means reducing them to the general level of their age; the level, that is, of modern histories, impersonal records, jealous contemporaries; of second-rate men and books, whether old or new. The one essential is that we keep the work of genius, in all its majesty and mystery, central. For the rest, the test is easy. All we have to ask is, Does this or that type of research assist, or retard, the unique revelation of the work under survey? Does it help us to focus the living reality *beyond*; the new dimension being shadowed, the mystery, the magic, the power, whatever we choose to call it?' (*Essays in Criticism*, Oct. 1953.) Of course that does not mean that no research is useful if it is concerned with the relation of poems and poets to their own contemporary world. But it does mean that the results of that research will be misleading if they are exclusive and are not kept in close contact with other results of research concerned with the less transitory and less occasional references in it.

The Homeric poems are on the whole like other poems of rare, and very great, poetic statement, which set a seal on a long age. But they are different in shewing some of the mysterious mechanism behind their power. They shew it because they appear before us without the self-assertive aspect of single authorship borne by other great poems. The Homeric poems can, of course, be read as unities with little thought of more than one author for them, and it is still possible even to argue that in some sense they were in fact both composed by a single poet. But even then there remains a sense in which their authorship is multiple, and indeed there are certain and undeniable signs of different dates for different passages. That is, there is at least some opportunity to watch the process by which, over centuries, the poetry grew to its final form. Other mature poetry has also grown through centuries; but the growth is not visible without special exploration, and the certainty of single authorship allows each text to be treated by itself, and even discussed, without any inevitable reference to sources or other antecedents which may have enabled the single author to create and form his poem. Single authors of great poems may be, and perhaps always are, 'many-minded' in their own way, containing their 'many minds' each in one brain. Homer, perhaps of all the most 'many-minded', contained the 'many minds' in more than one brain.

There were certainly 'two Homers', or two principal Homers. This is only part of the truth, but it is an important part. Nor is it a new or an eccentric belief; it was suggested much more than a century ago by Grote, and now something not very different is being argued by Mireaux. But the statement, and the arguments, which are probably the most conclusive and enlightening on this question were published by Sir William Geddes in 1878. They seem to have been neglected. But they are of very great value for the question how the Homeric poems acquired their power. They do not explain genius; nothing can. But they open one of the windows or inspection-panels to shew the mechanism by which genius works, or worked on this occasion.

When the *Iliad* and *Odyssey* reached their present form is still obscure; but at least it is certain, especially through the thorough researches of M. Jules Labarbe, that the text which Plato used is very much like ours. In the fifth century there is less reason to believe in a received text. The few notices suggest that our *Iliad* and *Odyssey* were not exalted so highly above all other epic as they soon after came to be, though of course old versions of stories, disagreeing with Homer's, were followed by many poets down to Quintus Smyrnaeus and beyond, and especially by Roman Augustan poets. What Peisistratus did to Homer is still uncertain. If the notices are correctly read without altering the text, they seem to mean quite simply that Peisistratus collected the Homeric poems together, and had them edited at Athens, because he needed them, and at that time they only existed in other places, where they were still remembered and recited, but perhaps with no complete and accurate text. Peisistratus may then have restored them successfully to their former condition, without adding, or altering, more than a very little. Unless Mireaux's extremely clever theory about him is true, and it is not proved and need not be debated now, Peisistratus probably acquired, regulated, and transmitted a text like Plato's and like ours. The big changes are most likely to have occurred earlier. There are now many trustworthy signs that much constructive work on the poems was done not long before 700 B.C., especially since the comparisons by Sir John Myres and Miss H. L. Lorimer of allusions in Homer to archaeologically known objects and techniques.

Of these comparisons some give these later dates. But other comparisons give earlier dates, some as early as the fifteenth century, and some interspersed in the generations between. Many are familiar, and for their observation W. E. Gladstone among others must be thanked. The Homeric poems have strata laid down in many different generations, at least since the heroic times of the fourteenth and thirteenth centuries when Achaean armies and fleets were in contact with the empires of Hittites and Egyptians. They even seem to remember the earlier Mycenae and the earlier Troy long before 1200 B.C., and to owe descriptions of cremation burials to nothing Greek but to Trojan practice observed by Achaeans at Troy at about, or before, that date. The Homeric picture of Troy attacked has lineaments clearly inherited from attacks on Babylonian cities at about 2000 B.C. The tradition is long, and not entirely obscure.

It has now become safe to recognize clearly a continuous tradition of Greek poetry, probably mainly oral and heroic, lasting from 1200 B.C. and earlier until the *Iliad* and *Odyssey* were finished, perhaps after or even well after 750 B.C. The reason is in the partial decipherment by M. Ventris and J. Chadwick of the Mycenaean tablets, found by Carl Blegen at Pylos in 1939, and dated about 1250 B.C., and in their convincing argument that the language is early Greek, akin both to the very early Arcado-Cyprian, already slightly known, and to the Greek epic dialect. The Greek epic dialect began no doubt in this early Greek of the Tablets. The Aeolic aspect of some expressions in epic seems to be a survival from either an early Aeolic, akin to the language of the Tablets or actually the language of the Tablets itself, which is like, or even is the same as, very early Aeolic. This language, originally spoken, evolved first as a spoken language and later as an artistic language no longer spoken. The main adventures which befell it were the acquisition of an Ionic colour and the artificial and mistaken creation of verbal forms by poets who had ceased to understand the old language exactly.

It was at some point in this long tradition that the two epic minds of the two Homers met. That is too simple, but it is true. Geddes gave the proofs, and they in themselves reveal the contrast between these minds. He divided the books of the *Iliad* and *Odyssey* into two groups, 'Achillean Books' which are early and primary, and 'Ulyssean Books' which are late and secondary, each group by a different poet. The Achillean Books are *Iliad* 1, 8, and 11–22. The other books of the *Iliad*, and all the books of the *Odyssey*, are Ulyssean Books. The differences are inescapable, and must be differences between different minds belonging to different times and places. The Achillean poet seems to belong to North Greece, perhaps Thessaly, and the Ulyssean to Ionia in Asia Minor. Scenery and weather-conditions indicate that. In the Achillean books Iris is the divine messenger, Charis is the wife of Hephaestus, Olympus is a mountain, horses are loved, dogs are not, and there is little thought of domestic harmony and happiness. In the Ulyssean books Hermes is the divine messenger, Aphrodite is the wife of Hephaestus, Olympus is or is becoming something like a sky heaven, horses are not much noticed, dogs are loved, and the ideal of domestic harmony and happiness is a cardinal motive. The spirit is very different. The Achillean books are fierce and harsh, with mockery of fallen foes but no kindly humour, and lacking sympathy for less admired characters. The Ulyssean books are more reflective and humane, less inclined to cruel mockery, and sometimes sympathetic to the less admired characters. The Achillean Achilles and Hector have no softer side; the Ulyssean have. The Achillean Helen is unredeemed, but not the Ulyssean. The Achillean Odysseus and Ajax are ordinary if effective heroes; the Ulyssean are far more individual, Odysseus strong, brilliant and undefeated, and Ajax valiant, but a little comic. With characterization goes some local feeling. The Achillean poet is Aeolic and Dorian, and the Ulyssean Ionic, in their sympathies.

Geddes is certainly on the whole right, and one result of his observations and arguments, given in great detail and at great length, is a light thrown on one of the reasons why the *Iliad* is great. Poetry has been defined as 'comparison and rhythm' and indeed that means simply 'comparison', since rhythm is itself a kind of comparison. And the two 'Homers' of the *Iliad* present a very effective comparison indeed, for between them they place in dynamic opposition two world-views and two tempers of mind, the heroic and the humane, or Hellenic. The *Iliad* epitomizes the heroic past, and matches against it another

M

epitome, an epitome of maturer and softer experience. Such constructive oppositions are normal in literary epic, especially Roman and Renaissance epic; but, in them, both terms of the contrast appear from a single poet's mind in his words. In the *Iliad* the effect is at least as great as in any other epic, and there may well be a gain in candour and sincerity, since both versions of the human plight are given from the heart. Hector and Andromache, seen together, are all the more poignant because they are framed in fighting of which some is told by a poet who did not so look into thoughts, and who presented Achilles of 'the unapproachable hands' without thinking of the heart which was subject to greater and softer things than the joy of battle.

Such is an important way to powerful poetic effect. Poets take in hand earlier poetry, see new possibilities in it, and develop them. Often they contradict or invert or reverse an older story or motive. The Achillean 'Homer' presents a fierce, single-minded, almost impious Hector, with a brother, Polydamas, milder and perhaps wiser, to oppose him with advice. The Ulyssean 'Homer' accepted and changed what he had received. He made Hector quite different, partly by blending Polydamas into him.

This is a small example, or at least a simple, although an important, example, of a method which can be detected again and again in the Homeric poems. The poets sometimes seem to agree closely with Goethe's saying that a poet ought to take over as much as possible from earlier poets, to alter everything, and always to alter it as little as possible. Mysteriously enough, this method appears to retain and compress the power of the old poetry which it always tries to use, and to produce new poetry which can be very new, and quite unrecognizable, because there have been so many alterations to the old material which is still richly retained. It is very much like the method disclosed in Coleridge by John Livingston Lowes in 1927, in Vergil by E. K. Rand in 1932 and by others then and later, and in Greek tragic poets by J. D. Denniston in 1942. There may have been many partial glimpses of this method in Homer during the last century; K. O. Müller seemed to suspect it in 1856. But it has only become clear and certain in the Homeric poems during the last thirty years; thanks are due in particular to publications of Ernst Howald, 1924, 1937 and 1946, T. W. Allen, 1930, Wolfgang Schadewaldt, 1938, Heinrich Pestalozzi, 1945, Renata von Scheliha, 1948, and J. Th. Kakridis, 1950. The detection of this method in the Homeric poems is important to any one trying to understand how so many rich contents of meaning are preserved in them and continually generate by their interaction new rich contents, with the result that 'Homer' is indeed 'many-minded'.

The Ulyssean books, then, were added to the Achillean. How many complications, and how many poets, are concealed under the simple classification into two groups of books, is hard to say now, but may be to some extent discoverable by further research. What is certain is that both groups of books were composed with help from this method of derivation and alteration; that is, the method of 'poetic integration', as I have called it, and the same method which is detected by the kind of research named by Kakridis 'neo-analysis'. This kind of research compares known texts with other earlier texts, extant or reconstructed, and notes every occasion when something strange, inexact, or untidy in the newer text can best be explained by something derived from some earlier text, where it was neat and organic, and next applied, altered, in the newer text without perfect adaptation. Howald and Pestalozzi shew clearly in their publications how the arguments are used. Most of the results are reliable, and can be used in general discussion.

The Ulyssean poet of the *Iliad* can be seen at work by comparing his books with the Achillean books and other material. It is hard to doubt that he constructed his character Diomedes by adopting poetry from the Theban cycle of epics, using it for the exploits of Diomedes, and making Diomedes himself as brave as his father Tydeus but otherwise quite opposite, faultlessly chivalrous whereas Tydeus was barbarously brutal. H. W. Stubbs most recently treated this question and further illuminated it. When the Ulyssean poet made his brilliant and undefeated Odysseus, he clearly took the Achillean Odysseus, already a nicer man than the Odysseus of pre-Homeric poetry, and elaborated him with characteristics of Palamedes, the good and ingenious hero whom the earlier Odysseus had treacherously killed. Perhaps he similarly combined the Achillean Ajax with the stupid and clumsy Coroebus of other old poetry to make his own valiant but slightly clownish Ajax. The Ulyssean poet put his heart into all three heroes. They are his own creations, and he made them by his own intuitive power to observe and to create. But they are the better made, and the richer, for the old poetry remembered, distilled, and infused into them. Another example is Antenor. Outside the Homeric poems he was a traitor to Troy. In the *Iliad* he has some slight inclination in favour of the Greeks and of peace. When Achilles has returned to the battle, Antenor wonders whether to fight or to flee, and in fact escapes, and survives. The Ulyssean poet made masterly use of this idea. For he made Hector himself ponder whether to fight or to flee, decide to fight, and then, nevertheless, flee; but not survive. Homer, as F. W. Clayton lately noted, liked incidents in pairs, as indeed did Vergil. Both use earlier versions of motives as a way to later, unexpected versions, and sometimes achieve in them supreme acts of power.

Not much can be said here about the *Odyssey*, but a little must be said about its guiding motive, harmony and fidelity in a happy home. There is a powerful message in that motive, a message discovered and confirmed by long experience and directed to the present and to the future, and perhaps to all the future, as long as humanity lasts. Apparently here too, the Ulyssean poet made his poetic discovery and decision by observing the Achillean books of the *Iliad* and no doubt other poetry also, and by inverting a statement which he found there. He chose the subject of Agamemnon and Clytaemnestra, in a home of wickedness and disaster. He, or possibly another poet very much like him, created, in contrast, the virtuous but also ill-fated home of Hector and Andromache. He then imagined the home of Odysseus and Penelope, this time a home both virtuous and happy also, a home which is to survive in harmony at least for some time; and he directed his material of heroic endeavour not to the destruction, from within or without, of a happy home, but to a happy home's preservation and restoration.

About this, two things are to be noticed now, the dexterous and simple turn by which new poetry of great power is made by poetic insight out of earlier poetry, and also the immensity of the material, acquired in long human experience, which may be released and used by a dexterous and simple turn given to older poetry.

True heroic poems appear to be most often tragic. Certainly the poet of the *Odyssey* had much tragic material to use. But clearly much of his available material was not merely tragic. Much of it was about other things besides disasters, whether it was used by the earlier poets to lead up to disasters or not. There are, of course, adventures and travels, little dramas of country life and fierce experiences of the sea, and an elaborate and complex repertory concerned with marriage customs. The poet of the *Odyssey* already knew and used for the situations and the events in and near the palaces of both Alcinous in Scheria and Odysseus in Ithaca stories, perhaps some of them far more than a thousand years old, concerned with the rituals of matriarchy and of magical kings; George Thomson and also Mireaux have suggested how they are to be identified, and W. J. Woodhouse shewed how these same stories, in a later form no doubt, as romances, were fitted together to make the *Odyssey*. The details are not for now, but the general fact is. The poet of the *Odyssey* included within it the contents of many minds by allowing the needs, the hopes, the fears, and the assumptions of older religions in a long succession through human development to persist in a newer story and enrich it, and to appeal to the inherited interests and inclinations, become almost instinctive, which the first hearers of the complete *Odyssey*, and readers of it today, must, however unconsciously, retain. The power of evocation, and the force of the poetic message discerned and delivered, can be traced to this freight of old, once strongly felt, and never quite forgotten, experience. And the combination of many motives in one poem is still in principle the same as the smaller adaptations. They are not absent from the *Odyssey*. Denys Page has shewn that the Homeric account of the Cyclops, and what Odysseus did to him, retains traces of several different versions of this well-known and widely diffused folk-tale. It is all part of the duty of great poets to reach out to reality and make contact with it over a great stretch of space and time.

Before this later poet, the earlier poet of the Achillean books in the *Iliad* worked by the same method. The scheme of the *Iliad* is based on the old eastern stories of attacks on cities, perhaps including one or more of the cities called Troy, and on another story, about the attack of Curetes from Pleuron in north Greece on the neighbouring city of Calydon, which Meleager refused to defend, because of his anger with his mother, until, after she and elders of the city had failed to persuade him, his wife, Alcyone or Cleopatra, finally succeeded, and he fought again. The poet of the *Iliad* knew poetry about Troy, in which Achilles was already a distinguished fighter, and probably had a quarrel, either with Agamemnon or with someone else. But the use of poetry about Meleager as a source surely made a far stronger story, because from it passionate loyalties and other emotional tensions could reinforce the Trojan tale. As usual the greater poem is less tidy than the poem which has been used to make it. The obvious example is the appearance in the *Iliad* that the Greeks are in a defended city, not a naval camp. The quarrel of Achilles is, then, shaped at first like the quarrel of Meleager but with a different motive. It proceeds with the substitution of Patroclus for Cleopatra, the friend for the wife, but, as Schadewaldt in particular noted, having the same name with elements reversed. For Patroclus, the Achillean poet used the motives of Antilochus, and of Achilles himself in another earlier poem. In the early poetry Antilochus, son of Nestor, saved his father but was killed by Memnon. Achilles was very fond of Antilochus, and killed Memnon in furious revenge. Later Achilles himself met death at the hands of Paris and of Apollo who helped him. There are plenty of recoverable details concerning the old poetry, and what happened is near enough to certainty. The Achillean poet, or a predecessor, blended Antilochus with Cleopatra to make Patroclus, a young man of whom Achilles was fond. Antilochus now is not killed, but he still provides a motive for the train of events leading to the fighting, and eventually the death, of Achilles by merely speaking a few words. Patroclus now persuades Achilles, not to fight immediately, but to let him fight instead of him. Patroclus is killed; his death is partly the death of Antilochus in the older poetry, because it leads Achilles to fight, and partly the death of Achilles himself as it had been represented before.

That is how Homeric poets derive motives from predecessors and redistribute them to form new and stronger stories. It is almost exactly the method of Vergil himself. Now this method enriches poetry by the contents of many minds who had contributed to the earlier poetry. Something is carried over into the new poetry, and retained there, condensed. How this works is hard to say exactly, but the Achillean examples may help to shew it.

This outline, much of it due to the discovery of others, is enough to recall the organic process by which Homeric poets developed and matured their poetry. It is certain, so far as it goes, apart from some doubtful details. But the question now is the use made of the method and the artistic impulses actuating it.

'Homer,' said E. V. Rieu, 'is not about heroes'. The paradox is revealing. The meaning, or part of it, must be that Homeric poetry is about real people as they live and act. Of course Homeric characterization is admittedly the best in all Greek literature. The personalities are strong and individual. They are not merely there for the sake of their grandeur, in their sense of honour, in their courage, and in dreadful dangers faced, and monstrous sufferings endured by them; that is how personalities tend to be in true heroic poems. But even the best characterization is not, by itself, enough in the best works. There has to be a strong and significant plot or myth; actions, sufferings, situations, and characters, must be in line, and set towards some kind of great significance. In fact, and perhaps necessarily, the subject of the poetry is many kinds of relation between personalities differently placed, personalities both human and superhuman. That is perhaps obvious, but it is not a simple matter and not without uncertainties.

The relations of people to one another are for us based on the patriarchal family. Children first grow used to other people in families. Their relations with people outside their own family are coloured by earlier experiences. Dispositions in family feeling towards obedience, self-assertion, dependence and protectiveness are diffused outside the family, and sexual or quasi-sexual love influences their diffusion. Gods and goddesses are seen as parents who provide and punish, and as impulses towards love, acquisition and hate. In the *Iliad*, which in this connexion is clearer for observation than the *Odyssey*, the poet or poets who gave it its final form took very great interest in shedding light on the relations between people, and people who are not types but individuals, created by conscious or unconscious intention to enact relationships, as significantly as possible, in situations of which some are carefully developed for this purpose. How elaborate is the planned development of action in the *Iliad*, with its long preparation for what is to come and its careful use even of details in the narrative, has lately been well recognized by, among others, Sir John Sheppard, Sir John Myres, E. V. Rieu, and, with especial concentration on this recognition, the late E. T. Owen.

This great success of Homeric poets can be traced in part to a long education in poetry forming a necessary base for direct observation of living people, and their acts, and their sufferings. It was art, like the art of Shakespeare, for example, not saga, nor heroic poetry, nor even, perhaps, normal Greek epic. Earlier Greek epic no doubt had shape, but on the whole it seems to have delivered plainer narratives, with, as usual, traditional conventions, like oral heroic poetry elsewhere. Motivation came from the story itself, as in the inferred poem about Meleager, not as in the *Iliad* from a source, and with incomplete adjustments to a changed story. In the earlier class moral significance is drawn from a situation and the assumptions of daily life. In the Homeric class of poetry it comes both from the assumptions of daily life, and also from literary resources. There were no doubt gradations, but the generalization is sufficient. One poetry is many-minded as another is not. The question is still subtle, and a comparison may help. There was a simple version of the murder of Agamemnon by Aegisthus, who married his widow Clytaemnestra, and was praiseworthily killed by Orestes, son of Agamemnon and Clytaemnestra. It is told by Zeus in the *Odyssey*, and he uses it for a simple moral; some mortals blame the gods for their misfortunes, when really it is all their own fault; that is how it was with Aegisthus. Obviously the story in its plainest outline needs to be enriched. It was enriched, especially by Stesichorus, Aeschylus, Sophocles and Euripides, and many after; and so successive poets, because they looked both into their own hearts and into the works of past poets, made the simple story sublime. It was also developed to greatness by an inversion; for the *Odyssey* itself is something like an inversion of just this story of Clytaemnestra the unfaithful. One of the best comparisons is offered by the *Philoctetes* of Sophocles; for even Sophocles could not have achieved the breath-taking brilliance of that play without the previous versions for him to alter beyond recognition by incomparable dexterities of touch. And again, without the past poets, and their heroines whom Vergil's Dido, in flash after flash, becomes, there could never have been a Vergil's Dido.

Greek epic clearly developed for many centuries, and became gradually more sensitively and humanely artistic. It probably developed as old Irish stories developed in the early Christian centuries. Some of them are known in several versions of different dates so that advances in sensitivity and moral tone can be observed. In many traditions of oral poetry and other story-telling it has no doubt been possible for many performers, in generation after generation, to contribute each a little alteration, and eventually to transform greatly the material transmitted. The decipherment of the Pylian Tablets makes it safer now to think that the tradition of Greek epic had lasted and changed continuously in a single language from Mycenaean times onwards. A certain change from a rougher to a more gracious and cultivated kind of art and thought is seen in the succession observed by Geddes, Achillean followed by Ulyssean books. It is also to the Ulyssean poet, or poets, that we owe the elaborate construction of epics in symmetrical patterns of responsions observed by Sheppard and Myres. It is still mysterious how this symmetrical construction was developed and worked into poems. But there is at least a sign of one earlier stage. The Achillean poet, or poets, seem to have used as a source an earlier poem which was a pre-Homeric form of part of the Cyclic *Aethiopis*. In this older poem, which Pestalozzi inferred and described, Achilles and Memnon, symmetrically opposed as heroes with divine mothers, fought. There are indications that the construction, not elaborate and on no great scale, was neatly and exactly balanced in pleasing unity. If so, the *Iliad* of the Achillean poet was untidy by comparison, and the final *Iliad* and *Odyssey* themselves, in spite of their patterned structure, are, like the greatest works generally, at least not everywhere smoothed to a uniform polish.

At what stage, if at any, before the Homeric poets worked, Greek epic was mere heroic poetry or mere saga is not yet known. But a stage between the Achillean books and the poetry about Meleager and Memnon can at least be suspected. Patroclus gives a sign. In the Achillean books he is a dear friend of Achilles, and apparently younger than he is. Once, however, he seems to be older; in a former poem he may indeed have been a kind of guardian to Achilles, like Phoenix in the *Iliad*. It is possible therefore that a poet before the Achillean poet had organized the *Iliad* roughly as it now is, and to do so had already transferred the part of Cleopatra, the wife of Meleager, to Patroclus, friend of Achilles. In any case there is a sociological interest, for friendship has grown in estimation to match ardent married love. Possibly, then, the start had been made; if so, the Achillean poet developed the friendship to greater fervour, perhaps making Patroclus younger, and presenting an association like the 'Greek love' of the fifth century. It is at least clear that Homeric audiences could accept with lively interest this kind of association; perhaps there had been a change since the poetry about Meleager and Cleopatra had been made.

The Homeric poems are full of rich messages of wisdom concerning human life. The new meanings, still highly valued, seem to be due to individual and 'many-minded' poets who evoked wisdom out of long experience by altering older poems with flashes of personal insight compatible, on the whole, with the assumptions, thoughts and ideals of hearers and other contemporaries. Here there is one of the approaches to an important problem, whether Homeric poets, as explorers of the moral and spiritual world, and as guides to it, for that is what poets should be, were subject to any ecclesiastical system, or were independent, or even humanistic. Of course they must have been, partially, both. They were anyhow subject as poets to Apollo and the Muses. But they sang what the Muses taught them, both directly by inspiration, and also by hard taskmastership in their craft.[1] Moralizing from doctrines of priesthoods has been left behind. These doctrines, weakly or strongly held, existed, and coloured social life. But they rather provided a framework than a picture. There was even a certain partisanship. Fernand Robert has very ably argued that the poets, men

[1] The part played by inspiration as opposed to art in Homer's poetry is acutely analysed in John Cowper Powys's *Homer and the Aether*, London, 1959.—J.D.C.

of Apollo, helped him in his drive against Poseidon whose
worship his own worship was in many cities seeking to replace.
But Robert also brilliantly shews that Homeric gods act on
men not according to theology but according to direct observation of life and an acute insight on the part of poets, who thus
gave material for an as yet unformulated theory of human
fortunes. It is true that there is more behind, in the past.
Charles Autran, surely one of the greatest of scholars, traced
Greek epic back in time, through a change of language, to
continuity with a tradition of Asiatic hymns to gods and heroes,
sung at temples as ritual. He noted that the great heroes of
Greek epic are also heroes of hero-cult; and he compared the
discoveries of J. Bédier concerning the ecclesiastical origins of
French mediaeval epic. Autran's discoveries are at least as
impressive. The eastern hieratic tradition does indeed seem to
be in the background, and so do the Greek hero-cults. But
humanization has gone far in the Homeric poems. Perhaps
many heroes had once been living human beings, had then
been equated with local *daimones*, and had later still been
restored to humanity by the poets, especially the 'many-
minded' among them who could keep some of the stored
enrichment of even that series of changeful and deeply felt
experience.

Great poets, said Mazzini, a fine scholar as well as a great
statesman and a great hero in the Homeric succession, stand
either at the close, or at the beginning, of an epoch, and their
poems either epitomize an age past, or prophesy an age to come.
The Homeric poems take both places, and achieve both tasks.
Their strict adherence to a form of thought and speech belonging, as Bruno Snell has penetratingly shewn, to an early age,
imposed a strain which strengthened them; their own restricted
language, creating new forms by positive mistakes concerning
the truth of words as demonstrated by Manu Leumann,
allowed them an autonomous esoteric pride of sovereignty.
They are both oral heroic poetry and mature literary works.
Such art forces wisdom forth. Very high claims have been made
for it. Simone Weil even wrote, 'The Gospels are the last
marvellous expression of the Greek genius, as the *Iliad* is the
first . . . But nothing the peoples of Europe have produced is
worth the first known poem that appeared among them. Per-

haps they will yet rediscover the epic genius, when they learn that there is no refuge from fate, learn not to admire force, not to hate the enemy, nor to scorn the unfortunate. How soon this will happen is another question.' We should not all agree entirely with those noble words. But we might agree that there must be reasons, however elusive, why Homer should have such power to lead Greeks and later men towards remote perfection, and nearer wisdom.

VERGIL AND HOMER

(*The Presidential Address to* The Virgil Society, *1950*)

No one man ever made a great poem. Inspiration, at least, is needed to help; or perhaps the Muses. The Muses are, or include within their significance, the whole store of earlier poetry which a great poet needs to actuate him; so they were interpreted by the late E. T. Owen. Inspiration from the Greek Muses was normally sane and wise, as Jonathan Tate has explained. But it was inspiration. 'The imagination,' said Petronius, 'will not act until it has been flooded by a vast torrent of reading.' It is a necessary duty of poets to set themselves in their right place within their poetic tradition, among the dead poets: T. S. Eliot's statement is familiar and famous. So are, or should be, the researches of John Livingston Lowes and Rosamund E. M. Harding. They all help to explain how it is that C. G. Jung is right to say that 'great poetry draws its life from the life of mankind'.

A living past continues biologically in the transmission of physical genes. The past lives equally in poetic transmission.

> The generations of all Time
> And all the lovely Dead are there.

The lines of Oliver St John Gogarty, continuing the thought of Propertius on the world beyond the gates of death, fit the world of poetry just as well.

'Poetry should be anonymous; but news should be signed.' For news is of the moment, and it is personal to the reporter. Poetry, on the other hand, should be even 'more philosophical than history' because it tells, not what happens, but 'just the sort of thing which would happen'. It is always hard to go beyond Aristotle, but some subsequent comments are enlightening. Among them is one by A. N. Whitehead in his *Adventures in Ideas*:

'Art has a curative function in human experience when it reveals as in a flash intimate absolute Truth regarding the nature of things. This service of Art is even hindered by trivial

truths of detail. Such petty conformations place in the foreground the superficialities of sense experience.'

There is much in the system constructed by Carl Kerényi
which, for those who accept it, can clarify the positive content
attributed to poetry in such announcements. Kerényi investi-
gates mythology. For him the mythical world of any people
has a reality and objectivity of its own, and awaits for its dis-
closure a mythical poet, just as the objective tonal world awaits
a musician. In a short survey of Kerényi's doctrine, Alexander
Altmann (*Philosophy*, 1949) notes that this objectivity is particularly obvious in folk-song and anonymous saga. The minstrels
rather experienced than created their mythical realm. He
recalls Michelangelo's saying that 'there is no thought which
the sculptor expresses in marble that does not exist there
already'. The known, reported experiences of many musicians
and poets, for example Mozart, Coleridge, Housman and Eliot,
offer confirmation within their limits; works of art are perhaps
regularly discovered, rather than constructed, by the artists,
and sometimes the totality of a work of art is given to an artist
all in a flash. Artistic discovery is often delivered during a mood
different from the mood of every day. Dante and Milton attributed their poetry to the inspiration of the divine Muse in the
night. Pindar, in a passage (*Nem.* 4. 7) praised by Gilbert
Norwood, and perhaps incomparable as a short account of the
whole matter, claimed that 'the speech which is fetched from
the deep of the mind, with chance of the Graces, has longer life
than any deed'.

Kerényi believes that there was at first a 'primordial stage of
inexpressible awareness of the divine'. The more profoundly
consciousness recaptures it, the more powerful a myth or work
of art is. This doctrine is not incompatible with Whitehead's
conception of absolute truth revealed in works of art. Perhaps
it does not go so far; perhaps it goes farther.

The decision rests with philosophy, not with poetic commentary. But poetic commentary must recognize that poetry
compresses experience and thought into generalizations.

E. V. Rieu once remarked to me that Homer is not about
heroes. He has also said that Homer never nods. That is, Homer
accurately tells the truth about the human world. He does not

tell mistaken stories about incomprehensible beings of long ago. Perhaps that goes beyond Aristotle: 'Homer is the only poet who can make his lies look like the truth.' Possibly they were not lies at all, but generalizations. Tennyson said that he had made the moated grange in his poem out of a great number of moated granges which he had seen. Such is the art, or the inspiration. But an appearance of contemporary momentary actuality must help. Indeed, Blake insisted on it, and denounced generalization. The eternal theme of martyrdom is the more eloquent at present when it is set in a modern society of cocktail parties and psychotherapy.

To be right a poem must agree with experience, and achieve very many true generalizations. If so, it will have poetic truth. An epic poem should clearly have the kind of poetic truth which was called by Shelley epic truth, and was implicitly attributed to Homer by him. This epic truth, a profound conception not fully to be understood in lack of any explanation by Shelley, must surely be truth reached from a very great number of generalizations from a very extensive experience. And in fact, as the late C. R. Buxton in particular explained, the great epics each express something like a whole age of human culture, with its questions, its answers, and its permanent gains. An age may sometimes be expressed in works which are not strictly poems, as according to Arnold Toynbee the age of the Roman Principate was expressed in the books of St Augustine. So Livy, in a prose epic, expressed the age of the Roman Republic. Perhaps Livy was unhindered 'by trivial truths of detail'; but A. Momigliano is right to insist that Livy reached the wider and deeper kind of truth, that is, the truth which comes by poetic generalization, for Livy's picture of old Rome included what mattered most. Augusto Rostagni has shown that Livy at first strongly influenced Vergil, and that later he was in turn influenced by him. They were, of course, harmonious. Livy expressed the older Rome, and perhaps more. Vergil expressed that Rome also, and he expressed, very certainly, much more besides.

There are reasons why poetry ought to be able to reach and to generalize more experience than is possible to works in prose. To attempt to list the reasons would be like trying to define poetry. Perhaps one of them is in the poetic faculty, helped by metre and other kinds of rhythm, of searching deeply in mental layers far below normal consciousness. Another may be in the poetic freedom to use symbols, and another in the eloquence of balanced structure. And poetry need not adhere to the particularities of any single time and place. That is, poetry is the more eloquent on account of conventions and anachronisms, if those old words still serve. It can be removed from any one system of actuality, and gains perspective at the start. Experience is foreshortened, and important lines stand out, as in air-photography. That is how, as C. M. Bowra shews, Camoens in *Os Lusiadas* reveals, in Vergilian patterns, the true issues, such as the issue between civilization and barbarism, which were important in the Portuguese expansion. Vasco da Gama himself, who knew neither where he was going, nor, after he had returned, where he had been, was too near to actualities to see the broad issues as they emerged, not long afterwards, in the poem.

'Many-minded Homer,' in the brilliant phrase of W. B. Yeats, expressed an experience long and rich indeed. Over two hundred years ago Giambattista Vico was publishing the opinion that Homer's birthplace was claimed by many Greeks because in fact Homer was the whole Greek people. In saying this Vico was as usual profound, whether in fact Homer was an individual, a committee, or a corporation, as L. A. MacKay expresses the choice. Certainly poetry can be made by a plurality of poets, as boys compose school plays by discussion, and as country people in Spain were lately said to compose ballads, debating variants with one another, so that it could scarcely be known who deserved credit for each line. It is fair also to cite radio-scripts, and indeed, as M. E. Hewlett recalls, the Bible itself. Even if Goethe exaggerated when he claimed that it is not genius, but sincerity, which is rare, Victor Bérard also tended towards some exaggeration when, believing in both multiple authorship for the Homeric poems and also in their artistic unity and grandeur, he found it hard to concede that interpolators or rhapsodists could be capable of such good poetry. They might well have been capable of it, being members of the Greek people at a period of self-expressive power. The thought of Vico, Gilbert Murray and Kerényi, in convergence or in succession, can clarify the obscurity. Keats might have

agreed, even if Homer can hardly now be identified as nothing
but a series of minstrels, each, as Keats puts it in his *Ode to
Maia*, 'leaving great verse unto a little clan'. The matter is
important. For, to read Vergil rightly, few things are so necessary as to understand that Vergil and Homer are peers, world-
poets in a single tradition.

Shelley called Homer the first epic poet. It is safe to say that
that means that in Homer, for the first time, sufficient human
experience was sufficiently distilled and reduced to epic truth.
To change the metaphor, Homer first drew succinct and precise
poetic conclusions from very many particulars. He spanned
many centuries and many cities and minds of men. That is why
the time and place of Homer have been so hard to fix. The
difficulty marks not the failure of the scholars, but the success
of Homer. It is exactly like the difficulty of fixing and limiting
the meanings of phrases in Vergil. The difficulty reveals not the
deficiency of the commentators but Vergil's intricate might.

The tradition of Homeric poetry looks more like the tradition
of the old Irish stories than any other. Our Homer is full of
memories gathered and retained during the centuries. As
W. E. Gladstone observed, Homer mentions Thebes in Egypt
as it had been in the fifteenth century, before power passed
from it. Allusions are however hard to fix, for example the
famous brooch in the *Odyssey*, and in the *Iliad* the Cup of
Nestor, to which Alberto Gitti has just attributed a post-
Mycenaean date, in support of his view that four to six centuries
cannot have elapsed between the events narrated by Homer
and Homer himself. It is here that the Irish parallel is instructive, for the Irish stories were developing for quite as long as
that before they were written down, and they, unlike the Greek
poems, have survived in great numbers, which allow comparison between variant versions of the same story. In the judgment
of Eileen Hall, the stories became, as time passed, less terse and
manly, they were more freely and boldly altered by the
minstrels, and they grew more artistic, with increased moral
interest, and elaboration of symbolism. Like the tale of Troy,
the favourite tale of Cuchúlain tended to supplant others.
Clearly the old material was made to express in many trans-
formations the changing thoughts, feelings, and intuitions of
many individuals in many generations. The old material is far

N

from being all that there is in the mature versions, but it has left its record in them. It is not one mind, or one group of contemporary minds, which is reflected in heroic story, and there is not one single point in time and space to which heroic story is fixed.

The Homeric poems also collected power through many transformations. Yet in them, and perhaps in all good epic, there is a point of focus. The judgment of one poet, or perhaps two or three poets, decided the form in which the Homeric poems, without many important changes afterwards, should survive fixed. The moderate estimate of the date, preferred by, for example, K. O. Müller long since, and by H. T. Wade-Gery now, is supported by various information, lately gathered, against late estimates, such as Bethe's, and the very early dates now proposed by Renata von Scheliha and Gitti. The new surveys of Homeric language by Paul Mazon, W. Bedell Stanford, and A. Severyns have decided that at least a few organic passages have Ionic forms which are not early, and which cannot be restored to any early original spelling. Another argument of Severyns is that the similes have the marks of a single mind, the mind of a man not princely or heroic, but used to ordinary life, and loving simple and domestic things. Perhaps the temper of this Homer is not far from the condition of the later Danai, still mainly lost to history, whose humorous, whimsical, half-European and half-Oriental sculpture was found in 1945 at Kara Tepe by a Turkish archaeologist, and reported, with assignation to the ninth century, by John Garstang in 1948.

In the metaphor of Sir John Myres, there was a time when the crucible and the mould came together, and many things lost the fluidity of becoming, and began to be, existing henceforward fixed in Homer's poetic system. Many enquirers are likely soon to bring that time nearer to the light of history, continuing for example the work of Charles Picard. There must have existed human societies on the frontier between Europe and Asia in which at least the form of the Homeric poems will soon cease to seem unnatural or surprising. Long narratives were there developed artistically from version to version, and, as in the northern custom lately described by Norah K. Chadwick, they were recited in order, during successive

sessions, on many days. There is no difficulty in understanding
that, as the ancient notices, if left unaltered, plainly admit,
the Homeric poems were not constructed, but reconstructed,
at Athens by command of Peisistratus (see pp. 147, 175
above).

But it is sufficient for the present argument that Homer's time
and place have been very properly doubted, even if now the
doubts are likely to be resolved. The doubts concerning the
times and the places in the represented world of the poems are
still more important. They are due to the artistic power of
generalization possessed by Homer or indeed by 'the Greek
people', with whom, at least in some partial sense, he certainly
shared an identity.

Francis Berry, a modern poet of considerable importance,
was contemplating a poem on his own experiences in Malta,
G.C. during the Second World War; and he quickly decided
to make the ostensible subject of the poem the siege of Malta in
A.D. 1565. Shortly defined, poetry is a way of saying two things
at once. It may compress together or superimpose very many
individual actualities, and consequently many people, things,
times and places may grow together into new identities, in
which afterwards some of the original facts may be noticed, to
the mistaken exclusion of others. The Homeric world can be
made to look even in detail very much like the Mycenaean
world. The agreement appears as impressive in the work of
Dörpfeld and of his successor, Heinrich Rüter. Renata von
Scheliha is not far from agreement with Andrew Lang, and an
early date is judiciously defended by Gitti. Émile Mireaux
finds an original for Agamemnon in Pheidon of Argos, and
supplies other correspondences to match this. Victor Bérard,
with great learning and skill, represented what to others is the
Mycenaean world of Homer as the later world of Greek
colonists in competition with Phoenician forerunners. Rhys
Carpenter finds in the *Odyssey* references to Egypt which for
him can only indicate Egypt at the end of the seventh century,
and in the *Iliad* he finds allusions which he takes to be not very
much older. Meanwhile, of course, he recognizes in the poems,
and sometimes successfully traces, other memories, some very
ancient indeed. These are all opinions recently advanced and
are modern, and the divergence, except that not much is now

heard of a sixth-century date for Homer, is almost as great as ever. The reason for the divergence is not solely that the scholars are fools or knaves, but that Homer was a great epic poet. He generalized experience so profoundly that his poetry suits situations six centuries, or more, apart. Rhys Carpenter even finds in the battle of Odysseus with the Laestrygonians a description of a battle, in the same place, which was fought in A.D. 1421. Homer could see and manipulate the 'permanent facts'. The great poems somehow 'cover everything'.

The characters in the Homeric poems are too human to be heroes, as E. V. Rieu observed. But, in two other senses, they are also too heroic to be human beings. Again difficulties of interpretation indicate poetic merit. One reason why the poems are so good is that their characterization is so good, far better than in any other ancient fiction. Another is that so much is represented in many of the characters. The old view that the heroes are 'faded gods' is, on the whole, truer than the naïve belief that they belong directly to history. J. A. K. Thomson's researches concerning Odysseus and Penelope are alone enough to shake that belief. The important heroes were on the whole very much as Pausanias represents them before they acquired the personalities which they have in Homer. They were super-human presences in shrines, as Helen is still a superhuman presence in Rhodes, and as she had been for a long time before she wept in Homer's Troy. Charles Autran has shewn the importance of priests and shrines in the generation of Greek heroic story. He, however, led by parallels such as the heroic tradition of Japan, is inclined to allow considerable historicity to the Trojan war. Whatever the exact truth may be, it is at least clear that a man may first live on earth and may then be tended as a hero after death. He may become a new hero or saint, or he may acquire some older identity. He may rise in the scale and he may descend again. The evolution of St George, as it was traced by Meta E. Williams, is instructive. He was once an early Egyptian god, pictured spearing a crocodile. He became a pre-Christian hero or saint with a shrine in the western desert. His cult became Christian and spread to Syria. In the early Christian centuries he acquired the name 'George' and a life-history as an officer of Constantine, supposed to have been finally martyred for his faith. His fame spread west, and grew, in iconography and sacred story, and is strong to-day. The biography, though it is sometimes believed literally, is fictitious, but the fame may have truth. There is nothing in any of his origins to disprove Lord Dowding's conviction that St George is now a living spirit, fighting evil.

Accordingly, Homeric heroes may have been men originally or they may not, and they may have undergone many trans-formations, so that it is hard to say, sometimes, whether a hero, so transformed, is really the same hero, even if he has the same name as before. The Achilles of Pausanias, who tore young maidens to pieces on the White Island, is scarcely the same person as the Achilles of Homer. Yet he is not entirely different. Even in Homer some of the ferocity remains, and becomes artistically eloquent, for the gain of humanity. In the poetry there is old and new together.

The ancient fear of the daemonic Achilles enriches Homeric poetry. So do other stresses and tensions, and among them in particular the stress and tension of change in social organization and discipline. In this there is no small interest. The change is a permanent fact in the living past of Homer, and of ourselves also, and the poetry turns it to enrichment by assimilation. But it has also a peculiar importance in that living past, for it, in particular, made the Greek present and our own.

'The whole of human history does not contain a single instance of a society which has advanced to the rationalistic condition unless its females have been born into an absolutely mono-gamous tradition; nor is there any example of a group which has retained its high position in the cultural scale after less rigorous customs have become part of the inherited tradition of all its members. A study of historical peoples reveals the fact that those societies which have adopted such customs as most nearly approach this compulsory lifelong association (which has never yet been achieved), and who have retained their rigid laws as to sexual conduct for the longest period, have advanced in the cultural scale to the highest position which any human society has yet reached.'

This is one of the conclusions reached by J. D. Unwin, after a thorough examination of eighty human societies.

Unwin's researches appear to prove that human societies

always increase in energy, memory and intellectual power in proportion as they have adopted stricter sexual discipline. Concurrently with this increase, there is a certain religious development, from conditions in which the dead are little considered, through the practice of tending individual dead men as heroes, to monotheism, and after that to rationalism. Unwin discusses the stages at length. An important stage is monotheism, and it is regularly associated with monogamy and monarchy. Without reference to the full argument, it is already clear that Homer's epic truth is the more comprehensive in that it expresses some immensely important steps in man's ascent. Homer arrays in artistic organization the pre-heroic, the heroic, and the divine. And Homer, in his only epigram, as Vernon Rendall calls it, praises as the best thing in life the happiness of a faithful husband and wife in their home (*Od.* 6, 182–5). Thus far Homer tells the story of secular mankind.

Homer is about heroes, and Homer is not about heroes. The question of Homer is interwoven with the heroic, perhaps in many senses of the word. Homer makes a spatial pattern of the temporal sequence in which imagined forms became heroes, gods, and human men very like ourselves, and in which, concurrently and causally, the relations of individuals in their societies altered towards civilization, with change of custom and law. Many time-sequences are scaled down almost until they are level. Some Homeric people and things are ultimately very old, but not all. Many may seem to be, or may even actually be, almost or quite historical, of one period or place. Homer's Troy itself is probably a blend, but Homer's Mycenae is Mycenae alone, at least in the core of its reference. The important people and things in Homer are normally poetic generalizations, inheriting something from many predecessors and resulting from recurrent actualities. Ritual begins the process of generalization which poetic art continues. Homer's myths are successors to ritual myths. They are versions of sacred stories told at shrines, at first in order to guide and to preserve, and later in order to explain, rituals performed at them. The myth-ritual theory has seemed inapplicable to Greek mythology. But that is because the origins in ritual belong to widely various places and times, and centuries of artistic alteration and re-alteration have overlaid them. Just what true historical tradition was transmitted from early to classical Greece is still hard to estimate. Alberto Gitti's warning that too few Greek historians have followed Beloch in learning from Niebuhr's critical approach to Roman history is probably salutary, and Lord Raglan is on the whole right to argue that in general the heroes of tradition are figures not of history but of ritual. Ritual, repeated often, amid violent hopes and fears, and necessarily remembered from year to year, is far more permanently and accurately transmitted than the recollection of historical events, which are even now easily confused or neglected, and which, in the past, were either soon forgotten, or recalled in increasingly inexact contaminations. The great stories everywhere are not usually about the historical figures concerned in great events. They are about imagined figures, generalized from ritual, itself perhaps originating from habitual currents of emotion, which create, in Kerényi's sense, an objective mythology, awaiting expression.

At many stages emotional charges from ritual dominated configurations in Homer. A full examination of the problem is due, but must be postponed. Identifications of ritual origins proposed by Rhys Carpenter, G. Rachel Levy, and Émile Mireaux may be hitherto controversial, but the direction is right. Compressed into Homeric poetry are the countless passionate memories, mystically transmitted and shared, which have descended down many long lines of ritual recurrence.

That may legitimately be said, but only provided that full weight is allowed to the celebrated critical arguments of H. J. Rose. Traces of old-fashioned barbarous and savage behaviours, thoughts, and superstitions among the Greeks are easily exaggerated, and have been lightly assumed to prove more than they can. It is necessary to face the critical arguments, but it is also necessary to adopt a long and wide perspective which admits the Ancient East to its view. Such a perspective is necessary so that the compressive power of Homer, and his parallel similarity to other epochal poets, may be rightly estimated.

To be classical, according to T. S. Eliot, a poet must command at least two languages. It was by a fine insight that he chose that requirement as one of four necessary conditions, fulfilled in particular by Vergil, who is pre-eminently classical.

But Homer fulfilled the condition too. He may not have known two languages, but interchange between more than two has helped to make his poetry. Charles Autran has been enabled by his incomparable erudition to make this fact much more clear and certain than before, and to shew its importance for the first time. The impact of two cultures on each other certainly fertilizes one or both. H. M. Chadwick associated the rise of epic poetry in many places with the impact on a less advanced of a more advanced culture, an impact which, for him, occurred when Greeks from the north met Mycenaeans. Opinions change quickly, and new complications are discovered, but this kind of dynamic contact certainly happened often. Many ethnic and cultural thrusts came from the east, and some from the north. Giuliano Bonfante and Benito Gaya Nuño have shewn from place-names the probability that the Philistines passed down the Adriatic coastland on their way to south-western Asia, and even left traces of themselves to the west of the Adriatic. L. A. MacKay has lately emphasized the important of Epirus and Illyria as origins of Greek peoples. Three generations ago Sir William Geddes, in a work of rigorous method, propounded a theory that the core of the *Iliad* was composed in Thessaly, and that the rest of it, and the whole of the *Odyssey*, are the work of a poet, or, less probably, poets, who lived on the coast of Asia Minor. Homer's Achilles has a temperament which has survived in exact likeness among modern Albanians, whose feuds, for example, have continued on the Homeric pattern.

Blended and compressed in Homer are not only ritual memories, but also memories of different human groups impinging on one another by various ways. If a long enough time is considered, very many can be relevantly identified; perhaps even, as G. Rachel Levy hints, the minds of the new and of the old stone age meet visibly together in the background of Homer. Most important of all, however, is the eruption southwards, from the steppes south-west of central Asia, of 'The Charioteers'. Again it is to Charles Autran that reference must be made for all this great topic. What is now known is different, sometimes subtly, from what had been said before. It is not exactly a question of north and south, or of Indo-European in distinction from other dialects of speech. But, before and after 2000 B.C., the Charioteers did indeed introduce southwards, with horse-warfare, a new kind, or new kinds, of mind and of culture too. Their Asia, as well as the hieratic Asia before them and the Asia of Geometric influence after them, affected the Greeks. The Achaeans themselves, with their names in -*eus*, came through Asia, from Arrian's 'Old Achaea' to the east of the Black Sea shore. There were other groups from Asia, too, principally perhaps great families installed in centres of religion and culture in Greece and elsewhere, and they created the rich and powerful Aegean world of which excavation has rendered splendid, but fragmentary, reports. Who among them were Greeks, and who were not, were questions which could not be asked until many centuries later. There may well have been fighting in Greece between steppic Charioteers, some arriving from the north and some from the east.

According to Ernst Robert Curtius, the Greeks of the full Hellenic centuries, unlike the Italo-Celts, retained very little of the religion of the earlier peoples who had spoken Indo-European dialects; their religion was Aegean, that is, apparently a religion of Asia, little changed by the Charioteers. Yet, not to mention early researches of Max Müller and others, A. M. Hocart found interesting fragmentary traces among the Greeks of a widely distributed dual system of ritual kingship, with its theology associated with Eurasian speakers of Indo-European, and reaching to Fiji and the African Yoruba. And now, however Greek religion itself may best be described, L. R. Palmer has been proving that Greek law and morality are rather northern than anything else. For Asia, E. Cavaignac has stressed the contrast between the old southern Oriental mind, and the mind of the Hittites, who first appear with a classical, or European, temper of thought obviously characteristic of them.

Rhys Carpenter may even be right to see in Homer's Odysseus some trace of an Odysseus who had once been a bear, superstitiously tended. But Homer's story of the Siege of Troy is notably modelled on sieges and sacks in and near Babylonia which occurred before 2000 B.C., for example operations against Lagash, Ur, and Babylon itself. There are the originals of 'the sacred veil', of the defensive city-goddess, and of the Apollo who in the *Iliad* shoots arrows of plague. Ishtar assembles the enemy against Erech, and Girra, the Plague God, is associated with an attack on Babylon; he is in part the same not only as Homer's Apollo, but also as his own Asiatic forerunners, and as the later St Sebastian, martyred with arrows, whom Rabelais knew as the saint who gave protection from the plague. In the tale of Troy there is eastern city-sanctity, and, old long before Homer, there is the strange motive of the wooden horse, which must ultimately be due to the Charioteers and to thoughts which they had, or occasioned in others, long before their descendants gave shape and manner to the fighters on the Trojan plain. Homer makes little of the older faiths, but they are there below his glittering surfaces. And they entered into his artistic blend.

The Charioteers spread their influence as far as Britain, North Africa, and Japan; and the pre-history of Trojan narrative can sometimes be traced back through their story. So it is that the adventures of Menelaus and Helen are paralleled by variants from India and Java, and so it is that one of the ritual stresses which have left a mark, the stress of change in marriage-customs, has moulded both Indian epic and the *Odyssey*. In Indian epic there is a unique incident, in which, contrary to the law of the Charioteers, a princess has to choose her own husband. In the *Odyssey* Penelope is clearly wanted to choose for herself a husband from among the suitors. Yet the suitors themselves gather just as if they are to take part as candidates in betrothal assemblies of later Greece, at which of course the choice rested with the girl's father. This transition, identified in Homer by Renata von Scheliha, and the conflict which it brought, may be very ancient, but in Greece, as elsewhere, the effects have survived. Their vitality in classical Greece has been rightly emphasized for different reasons by both George Thomson and Colin Hardie. Clytaemnestra and Oedipus had interest for Athens, for, however old was the change from matrilineal to agnatic organization, the extant marks of it are alone enough to attest it, at least for some people in some places. It looks like a common inheritance in Greece and in India. In India, as John Gordon Vernon recalls, Sita's father, Janaka, said in the story 'I have a daughter Sita, not born of men, but sprung from the furrow as I ploughed the field and hallowed it. On him who bends the bow, I will bestow my daughter'. And Rama did so. Such was the material open to Homer and his predecessors. The social stresses of the conflict, having ritual importance, must have been severe. They enriched the Homeric blend.

Homeric epic mattered long ago, and as E. V. Rieu's translations have proved matters still. That is because it is about things which matter and which have mattered. Among those things are love and marriage, on which both the *Iliad* and the *Odyssey* turn, marking the ancient and enduring fight for the happiness of home. The poems represent the approach to monogamy and monotheism in the scheme of J. D. Unwin. They are salutary still, in an age when, as Lady Violet Bonham-Carter says, average behaviour is not enough. The poems are the more salutary, because their art is delicate and profound. Edmond Beaujon, investigating the subtle secret of it, has shewn that Homer presents the right order of society and of home as a ritual truth, at once symbolic and effective. Behind Homer, and indeed in Homer, is the ancient sacred marriage, which makes the flowers grow. Greek myth, as Gilbert Murray has proposed, remembered and unified it from many local rites, of which by no means all need have been performed in Greece. The old superstition, if that is the right word, is in Homer transformed, and made human. The secure union of a very human king and queen brings peace, plenty, and happiness, as by a ritual stability. The human people of Homer are heroic at least in Beaujon's sense, for they achieve what only heroes can achieve—'Symbolic Action'.

In Unwin's scheme, monogamous phases are succeeded by rationalism and decadence, with perverted emotions. Inflamed friendship, characteristic of classical Greece, is hinted, as H. J. Rose lately recalled, in the *Iliad*. The loyalty between Achilles and Patroclus should have been creative, but, since it was feverish, it was destructive. It is because Achilles himself, at his worst, was childish, that he saw Patroclus as a little girl, running in tears to her mother. The *Iliad*, therefore, very subtly marks the danger of decadence, a danger which the *Odyssey* strongly meets. How subtly Homer, or a predecessor, went to work is brilliantly suggested by Wolfgang Schadewaldt and Renata von Scheliha. The suggestion is that the poet invented Patroclus, and invented a name for him; the poet himself was the 'father' who brought Patroclus 'fame'. Now Patroclus in the *Iliad* derives his dramatic part from Cleopatra, the wife of

Meleager, in an old poem now lost, who persuaded Meleager to fight, when others could not persuade him. Homer or another, building the *Iliad* on the plan of the *Meleagrid*, may therefore have neatly inverted the syllables of Cleopatra's name; and the message is there, for those who have ears to hear. If so, nothing more Vergilian has yet been recognized in Homer.

The latest publication on this question is by J. Th. Kakridis, who compares ancient and modern versions of the story, and who proposes the term 'neo-analytic' for the method by which scholars now trace the process used by great poets in combining earlier poems, and redistributing their elements, for their own new expression. T. W. Allen, W. Schadewaldt, E. Howald, H. Pestalozzi, D. L. Page and J. A. Davison have helped to shew that Homer created his poetry in that way. Meanwhile, the same process had been discovered in Vergil, and called 'integration', some years ago; it was E. K. Rand who suggested that Vergil and Coleridge worked in similar ways. Colin Hardie has now shewn that Dante 'integrated' passages of Vergil in new combinations, and Kenneth Muir has proved that Shakespeare himself so treated his sources. It is now possible to trace backwards into the past the sources of the *Iliad*, and, in turn, their sources. For generations the integration of older poetry had been practised. The death of Patroclus in the *Iliad* is based on the death of Achilles himself in an earlier poem. One of Homer's sources was a neatly symmetrical *Memnonid*, in which the battle was between Achilles and Memnon. The pattern of the *Iliad*, described by J. T. Sheppard and Sir John Myres, is far more elaborate, but not so neatly precise. In Homer, greatness broke through the symmetries of form and fact in which the tales of Memnon and Meleager had been framed. Homer stands at this artistic culmination, as he stands too at the social culmination, in which emotional life, canalized in monogamy, next dangerously overflows. It is not insignificant that Patroclus replaces Cleopatra, and that Achilles, able to face authority neither in himself nor in Agamemnon, relies on his divine mother, herself a sharp inversion of Meleager's mother, for protection.

Homer's imagination, actuated by a 'vast torrent of reading', or rather of listening, could do its own part. It was, as Ernst Howald says, by 'a supreme sensitivity to the imponderables of the human spirit', a sensitivity which goes far beyond the limits of conscious thinking, that 'Homer made his lies look like truth'. The subtlety of his art has been becoming continually clearer, especially lately through the acute exposition of E. T. Owen. He shews how everything in the *Iliad* acts on the percipient emotionally, and exactly right, expanding what has gone before, preparing what is to come, and delivering, at each moment, just the impact which the whole great poem demands. Every reaction to Agamemnon's folly, and even every death dealt by Achilles, is eloquent and indispensable.

All is part of the unitary Homeric world, a world, as Mark Van Doren notes, in which everything is moving and alive, as in no other poet's; a world where everything ripples and quivers, the leaves of Mount Pelion as the waves of the sea and the ranks of standing men. Humanity is still living as an organ of a living world.

Past, present, and future are clasped and focussed in Homeric poetry. There is no sign that it will become obsolete. Odysseus, so far from being, as he has been thought, and not only by Vico and Voltaire, morally out of date, offers rescue for many living now, and Achilles, and Hector too, are hard to match for illumination of the permanent facts which are to-day most urgent. Simone Weil, writing according to Herbert Read 'in the accents of genius', maintained that only Homer, and successors entirely dependent on Homer, have presented a moral system simple and true enough to save contemporary humanity. In recent poets the generality must be less and the irrelevances and misleading differentiations more, so that an earlier poet is a more useful guide. The matter is explained by Fernand Robert with great penetration and clarity. As he says, sailors are better trained on sailing ships than on modern ships, and science learnt forty years ago is now very much more out of date than is any of Homer's poetry which was read at the same time.

It is still poetically true that when evening has passed, 'the black of night has stolen all colour from the world' (*Aeneid* 6. 272). Yet in fact more colours are visible, in the sky at least, on a dark night than in bright daylight. It has been argued that perceptions, or the mind's reception of them, have changed or varied.

A totality seems to be directly presented in palaeolithic cave-painting and in Shakespearian verse. Homer's verse is formulary, and his descriptive repertory is discrete or fragmentary, like geometric drawings on vases. A statement is built up by adding part to part. There are not enough general words and there are too many particular words, for example, nine nouns for 'strength' and eight verbs for 'see'. Bruno Snell has argued this question, and shewn how the structure and content of thought and language changed by stages from Homer to Vergil. From the time of Archilochus individuals were conscious of their own souls, and sought a new relation between themselves and the world, perhaps in some observation of a fixed rhythm of life, or in a philosophy of individual or collective history, since the old ritual unity had been lost. Presently the naïve belief in myth was also lost. But Vergil was nevertheless in sharp contrast with the great Greeks when he consciously used myth for symbolic expression. One of his first innovations was his construction, out of a passage in Polybius, of the mythical poetic Arcadia. Already in the First *Eclogue* Vergil was doing something very new indeed in his solidly responsible blend of mythic configuration with actualities of his own day. He was also fixing poetry for centuries. Furnishing a continuation of Snell's narrative, Ernst Robert Curtius has proved that the new Vergilian landscape of the First *Eclogue* became a convention dominant in Romance languages, just as their epic form reached them through Vergil from Homer. But Vergilian myth reaches farther than that. Luigi Alfonsi has profoundly seen that Propertius, with Roman concentration and Roman sense of time, completely altered the mythic resources which he inherited from Hellenistic poets, and made of myth a device for consolidating the present by transmission from the past, for securing the future by a directed will, and for penetrating beyond the veil, all passion burnt away. The Propertian sequence of personal love, patriotic ardour, and mystic vision marks him as one of the great poets. And Vergil trod his way.

Macrobius, as Vernon Rendall recalls, has left the first extant comparison of Vergil and Homer, and his match of phrase with phrase may stand. In addition, the poets are alike as world poets, or epochal poets, who by integrating past poetry distil and condense a vast experience. Both generalize, and focus a resultant. They are not inclined to present single facts actual in one moment of time, whether an actual Troy of history or an actual landscape. Vergil often preferred a conventional and literary description even when he could have described a scene naturalistically, but in this subtle matter, where the exact truth is elusive, the researches of Anna G. de Tollenaere-Blonk and Curtius must now be set beside the researches of Bernhard Rehm and Bertha Tilly. At any rate Vergil carried his generalization so far that in the *Georgics* he may even have integrated an imaginary bird, a 'sea-coot', from Cicero and Aratus. That, and several other examples, are furnished by L. A. S. Jermyn, who can be said to have proved that the *Georgics*, in spite of their practical aspect, are not immune from the Homeric law. A good example in the *Aeneid* is the Sibyl at Cumae. J. H. Waszink has proved that Vergil created her out of elements derived from earlier sibyls. There had been no Cumaean Sibyl in the story, though perhaps a death goddess, such as the Calypso investigated by Hermann Güntert, had long been revered near Cumae. Vergil is like Homer in this condensation of reminiscences, poetic or literary, or poetic and literary, into new and intense significations. Sometimes there is a neat inversion, of immense effect. Such is Vergil's use of Lucretian phrases to express the opposite of Lucretian doctrines, observed in particular by Agnes K. Michels, and Vergil's attribution to the High God himself of the advances in civilization which in Hesiod are due to Prometheus, and which offended Zeus, a characteristically Vergilian decision which L. P. Wilkinson has just noted. Enough is known of Homer to justify a claim that here, too, he and Vergil are alike. Both find such ways to make dynamic and new the long experience which they generalize and condense. Homer lays a claim to the universality which T. J. Haarhoff asserts of Vergil.

It is easy to distinguish too sharply Vergil's Latin from Homer's Greek. Certainly, Vergil's words are burning atoms of inextinguishable thought, but hardly Homer's; and some of them contain the rippling vitality and expansive truth, self-dependent, or in mutual reflection, which in Homer characters may have, but not often individual words. And for Vergil, as for no poet before, time, in the words of Father E. J. Stormon, S.J., is a constituent part of reality. Vergil's phrases are shot with it, iridescently. Homer on the other hand composed by formulae inherited from far back in eastern hieratic tradition. The researches of Charles Autran have already proved that Homeric poetry is, ultimately, at least as bilingual as Vergilian. T. S. Eliot's insight is justified for both; and a way is opened for a new analysis of Homeric language, evolved, like Vergil's, under stress of forcing significance out of inadequate verbal forms. Nor is it clear that Greek epic style is in all senses very much more formulary than Latin. Latin poetic styles are formulary, too, and so is modern English. For example, in the broadcast report of the Budget in 1947, almost everything was expressed by what could well be called formulae. Perhaps Vergil did what Homer did, but for a different mental world. Homer reconciled ancient wisdom with the beginning of analytical European thought and sentience. Vergil's reconciliation extended farther than can yet be said.

Homer had the immense problem of building incidents in contrast and balance to reach his human revelation. Vergil's mature art was not limited to that. He had learnt from Greek epic the two great lessons of construction by integration of earlier poetry in new, bold, combinations, and of right balance in dualities which would be the better if not exactly symmetrical. The first lesson Vergil applied not only to stories and characters, but to everything else also, including the internal intricacies of words, and minute complexities of thought. The second lesson, so like St Augustine's belief that even balance and equality, especially if not quite exact, are the most divine of earthly merits, has been illuminated after long obscurity by R. W. Cruttwell in a work of great intellectual power. The *Aeneid* is constructed in an elaborate symbolic language, which intertwines comparisons to sustain heavy charges of significance. By this method Vergil superimposed contemporary on earlier Roman history, and the whole conception of Rome on the conception of Troy. A suggestive phrase may reveal an expressive equation. Vergil's 'ancient mound of Ceres' is adapted from Homer's queer reference to the 'barrow of Myrine' or 'Batieia'. Now Dardanus is central in the scheme of the *Aeneid;* and Dardanus was reported to have been married to Bateia, and his brother to have lain with Demeter or Ceres, in a furrow. Dardanus was for Vergil the link between Troy and Italy; and his name contains as an element an old word meaning 'bee'.

He, therefore, is recalled by the portent of the bees swarming in the citadel of Latinus. The Etruscan-Roman contacts of Aeneas, as lineal heir of Dardanus to the cult of Vesta, result in the *Aeneid* directly from his Cretan-Trojan contacts as Teucer's lineal heir to the cult of Cybele. Vergil applies the same terms both to the Trojan contacts of the Etruscan Dardanus, and to the Etruscan contacts of the Trojan Aeneas. In the prophetic welcome of Tiberinus, the 'Etruscan Tiber', Aeneas is seen as equivalent to a returning Dardanus, who brings back with him once more from Phrygia an originally Etruscan 'Troy Town'. Of the enormous significance, in facts beginning to emerge, and in their poetic resonance, of the Etruscan and Asiatic past of Rome, it is, once more, for Charles Autran to speak.

In this method Vergil exploited according to his own invention the Homeric power of condensed suggestion. Vergil exploited the simile comparably. W. Elmslie Philip has shewn that he used similes to regulate his material, to bring out contrasts of character and situation, and to emphasize the human and emotional qualities concerning which, in the narrative, Vergil is more reticent than Homer. The similes are knit with the context, and simile is linked with simile, until at the end of the *Aeneid* they are massed in full power. There is a strange parallel with Homer. The direct content of the *Georgics* gives material for similes in the *Aeneid* rather as the direct content of the *Odyssey* corresponds to the similes in the *Iliad*, as A. Severyns has argued. Vergil does not forget Homer for long.

Perhaps Homer gives all that mankind should need, but it was left to Vergil to give much that mankind does in fact need. Vergil reaches, as Homer does not, into the organization and the complexities of the later and the modern world. He thought through politics to mystic perception, and passed beyond pure epic tragedy. Perhaps he could succeed because he also reached farther back in time than Homer. He remembers the old Aegean world and its oriental pre-history more clearly, and often he restores something which in Homer is a broken tale. A safe and sufficient example is provided by the city-sanctities at Troy; on such matters it is proper to wait until evidence is arrayed for a full statement, but fragments of support are always occurring. Vergil's emphasis on Buthrotum, where, as Leaf humorously noted, he made no attempt at topographical

o

accuracy, fits the distant truth concerning the passage of the Philistines indicated by Giuliano Bonfante. John Garstang has reported from Syria a Hittite statue of the eighteenth century B.C. with a face of stern, responsible lineaments, representing some governor, clearly a man under authority living as by law of European duty. Such a man is not Homeric. He is Vergilian. But most important is Vergil's progress towards the Divine. For him the human is not enough. Vergil won the conviction that, in words used by Father E. Watts, and quoted by Murray Hickey Ley, 'God is not niggardly in his revelations' and that 'in every moment is an eternity'.

Perhaps this is to misunderstand Homer. Alexander Pope was right to say, with a Vergilian depth of meaning yet to be explored, that Vergil found that 'Nature and Homer' were 'the same'. But Vergil did discover, as Theodor Haecker saw, and indeed discovered in reaching back to old Egypt and reaching forwards too, that the centre for European man is the family, which is a Holy Family, Homeric but also Divine.

SELECT BIBLIOGRAPHY

For further references to works on Homer the reader should consult:

ALBIN LESKY, *A History of Greek Literature*, London, 1966
SIR JOHN L. MYRES, *Homer and his Critics* (ed. Dorothea Gray), London, 1958

For the main Vergilian works referred to in the Appendix see the author's *Roman Vergil* as listed below.

CQ = *Classical Quarterly*
CW = *Classical Weekly* (now *Classical World*)
$G\&R$ = *Greece and Rome*
JHS = *Journal of Hellenic Studies*

ABBOTT, G. F., *Songs of Modern Greece*, Cambridge, 1900
ALLEN, T. W., *Homer: The Origins and the Transmission*, Oxford, 1924
AUTRAN, C., *Homère et les origines sacerdotales de l'épopée grecque*, 3 vols. Paris, 1938–43 (Reviewed by W.F.J.K. in *JHS*, 1952)
BASSETT, S. E., *The Poetry of Homer*, Berkeley, 1938
BEAUJON, E., *Acte et passion du héros: essai sur l'actualité d'Homère*, Neuchâtel, 1948 (Reviewed by W.F.J.K. in *JHS*, 1949)
BÉRARD, V., *Les Phéniciens et l'Odyssée*, 2nd edn. Paris, 1927
BETHE, E., *Homer: Dichtung und Sage*, 2nd edn. Leipzig, 1927
BLAKEWAY, A., 'The Date of Archilochus', in *Greek Poetry and Life*, Oxford, 1936
BOWRA, C. M., *Tradition and Design in the Iliad*, Oxford, 1930
Heroic Poetry, London, 1952
Homer and his Forerunners, Edinburgh, 1955
BRADFORD, E., *Ulysses Found*, London, 1964
CARPENTER, R., *Folk Tale, Fiction and Saga in the Homeric Epics*, Berkeley, 1946 (Reviewed by W.F.J.K. in *JHS*, 1946, and *G&R*, 1947)
CHADWICK, H. M., *The Heroic Age*, Cambridge, 1912
CHADWICK, NORAH K., *Poetry and Prophecy*, Cambridge, 1942
DAVISON, J. A., 'Homer and the Modern World', in *Pro Antiquitate Viva*, Prague, Statni Pedagogické Nakladatelstvi, 1967
VAN DOREN, M., *The Noble Voice*, New York, 1946
FORSDYKE, J., *Greece before Homer*, London, 1956
GEDDES, W. D., *The Problem of the Homeric Poems*, London, 1878
GITTI, A., *Mythos*, Bari, 1949
GLADSTONE, W. E., *Studies on Homer*, Oxford, 1858
HALL, EILEEN, *Cuchulain, The Hound of Ulster*, London, 1925
HARDIE, C., 'In Defence of Homer', *G&R*, 1956

HARDING, ROSAMOND E. H., *An Anatomy of Inspiration*, Cambridge, 1948

HOWALD, E., *Der Dichter der Ilias*, Zürich, 1946 (Reviewed by W.F.J.K. in *JHS*, 1946, and *Erasmus*, 1947)

JACOBY, F., 'The Date of Archilochus', *CQ*, 1941

KAKRIDIS, J. TH., *Homeric Researches*, Lund, 1949

KIRK, G. S., *Homer and the Epic*, Cambridge, 1965

KNIGHT, W. F. J., *Roman Vergil*, revised and augmented edn., Peregrine Books, Harmondsworth, 1966
Vergil: Epic and Anthropology (ed. J. D. Christie), London, 1967

LABARBE, J., *L'Homère de Platon*, Liège, 1949

LANG, A., *Homer and the Epic*, London, 1893
Homer and his Age, London, 1906
The World of Homer, London, 1910

LEAF, W., *Companion to the Iliad*, London, 1892
Iliad, 2nd edn. London, 1900–2
Troy, London, 1912

LEUMANN, M., *Homerische Wörter*, Basel, 1950

LORD, A. B., *The Singer of Tales*, Cambridge, Mass., 1960

LORIMER, Miss H. L., *Homer and the Monuments*, London, 1950

MACKAY, L. A., *The Wrath of Homer*, Toronto, 1948

MAZON, P., *Introduction à l'Iliade*, Paris, 1942

MIREAUX, É., *Les Poèmes Homériques et l'Histoire Grecque*, 2 vols. Paris, 1948–9

MURRAY, G., *The Rise of the Greek Epic*, 4th edn. Oxford, 1934

MYRES, J. L., *Who were the Greeks?* Berkeley, 1930
'The Last Book of the *Iliad*', *JHS*, 1932
'The Pattern of the *Odyssey*', *JHS*, 1952

NILSSON, M. P., *The Mycenaean Origin of Greek Mythology*, Berkeley, 1932
Homer and Mycenae, London, 1933 (Reviewed by W.F.J.K. in *CW*, 1936)

OWEN, E. T., *The Story of the Iliad*, Toronto, 1946

PAGE, D. L., *The Homeric Odyssey*, Oxford, 1955
History and the Homeric Iliad, Berkeley, 1959

PALMER, L. R., *Achaeans and Indo-Europeans*, Oxford, 1955

PARRY, M., *L'épithète traditionnelle dans Homère*, Paris, 1928
'Studies in the Epic Technique of Oral Verse-making', *Harvard Studies in Classical Philology*, 1930 and 1932

PESTALOZZI, H., *Die Achilleis als Quelle der Ilias*, Zürich, 1945 (Reviewed by W.F.J.K. in *JHS*, 1946, and *Erasmus*, 1947)

POLLARD, J. R. T., *Helen of Troy*, London, 1965

Powys, J. C., *Homer and the Aether*, London, 1959

Raglan, Lord, *The Hero*, London, 1936

Rieu, E. V., *Homer: The Odyssey* (translated), London, Penguin Books, 1945

Homer: The Iliad (translated), London, Penguin Books, 1950

Robert, F., *Homère*, Paris, 1950

Schadewaldt, W., *Legende von Homer dem fahrenden Sänger*, Leipzig, 1942 (Reviewed by W.F.J.K. in *JHS*, 1953)

Von Homers Welt und Werk, 3rd edn. Stuttgart, 1959

von Scheliha, Renata, *Patroklos*, Basel, 1943 (Reviewed by W.F.J.K. in *JHS*, 1946, and *G&R*, 1948)

Scott, J. A., *The Unity of Homer*, Berkeley, 1921

Severyns, A., *Homère*, 3 vols. Brussels, 1945–8 (Vols. 1–2 reviewed by W.F.J.K. in *JHS*, 1946)

Sheppard, J. T., *The Pattern of the Iliad*, London, 1922

Snell, B., *The Discovery of the Mind*, Oxford, 1953

Stanford, W. B., *The Ulysses Theme*, Oxford, 1954

Homer: The Odyssey (edited), 2nd edn. London, 1964

Steiner, G. and Fagles, R. (editors), *Homer: A Collection of Critical Essays*, Spectrum Books, Englewood Cliffs, N.J., 1962

Stubbs, H. W., 'Homer, Thebes and Argos', *Proc. Classical Soc.*, 1953

Thomson, G., *Studies in Ancient Greek Society: The Prehistoric Aegean*, London, 1949 (Reviewed by W.F.J.K. in *JHS*, 1952)

Thomson, J. A. K., *Studies in the Odyssey*, Oxford, 1914

Unwin, J. D., *Sex and Culture*, London, 1934

Ventris, M., and Chadwick, J., 'Evidence for Greek Dialects in Mycenaean Archives', *JHS*, 1953

Documents in Mycenaean Greek, Cambridge, 1956

Wace, A. J. B. and Stubbings, F., *A Companion to Homer*, London, 1962

Wade-Gery, H. T., *The Poet of the Iliad*, Cambridge, 1952

Webster, T. B. L., *From Mycenae to Homer*, London, 1958

Weil, Simone, 'The Iliad, or the Poem of Force', *Cahiers du Sud*, Marseilles, 1940–1; translated by Mary McCarthy, Politics Pamphlet No. 1, New York, 1945, and also in *The Mint*, No. 2, London, 1948

Welcker, F. O., *Der epische Cyclus oder die Homerischen Dichter*, vol. i, 2nd edn. Bonn, 1865; vol. ii, Bonn, 1849

Whitman, C. H., *Homer and the Heroic Tradition*, Cambridge, Mass., 1958

Williams, Meta E., 'Whence came St George?' *Bulletin de la Société Royale d'Archéologie d'Alexandrie*, 1936

Woodhouse, W. J., *The Composition of Homer's Odyssey*, Oxford, 1930

INDEX